THE BALANCE SHEETS
OF IMPERIALISM

———

PUBLISHED FOR

THE CARNEGIE ENDOWMENT
FOR INTERNATIONAL PEACE

DIVISION OF ECONOMICS AND HISTORY

THE
BALANCE SHEETS
OF
IMPERIALISM

FACTS AND FIGURES ON COLONIES

BY

GROVER CLARK

NEW YORK / RUSSELL & RUSSELL

PREFACE

Even the man who reads nothing beyond the newspaper headlines knows in these days that the present colonial situation is satisfactory neither to the "haves" nor to the "have nots" nor to the people in the territories controlled. He is beginning to suspect, too, that the old arguments which were put forward to justify the taking of colonies were not such incontrovertible truths as formerly they were thought to be.

In that suspicion he is entirely correct. Three main claims have been made as to the value of colonies: that they provided important outlets for population; that the possession of them gave important opportunities for profitable trade which otherwise would not be available; that control over the sources of raw materials in colonies added to a nation's security in time of war and give it important advantages in time of peace. The actual record of colonies, especially for the past half century when the taking and administering of colonies has gone on under modern conditions, demonstrates conclusively that each of these three claims is essentially fallacious.

The West has been expanding for four hundred years. But the experience with colonies in the first three of those four centuries, up to roughly 1800, can throw little light on present-day colonial problems because the conditions of the world generally and of expansion in particular were so radically different then from what they now are.

In the eight decades following 1800, conditions began to become more nearly like those of the present, especially in the latter part of this period. From the record of these decades, we can get suggestions for dealing with our present problems, particularly from the writings of Bright, Cobden, and the other British free trade advocates. The process by which the British Dominions-to-be secured successive advances toward independence also is illuminating.

By the time the 1880's started, modern industry, transportation, and communication had become well established. The new need for markets and raw materials, and the new facilities for reaching them, were important factors in bringing on the new outburst of rivalries for overseas territories. General economic conditions throughout the world were much more nearly like those of today in the period during which the "new imperialism" got under way than in the earlier periods of expansion. The records of the expanding nations in the half century since 1880, therefore, are much richer in data pertinent to present-day colonial problems than those for the preceding periods.

The records themselves, too, are much more complete for the recent years than they are for the earlier, though there still remain many gaps.

This is why this study has been concentrated almost entirely on the records of the past half century. Limitations of time and opportunity, too, have made it necessary to go mainly into the records of the five countries which have been most active in the expansion (Britain, France, Germany, Italy, and Japan), though some attention also has been given to the other colony-holding countries.

The corner stone of the "Conclusions from the Evidence," which are given in the first section, is the statistical material brought together in the tables in this volume—and the considerably larger volume of statistical material which was analyzed but is not reproduced. The raw material for these tables has been taken mainly from official publications of the several governments whose colonial experience is considered (Britain, France, Germany, Italy, and Japan chiefly, but also Belgium, the Netherlands, Portugal, Spain, and the United States), or from the League of Nations publications for recent years. Some of it is drawn from statistical compilations such as Ferenczi's monumental collection of migration statistics in *International Migrations*, Vol. I, which brings together all the available migration data for the years prior to and including 1924.

No table in the present volume, however, is a direct or even approximate reproduction of a table published elsewhere.

The purpose here has been to bring the material together in such a way as to show proportions and tendencies, rather than absolute amounts. Hence percentages have been calculated and are used in the tables, very generally. The absolute figures also are given, in most but not all cases. Wherever possible, exactly comparable year periods have been taken, but lacunae in the original material sometimes have prevented making exact comparisons; the years for which migration statistics are available in the different groups used, for example, vary considerably, and there are gaps in the official trade and financial statistics of some of the countries. These variations in years and these gaps have been noted.

Each table is preceded by a brief summary indicating the significant points in it. The sources from which the collections have been made are given, together with such footnotes as seemed desirable.

The material on the "Political Status of Colonized Territories, 1935," which follows the statistical tables, has been gathered from various sources specially for this study. No such compilation is available in published form elsewhere in nearly as complete or as up-to-date form.

The list of treaties relating to colonies brings together in convenient form the references to this kind of material bearing on colonies.

The bibliography gives most of the official periodical publications containing statistics relating to colonies and cognate subjects, for the principal colony-holding countries, and lists some of the non-periodical official studies which contain pertinent data. The list of books by individual authors, in the bibliography, by no means includes all the books containing material on Western expansion and colonies; a complete list would fill a large volume. But it gives most of the more important modern books and some of the older volumes, and it is reasonably representative of the different points of view.

This volume on the *Balance Sheets of Imperialism* contains the more important parts, but not all, of the statistical material which was gathered from official and other sources as the first and foundation part of the study. The conclusions from this, and from other material drawn from original sources, are summarized concisely in the introductory section on "Conclusions from the Evidence." This basic material also underlies the more general and less technical discussion of imperialism and colonies, including a brief history of Western expansion, which is being published by the Macmillan Company under the title *A Place in the Sun*. Although published separately, *The Balance Sheets of Imperialism* and *A Place in the Sun* are companion and mutually supplementary though not mutually dependent volumes.

Grants from the Carnegie Endowment for International Peace have made possible this study of one phase of the problem of colonies, and the publication of this volume. Dr. James T. Shotwell, Director of the Division of Economics and History of the Endowment, has been primarily responsible for making the arrangements for the study. His advice and counsel in the preparation and presentation of the material have been exceedingly valuable; these, and even more the warm friendliness which he has shown throughout, are only very inadequately acknowledged by this brief word of appreciation and gratitude. Dr. Denys P. Myers, of the World Peace Foundation, assisted in gathering some of the documentary material. He compiled the list of treaties. Miss Marie Carroll, also of the World Peace Foundation, and Miss Miriam Farley, of the Institute of Pacific Relations, aided in collecting the statistical material, and Miss Carroll's knowledge of League of Nations documentary sources proved a valuable help. The members of the staff of the Economics Division of the New York Public Library made the work much easier by their constant readiness to place the resources of that great institution at the disposal of the writer. The British Library of Information in New York was generous ·in letting the writer use its material. The writer's most constant helper, and the one to whom his gratitude goes out especially, has been his wife, Kathryn B. Clark.

To the Carnegie Endowment, and to these individuals and others who have assisted in the study, the writer expresses his sincere thanks. The responsibility for views expressed, and for errors, is his, not theirs.

New York
May 15, 1936

GROVER CLARK

TABLE OF CONTENTS

LIST OF TABLES

THE BALANCE SHEETS
OF IMPERIALISM

CONCLUSIONS FROM THE EVIDENCE

Western expansion in the past four centuries, culminating in the swiftly moving drive during the three decades which just preceded the World War, undoubtedly has brought certain substantial advantages to the Western peoples. But, especially in the decades just before and since the World War, this expansion also brought heavy costs, in money, in lives, and in past and present antagonisms. These costs are the debit entries which must be made in the ledger of imperialism.

For the three centuries up to 1800, the record, if it were available—as it is not, except in very general terms—probably would show a cash profit to the Western governments and taxpayers, provided no money value were put on the lives lost, in the taking as well as in the taken countries.

For the eight decades preceding the new drive for colonies which started in the 1880's, the governments as such spent considerably more on expansion than they received directly from it. These losses ultimately fell on the taxpayers. But private interests were making good profits on trade with the overseas territories, and the governmental expenditures were much less than they came to be later. Perhaps the private profits roughly equalled the governments' losses. In any case, between 1800 and 1880, the balance for the people as a whole in the colony-holding countries was not large on either the debit or the credit side of the ledger.

Since 1880, however, the cash costs to the countries which have used force to get or keep control of colonies unquestionably have been very substantially more than any possible cash profits derived from the trade with

¹ Compare Tables VII to XVI.

the territories controlled.¹ Germany and Italy have spent more directly on their colonies than the total value of the trade with them; Italy's margin of expense over trade value was very large, even before the present drive into Ethiopia started. Japan has not spent as much directly on getting and keeping her colonies as the total value of her trade with them, but considerably more than the possible profits on that trade. The direct colonial expenses for France and Britain probably have been some, but not much, more than the profits on the trade with the overseas territories, especially if the trade with the Dominions be counted in the British total.

For all these countries, however, the direct expenditures on the colonies are only a part of the real colonial costs. A part of the general naval and military defense expenses must be charged against the colonies, since not one of these nations would feel required to maintain such expensive armed forces if it did not have the overseas territories. If a conservatively estimated share of the general expenditures for defense be allocated to the colonies as their proper share of the "overhead" expenses of keeping up the nation's armed forces, the ledgers of the colonies show a large red ink balance for every one of the principal colony-holding countries. And this debit balance for the cash accounts includes no portion of the expenses of the World War, even though the jealousies aroused by the drive for colonies were so important a factor in bringing that War about.

The record shows, too, that the gains in other than direct money terms which frequently are claimed to result from the possession of colonies have not been anything like enough to compensate for the heavy cash losses which the ledger records.

In spite of all that was said about the value of colonies as outlets for population, and as places to which people could go without being lost to the "fatherland," the number of those who left all Europe permanently to live in the overseas territories controlled by European governments—which does not include the British Dominions—in the past half century has been extremely small compared either with the increase in population at home or with the migration to regions which were completely independent or, like the Dominions, practically so.[2] Europe's population in this period has increased about 173 millions. The net emigration from Europe has been about 19.3 millions. The net emigration to the territories controlled from Europe has been about 500,000—which is less than 0.3 percent of the population increase in Europe, and only 2.6 percent of all the permanent emigrants.

In spite, too, of the insistently repeated assertion that the possession of colonies and the consequent control of raw materials in them materially increases a nation's security in time of war and gives it substantial advantages in time of peace, the records show that this claim, like the claims that colonies provide important outlets for population and yield large and profitable trade to the holding country, is fundamentally fallacious.

The wartime situation is obvious enough. Access to the sources of raw materials depends on the ability to keep communications open with those sources, not on the presence or absence of political control over the territories where the sources are.

In times of peace, substantial advantages can be derived from "ownership" of the source of any particular raw material, in insuring either supplies or large profits for the "owning" country's nationals, only to the extent that something approaching monopoly control can be maintained of all the sources of supply. But through the development of new sources, or of substitute products, for all the important raw materials, whether agricultural or mineral, it has become practically impossible for any country today to keep anything like monopoly control of any raw material. The tendency, as the record clearly shows, is strongly toward, rather than away from, increased competition in the world's raw materials markets.[3]

Furthermore, the fallacy of the claim that a country really can make itself materially less dependent on foreign sources of supply, and on foreign markets, by adding to the territory under its control is strikingly demonstrated by the actual trade record of the colony-holding countries.[4]

Not one of them does as much as a fourth of its trade with its colonies. Japan has the best record in this respect, but even she, and even in 1929-1934 when her trade with her colonies was at its highest in proportion of her total trade, did only 22 percent of her external business with the lands under her control. Even if all the British trade with the Dominions be included, the United Kingdom, even since the Ottawa Agreements of 1932, has done with all the British countries just over a third of her external trade, and the share with the British territories under London's control has been only 15 percent of the total.

Nor does one of the colony-holding countries get from the overseas territories which it controls as much as a fifth of the raw materials and the foodstuffs which it requires, or sell to these regions as much as a third of the products of its factories.[5] Even includ-

---

[2] Compare Tables XVII to XXVIII.
[3] Compare Tables XLIX and L.

[4] Compare Tables XXIX to XLVIII.
[5] Compare Tables XLI to XLVIII.

ing the trade with the independent Dominions, the United Kingdom gets only a little more than a third of its food and raw materials imports from within the British Commonwealth, and sells less than half its exported manufactured goods to the British countries.

In brief, every country depends far more on foreign sources of supply and foreign markets than it does on overseas territories and sources under its own control—in spite of all the claims that have been made to justify the taking of colonies, and in spite of all the money and lives that have been spent to get and keep colonies.

Moreover, no country gets *all* of its trade with its colonies, or with any colony, *because* it has political control. Control gives some advantages in getting trade, but the very fact that all the colonies trade with other countries than the one in control demonstrates that the controlling country could and probably would get a fair amount of trade with the regions which make up its colonies even if it did not have control.

Obviously it is impossible to determine precisely what proportion of the trade, in any particular case, goes to the holding country because it has control. But it is interesting to observe the British record in this connection. In the past half century, the share which the territories controlled from London have had in the trade of the United Kingdom has decreased, while that of the self-governing Dominion areas has increased. The record of the overseas countries tells the same story: the share of the United Kingdom in the trade of the regions which it controls has fallen off, while that in the trade of the Dominions has increased. On its face, this record suggests that the trade importance of the British overseas countries has been in inverse, not direct, ratio to the amount of political control. But to draw that conclusion would be to give far more weight to the influence of political control in determining the movement of trade than the facts warrant.

Stated briefly, these are the conclusions which are inescapable from a careful analysis of the record for the past half century of what their colonies actually have meant to the principal colony-holding countries. The three main arguments for possessing colonies turn out to be three great fallacies—and they are seen to be dangerous as well as costly fallacies when account is taken of the results of the struggle for colonies not only or even primarily in cash but in lives lost, in wars caused, and in the pyramided hatreds which so gravely threaten new wars.

TERRITORIAL EXPANSION

One part of the record of expansion is that which relates to the amount of territory taken. This shows the amazing extent to which the Westerners have extended their political control over the earth [6]

By 1800, three centuries after the modern period of expansion from Europe started, the Western nations had staked out claims to about 28,000,000 square miles of the earth's 51,100,000 square miles of land. This included Europe, the Americas, most of India, the Russian part of Asia, parts of the East Indies, and bits along the coasts of Africa. The Westerners actually occupied or controlled, however, somewhat less than 18,000,000 square miles of this, including the 4,400,000 square miles in Europe. Even so, they controlled 35 percent of the earth's surface, while their claims covered 55 percent.

By 1878, just before the new drive for

[6] For data on territorial holdings, see Tables I to V.

colonies started, the Westerners had added 6,500,000 square miles to their claims, mainly in Oceania and North Africa, and had consolidated their hold both on this new territory and on the regions they had claimed by 1800. This gave them 34,500,000 square miles, or 67 percent of the earth. The expansion of claims, for this 78 years, had been at the rate of about 83,000 square miles a year; that of territory actually controlled or occupied, at the rate of some 216,000 a year.

Between 1878 and the start of the World War, the Western powers increased their holdings by 8,653,000 square miles, bringing the total to 43,125,00 or 84.4 percent of the world's total. In this 36 years, the borders of Western authority were pushed outward at the rate of 240,400 square miles a year, on the average—an addition each year of territory somewhat larger than the whole ·of France.

Since 1914, Western holdings have been increased only some 104,000 square miles, all of this being territory formerly under Turkey but now held as mandate areas. This gives the West, today, 84.6 percent of the earth's surface.

Since 1878, Japan has come to the fore among the expanding countries, the first of the non-Western nations to do so. Possessing only 148,000 square miles in that year, she added 115,000 square miles by the beginning of the War, and has secured control over another 502,000 square miles since then, including the puppet state in Manchuria.

ECONOMIC OPPORTUNITIES AND POLITICAL CONTROL

As a result of the expansion during the past four centuries, a large share of the earth and its people have come under Western control. Yet the acquisition of more square miles of land and of rule over more millions of people has been, in itself, by no means the sole motive for the expansion, though the desire for the "prestige" of "owning" extensive areas undoubtedly has been an important influence.

When the expansion started, and well on toward the end of the eighteenth century, those who sailed across the seas from Europe, and those who furnished the money for their trips, scarcely had a thought for acquiring territory as such. What they were after was trade, or loot, or both—and in many cases they were none too scrupulous about the methods they used to get what they wanted. The great trading companies, like the British, French, and Dutch East India Companies and the Hudson Bay Company, which were responsible for so large a part of Western expansion in the seventeenth and eighteenth centuries, were primarily and, in intention at least, almost exclusively trading concerns. Even the Puritans, the Cavaliers, the Dutch merchants, the French fur traders and Huguenots who went to North America did not go to the new country primarily to add to the territory of their kings. They sought religious freedom, or economic opportunities, or other objectives; the taking of land, when it was taken, and the establishment of governments, when they were established, were incidental to the achievements of these purposes. The Spanish and Portuguese went into Central and South America, too, not chiefly to establish colonies or to get new territory, but rather to get the gold and silver which was in the territory. The assumption of political control and the creation of local administrations came when they found that it was "necessary" to overthrow the local authorities and take control into their own hands to get what they wanted.

So, too, in India and the East Indies, the political penetration and the development of the political administrations of the great trading companies came as an incidental result of the economic penetration. Conditions were disturbed and the local authorities could not or would not maintain "order." The methods used by the penetrating Westerners aroused active opposition which it was "necessary" to suppress. So troops were brought in, and control was taken of the political administration, either directly or through puppets.

But as overseas trade developed, as competition for economic opportunities grew, and armed clashes occurred more and more frequently, the home governments found themselves increasingly drawn into the struggle. They had chartered the trading companies, and thereby assumed a certain measure of responsibility for them and their interests. They derived revenues from the companies' business, and so were interested in seeing the trade increase. Thus by the first part of the nineteenth century, the political side of the expansion was passing rapidly into the hands of the governments.

With the assumption of this political responsibility and control, the governments took over the expenses of maintaining the armed forces which they thought were necessary to "protect" and extend the interests which had been developed. In the earlier period, the trading companies had furnished their own soldiers and warships, and paid the costs as part of the normal expenses of doing business. This was why, until around 1800, the expansion from Europe, on the whole, was a source of revenue rather than of expense to the governments and the taxpayers generally, even though in some cases, like that of the British in North America, the costs of protection and maintaining control fell in large part directly on the governments instead of being paid by trading companies or out of local taxes. But the governments' costs in connection with the expansion

jumped at once when the big trading companies unloaded onto the governments the political side of their activities. Unfortunately for the taxpayers, the governments did not, along with the expenses, take over from the trading companies the profits on the trade.

Political control as such acquired a new importance when it became useful as a means of defending interests or opportunities from European rivals. This stage was reached in the latter part of the eighteenth century, particularly in the Americas.

About this time, too, the "mercantilist" theory secured a strong hold in the expanding countries: the theory that the overseas territories should be developed economically simply as feeders for the economic system of the holding country; that all their trade should be with the "owner"; that no manufacturing or other growth should be permitted which would compete with industry at "home." To secure these mercantilist objectives, political control obviously was necessary, as a means both of regulating affairs within the colonies and of shutting others out from access to economic opportunities in the colonies or trade with them.

The British first, and then the Spanish, discovered that the attempt to apply mercantilist policies too rigidly led to revolt in the regions settled by Europeans. After England had lost the thirteen colonies which became the United States, she changed her attitude and granted local self-government in progressive stages as the inhabitants of what have come to be the Dominions demanded it. But the Spanish never did learn the lesson, and, in the first decades of the nineteenth century, they lost by revolution all their colonies in Central and South America, though they kept a few small islands in the Caribbean and the Pacific until the war with the United States in 1898.

Toward the middle of the nineteenth century, too, "free trade" ideas became dominant in England.[7] The expenses of keeping political control in the colonies were mounting. The rapid development of modern industry gave Britain a great advantage in trade over the other countries in which this development was slower. Trade with the independent United States grew rapidly, and that with the British countries in the Americas increased most satisfactorily after strict mercantilism had been abandoned. Altogether, the weight of evidence all seemed to be on the side of those who argued, with Adam Smith, that the largest profits would be secured from the free movement of trade.

Such ideas also spread onto the continent, though they did not become as dominant there as in Britain.

For a time after the Napoleonic era, too, the European powers were absorbed with affairs at home, and the people were busy pushing forward the remarkably rapid economic reconstruction which followed the successful development of the use of power-driven machinery. The middle decades of the nineteenth century also saw important political changes in Europe.

For these and related reasons, the interest in the extension of political control over territories across the seas died down, though France did take Algeria in 1830 and Britain consolidated her position in some of the British areas.

Then industry developed to the point where Europe could not consume the products of the factories and overseas markets became highly desirable. Bismarck welded the German states, weak in their separateness, into the powerful and aggressively ambitious German Empire, seeking the "place in the sun" to which its leaders said its greatness entitled it; a place not only in the councils of Europe but also among the holders of lands overseas, which would provide outlets for its population, markets for its goods,

and raw materials for its factories. Italy also became united at this time, and began trying to climb the ladder to "greatness" both in Europe and overseas.

When the Congress of Berlin met in 1878, the principal questions before the representatives of the powers concerned the Balkans and other regions within Europe itself. Colonial questions were considered only quite incidentally. Then Italy took Eritrea in 1883, and in the next year Bismarck laid claim to all except a small part of the territories which were to become the German colonies. The new scramble for colonies had started.

As in the earlier stages of expansion, the desire for extension of territory was only one of the motives. At least equal in influence, and perhaps more potent even in the three pre-war decades, was the desire for economic opportunities. These might be secured by getting the right to trade at various ports, as in China, or by marking out "spheres of influence" in which special and partially or wholly exclusive trade and other economic privileges would be enjoyed, as in China or Persia or Turkey, by investments which gave opportunities for developing mineral resources or other profit-making enterprises. Sometimes these opportunities could be secured without taking actual political control. In such circumstances, the expansion remained primarily economic, and did not proceed to the formal establishment of political control.

But the same two influences were at work that had been earlier, tending to transform economic penetration, however peacefully intended at first, into political domination.

One was the conviction of the Europeans that they had the right to go where they chose, and to insist that conditions where they went should be satisfactory to them. Unpaid debts, local disturbances, and various

[7] Compare the writings of Cobden, Bright, and others of the free trade advocates.

such results of local administrative "inefficiency" or corruption, or of resentment against Western penetration, furnished the excuse for taking control more or less completely. Many of the Westerners were sincerely convinced that such incidents made it necessary to take control. Improvement in living conditions for the common people which sometimes followed the establishment of European control served as further justification for the political expansion.

The other influence working toward the assertion of political claims was the desire to keep some other country from getting the land and whatever trade or raw material or other economic benefits eventually might be secured from it. This motive had appeared in the eighteenth century. It became strong again after the 1880's, when not much was left unclaimed in the world except in Africa. The decrease in the possible spoils made it seem highly desirable to take what could be taken before they were gone altogether. Precise boundary delimitation of territories claimed, for example, did not become important until serious conflicts arose because claims overlapped. And it was only after comparatively little was left to be claimed, in the 1880's, that the expanding powers found it necessary to agree among themselves that "effective occupation" rather than mere assertion of a claim was necessary to validate a country's right to "backward" territory.

The progressive concentration of the energy of expansion within a steadily decreasing area in any case would have brought progressive intensification of the rivalries. But the need for new markets and the emergence of new claimants in the last quarter of the nineteenth century materially increased the energy of expansion. The developments leading to these various economic and political changes had been gathering headway for some time before the 1880's. Almost simultaneously, they reached their climaxes, and the principal powers were swept into new and feverish competition, partly in Europe and partly in the rest of the world, which carried them on into the World War.

The competition for overseas trading and other economic opportunities, and for overseas territories both as a means of securing these opportunities and for "prestige," previously had been closely associated with rivalries within Europe. In the three pre-war decades, the intra- and extra-European phases of the rivalries were more intimately related than ever, largely because the development of swift and cheap means of transportation so greatly had reduced the effective size of the world and brought its several parts so unprecedentedly close together. Hence it is impossible to draw any hard and fast line between the parts which the colonial rivalries and the rivalries in Europe played in bringing on the catastrophe of the War. Hence, too, it is impossible to determine how much of the costs of that War, and of the minor wars and preparations for war which preceded it, properly should be charged as part of the costs of colonies. But it is well worth while to keep in mind the fact that the intensification of the struggle for colonies was part and parcel of the development of new and more active rivalries in Europe, and that the jealousies aroused in each field added to the antagonisms in the other.

THE POPULATION FALLACY

The evidence showing the fallacy of the claim that colonies provide important outlets for population is so devastatingly clear that it can be dealt with briefly.[8]

8 For data on migrations, see Tables XVII to XXVIII.

In 1913, twenty years after Germany got most of her colonies, there were fewer than 20,000 Germans of all occupations in all the German colonies. This is considerably less than half the number of Germans living in 1930 in the Bronx Borough of New York City—the borough which has the smallest German population of the four principal boroughs.[9]

In 1931, there were less than half as many Europeans of all nationalities in all the Italian colonies than there were Italians on the island of Manhattan in New York.[10] Since 1886, the total net Italian migration to all of Africa has been just about 7,000.[11]

Between 1865 and 1924, over 17,000 more Hollanders *entered* the Netherlands from the Dutch colonies than left for these colonies, even though the Netherlands is one of the most thickly settled countries in the world.[12]

All the Europeans of all nationalities, plus the so-called "assimilated" of the local peoples in the French colonies in Africa,[13] today are only a few hundred more than the Italians who have settled in France since the World War: roughly, 1,200,000.[14]

Between 1925 and 1933, Japan's population increased eight millions. The total net emigration from Japan to all her colonies in that same period was less than 294,000,[15] and the net emigration to all the world outside of Japan Proper was only about 350,000.[16] Sweden, with a present population of six millions compared with Japan's sixty-five millions, has sent abroad in the past fifty

years half again as many permanent emigrants as Japan.[17]

Of the 28 millions of all nationalities who sailed to other continents from British ports from 1886 to 1933, precisely 5.0 percent went to the British territories other than the Dominion areas; to the regions where Britain had real control, that is to say.[18] The Dominions got 38.8 percent, and the United States 51.6 percent. For the 118 years, 1815 to 1933, only 3.5 percent of those who departed from British ports for overseas destinations had British territories other than the Dominions-to-be as their destinations.

The net emigration from Europe in the past fifty years has totaled about 19.3 millions.[19] Of these, about 16.7 millions migrated to the Americas—86.7 percent, though the European-controlled territory in the Western Hemisphere is less two percent of the area controlled from Europe. The United States got 9.3 millions of these migrants, chiefly from northern Europe. Central and South America took 5.7 millions, mainly Spanish and Portuguese but with a considerable number of Italians. Canada absorbed only 1.7 millions. Only about 2.6 millions went to all the rest of the world.[19]

In 1930 the number of foreign-born whites living in New York City was more than seven times the total of the European emigrants who have settled permanently in Africa in the past century: 300,000.

There are more foreign-born whites living in the state of New Hampshire than all the

---

[9] Table VI-B.
[10] Table VI-C.
[11] Table XIX-A, deductions being made from the gross emigration to get the net emigration figure, in accordance with the proportions shown in the Algerian figures, Table XXV.
[12] Table XXIV.
[13] Table VI-A.
[14] Table XXIII.
[15] Table VI-D. Net migration calculated by deducting from increases in Japanese population in the colonies, the increase attributable to excess of births over deaths calculated at 15 per 1,000 per annum.
[16] Table XVIII.
[17] Table XVIII.
[18] Table XXI.
[19] These figures of net migration were calculated from data in the migration tables supplemented by data in the sources there cited.

Europeans who have gone to stay in Asia in the past fifty years.

In the face of such a record the absurdity of claiming that politically controlled colonies have been important as outlets for population is too obvious to need further discussion.

The record shows that the presence or absence of political control has had practically nothing whatever to do with determining the destination of emigrants from Europe. Those who left their home lands went where they thought they would find better opportunities, or more freedom, or easier conditions of life. The Americas, Australia, and New Zealand offered room and freedom and opportunity in the past fifty years and more. So the emigrants went there. The other parts of the world were filled up, or had climates unsuitable for Europeans. So only those went there who had very compelling reasons.

THE TRADE FALLACY

The trade and costs record is even more discouraging than the migration record, for those who say that colonies are necessary.

All of Italy's trade, imports and exports together, with all of her colonies, from 1894 to 1932, was worth 5,561 million lire. This was less than one percent of her total external trade in the same period. In the twenty years, 1913 to 1932—the records do not go further back—Italy spent on her colonies 6,856 million lire.[20]. **The direct colonial expense in twenty years thus were 1,300 million lire more than the value of all the colonial trade in forty years. And a recent announcement had it that Mussolini has spent, in the first six months of his Ethiopian campaign, over 10,000 million lire.**

Germany's record of colonial costs and trade is not quite as bad as Italy's, but it is bad enough.[21] In the last twenty years that Germany had colonies, 1894 to 1913, her trade with all of them, including Kiaochao, was 972 million marks. In the same period, her colonial expenses, not including those for Kiaochao, were 1,002 million marks. The colonial trade was less than 0.4 percent of her total trade. Furthermore, while Germany's share of world trade increased between the decades 1894-1903 and 1904-1913, her share of the trade of her own colonies fell off from 35.2 percent to 26.6 percent. The total trade of the colonies, in other words, developed much more rapidly than their trade with Germany, in spite of Germany's "ownership" and of the marked German efforts to maintain strictly mercantilist control.

Japan has spent, altogether, directly on getting and keeping her colonies, about 2,860 million yen.[22] This is 18.4 percent of all her trade with all her colonies from her first acquisition of overseas territories.

But it is by no means all the colonies have cost her. A very substantial part of the expense of creating and maintaining her large navy and army is due directly to the fact that she has sought and taken colonies; how much of the total expense, it is impossible to say. But if we divide Japan's military costs in the same proportion as her external trade is divided between foreign and colonial, we shall get a figure which will be distinctly too low rather than too high.

Japan's trade with her colonies, 1894 to 1934, was 15,551 million yen, or 15.4 percent of her total external trade. This pro-

[20] Tables IX, XIV, and XXXIII.
[21] Tables VII, XIII, and XXXII.
[22] Tables X, XI, XV, XXXIV. Russo-Japanese war costs calculated at 1,800 million yen; Manchurian expenses since 1931, at 500 million yen.

portion of her total military expenses, not including World War costs or the direct colonial costs already mentioned, is 2,379 million yen. Taken with the direct colonial costs, this gives 5,329 million yen as a distinctly conservative estimate of what Japan's colonies have cost the Japanese taxpayers. This is just over a third of all her trade with all her colonies in the same period. There is no doubt whatever that even the direct colonial costs of 18.4 percent of the trade, to say nothing of this 33.7 percent of direct and indirect costs, have been a good deal higher than the average net profits on that trade. While some big business interests have found Japan's colonies profitable, the taxpayers of the nation as a whole have paid heavily for acquisition and possession of these territories.

France has done a little better than Japan.[23] No French government finance figures are to be had for the years 1918 to 1921, inclusive. Direct colonial expenses for the rest of the time from 1894 to 1934 were 8,814 million francs. This was 4.6 percent of the colonial trade for the same period, which was 193,461 million francs or 14.7 percent of the total trade. Dividing the total defense expenditures in this same proportion, we get 32,134 million francs as the proportion indirectly chargeable to the colonies. With the direct colonial expenses, this makes 40,948 million francs, or 21.1 percent of the colonial trade in this period. If we leave out both trade and expenses for the World War years and through 1921, the record shows: colonial trade 185,403 million francs, or 15.0 percent of the total trade; direct colonial expenses 8,223 million francs, or 4.4 percent of the colonial trade; colonial share of total defense expenditures, 22,105 million francs; total direct and indirect colonial costs, 30,328 mil-

lion francs, or 16.3 percent of the colonial trade.

Thus, however the figuring is done, a conservative estimate shows that the French taxpayers have paid for the French colonies around 15 percent of the value of all that France has bought from her colonies and all she has sold to them in the past forty years. Something of what the French consider a reasonable return on investments is indicated by the fact that French government bonds yielded 3.9 percent on the average, 1930 to 1934.

The British records also show that overseas territories have cost more than they have been worth in trade, especially the territories over which Britain has control—which does not include the Dominions.[24]

Figures of direct colonial expenditures which mean anything are impossible to get. The only thing we can do in estimating costs, therefore, is to divide total British defense expenditures in the same proportions as the total external trade is divided. In Britain's case this obviously will give a decidedly low item of costs chargeable to relations with overseas British countries, because so nearly all of Britain's naval expenses are due directly to the fact that the British flag floats over such far-flung territory.

From 1894 to 1934, the United Kingdom did with the other British countries, including the Dominions, a total business, imports and exports, of £18,018 million.[25] This was 31.1 percent of all her external trade. For the same years, this proportion of her ordinary defense expenditures, not including the special World War costs, was £1,295 million, or 7.2 percent of the trade with the British countries.[26] If the World War expenses be included, 31.1 percent of the total defense costs would be £3,888 million, or 21.6 per-

[23] Tables XII, XXX, and XXXI.
[24] Tables XVI, XXXVIII, XXXIX and XL.
[25] Table XXXVIII, particularly.
[26] Table XVI.

cent of the trade with the British countries. British government bonds yielded, in 1930 to 1934, an average of 3.8 percent, or only a little more than half the proportion even of the ordinary defense expenses to the trade with the British countries. Thus even if nothing whatever be charged against the colonial trade as direct colonial costs, the United Kingdom's costs of having an empire on which the sun never sets have been considerably higher than any possible profits to the nation as a whole on the trade with other parts of that empire.

But there were heavy expenses, for fighting in Africa, for the defense of India, for naval bases and other defense purposes at Singapore, Hongkong, and other Far East-ern outposts. Part of the costs of these were paid out of local revenues; just what part it is impossible to discover from the published records. But a considerable share came directly out of the pockets of the taxpayers of the United Kingdom.

Thus even though it is impossible to get exact figures of what their colonies have cost the principal colony-holding powers, the official records themselves show clearly that the direct and indirect expenses of the colonies in the past half century have been a good deal more than any possible profits in all the trade with them—allowing nothing for the human lives lost, the human misery caused, and the bitter hatreds engendered by the scramble for colonies.

TRADE AND CONTROL

It is obvious enough that the holding countries would have secured at least part of the trade with the colonial regions even if they had not had political control. There is no basis, in most cases, even for speculating as to what proportion of the trade has been secured *because* of the political control, but the record shows some facts which are most discouraging for those who say control is necessary to get trade.

Every colony-holding country does more business with the territory it controls than it did fifty years ago. But so do the other countries do more business with these colonies. Mere increase of trade between the holding countries and their colonies thus proves nothing about the effect of political control on that trade.

In the case of Japan and France, political control does seem to have given some trade advantage.[27] Both the proportions of the trade of the colonies with the holding country, and of the holding country with the colonies, has increased in recent years. Japan, in

[27] Tables X, XXX, XXXI, and XXXIV.

practice though not officially, has applied the mercantilist technique of regulating the economic development of her colonies to make them fit into her own economic system rather than to give them a rounded economic life of their own or to allow equality of economic opportunity in them to all countries. France has been somewhat less specifically mercantilistic in handling her colonies, but she too has not noticeably kept the economic door open to the other nations. The costs of the colonies, as we have seen, however, have been greater than the profits on all the trade with them, for both these countries. Necessarily, therefore, the ratio of costs to trade has been considerably higher for the trade which has been secured because of political control. Even in these two favorable cases, therefore, it is clear that the acquisition and holding of colonies have meant a substantial net money loss rather than a financial gain to the nation as a whole.

In Italy's case and in Germany's, since the costs amounted to more than the total trade, obviously colonies have been a heavy liability.

Britain's record on its face points to the conclusion that the amount of trade is in inverse rather than direct ratio to the amount of political control, since the figures for the United Kingdom's trade back to 1894 show that of the trade with the overseas British countries a steadily increasing share has been with the Dominions which are self-governing, and a steadily decreasing share with those regions which are controlled from London.

In 1894, only 49.0 percent of Britain's trade with all the British countries was with the self-governing parts of the Empire.[28] In 1913, these regions' share had risen to 50.9 percent. For the five years 1929 to 1933, their share was 54.5 percent, and in 1934 it was 59.9 percent. Thus the proportion increased nearly 11 percent.

By 1894, Canada, Australia, and New Zealand had secured practically complete control of their own finances and tariffs. In the years which followed they and the other Dominions freed themselves from the last remnants of any control whatsoever from London. And in these same years, the Dominions' share in Britain's trade increased from less than half to only a little under two-thirds.

On the other hand, the share of India, British Malaya, and Ceylon in Britain's trade steadily decreased in this period. Britain has had complete control of these regions since well before 1894. She has spent many millions of pounds developing them. Yet from the trade point of view they are relatively only a little more than half as important to her now as they were forty years ago. Their proportions of Britain's intra-Empire trade were: 43.5 percent in

1894; 39.6 percent in 1913; 25.0 percent in 1929-1933; 24.2 percent in 1934.[29]

Yet it would be quite incorrect to conclude that the Dominions' share of Britain's trade has increased *because* political control there has decreased. The truth is, of course, that in 1894 the Dominions were comparatively undeveloped, and that they have developed economically very much more rapidly since then than have India, Malaya, and Ceylon. Consequently, the opportunities to sell British goods, and to get goods which Britain needs, have increased relatively faster in the Dominions than in the British Asiatic countries. The presence or absence of political control has had only an incidental influence, if any.

The other side of the picture, the side of the overseas British countries, is equally unpleasant for those who believe that political control insures exceptional trade opportunities.

The British countries as a whole now do with Britain a considerably smaller share of their total trade than they did in the middle of the nineteenth century, or in 1894: 36.1 percent for 1929-1933, compared with 48.7 percent for 1854-1863, and 47.3 percent for 1894-1903, for example.[30] But the share of the self-governing countries' trade which is with Britain has fallen off much less than that of the other parts of the Empire. It was exactly 50.0 percent in 1854-1863; 56.2 percent in 1894-1903; 47.8 percent in 1913; and 42.3 percent in 1929-1933. India, however, did 52.1 percent of her trade with Britain in 1854-1863, but the proportions dropped to 44.5 percent, 42.3 percent, and 32.2 percent in the successive periods already mentioned. In other words, in 80 years the United Kingdom's share of India's trade has decreased from more than half to less

[28] Table XXXIX-B. Note that this is the proportion not of Britain's total external trade but of her intra-Empire trade.
[29] Table XXIX-B. Also see Footnote 28.
[30] Table XL-A to XL-L.

than a third, while her share of the Dominion areas' business has decreased only from exactly a half to just over two-fifths. But political control has not caused this.

Besides the disappointment to the control-brings-trade enthusiasts, this record reveals a significant fact. All the overseas countries, and especially the countries over which Britain has had and still has control, are distinctly less dependent economically on Britain than they were eighty years ago or even just before the World War. Britain, on the other hand, is substantially more dependent on the British countries, especially on the self-governing Dominions, than she formerly was.

JAPAN'S TRADE IN MANCHURIA

Japan's recent experience in Manchuria supplements and confirms the conclusions from the trade record of the other colony-holding countries for the past half century.[31]

In the four years 1932-1935, Japan exported to Manchuria and the Kwantung Leased Territory 641 million yen worth more of goods than in the four years 1927-1930. In the second four years, she invested 800 million yen in this area, or 159 million yen more than her increase in exports. Political control is not necessary, to get export increases, if a country is willing to pay for those exports out of its own investments, as Japan has done. And besides these investments, Japan has spent around 500 million yen on her military adventure since 1931. Expenditures: 1,300 million yen. Increase in exports: 641 million. Profits: ?

Furthermore, one of the principal excuses for going into Manchuria was that Japan needed raw materials from there. But in 1932-1935, Japan's imports from Manchuria were 152 million yen *less* than in 1927-1930 —while her imports from the world as a whole were down only 34 million yen. From Manchuria, which was supposed to be peculiarly a source of supplies, Japan bought 152 million yen less, while she was buying 118 million yen more from the rest of the world.

The record is even more discouraging from the expansionist point of view if the trade of the whole territory occupied by Chinese be considered. Japan's exports to China Proper dropped, 1932-1935 compared with 1927-1930, by 586 million yen. Her imports from China Proper fell off 186 million yen. So her exports to China and Manchuria together were up only 55 million yen, while her imports from this area were down 338 million yen. Her total trade with Chinese-occupied territory decreased 283 million yen, while her world trade increased 325 million yen. Japan did 608 million yen more business with the rest of the world while she was doing 283 million yen less business with the part occupied by Chinese. She paid— and more—in China for what she gained in Manchuria.

THE RAW MATERIALS FALLACY

The argument that political control is necessary to secure raw materials has no more foundation in fact than the other two chief arguments for taking colonies.

The security-in-war argument can be disposed of very briefly by pointing out, as has been done, that access to raw materials anywhere, whether in the colonies or in foreign countries, depends on the ability to keep communications open with the regions where

[31] Tables XXXVI-A and XXXVI-B.

the raw materials are. Political control or its absence has nothing to do with this. Germany's experience proves the point entirely adequately. Even if her colonies had been made entirely of rubber, cotton, nitrates, vegetable oils, and the various other raw materials which she came to need so badly as the World War progressed, they would have been no use whatever to her because she could not maintain contact with them—any more than she could with the foreign overseas countries from which she might have secured the necessary materials.

Even in peace time, political control gives only minor advantages in access to raw materials.

If the raw materials are to yield a profit, they must be sold. Coal in the mine, and rubber ungrown, pay dividends to no one. But as things now are in the world, if political control be used to raise prices to foreigners exorbitantly, the foreigners can and will go elsewhere to buy. The profits to the private owners of the sources will be reduced correspondingly, and these owners will put pressure on their governments to be "reasonable."

When raw materials are developed for other than commercial purposes, and the development is continued even if the costs are considerably higher than the current world prices for the product, a special situation exists, of course. This is the case with the oil production by the Japanese at the Fushun Collieries in Manchuria, for example. Japan could buy oil distinctly more cheaply than she can produce it, at present, at Fushun. She has sunk a large investment into the distillation plant, and produces oil at excessive costs, for her navy. This is bad business for the Japanese taxpayers. But the Fushun oil losses belong in the same "unproductive" class as the expenses of Japanese battleships. Even in the case of war, however, the Fushun oil would be useful to Japan only if she could

[32] Tables XLIX-A to XLIX-C and L-A to L-K.

keep the plant going and keep control of communications with it—which, quite possibly, she would have trouble doing.

In the field of raw materials as valuable business assets, it now is substantially less practicable for any country to try to use political control to get monopoly profits than it was even a few years ago, for two principal reasons: synthetic substitutes have been and are being developed to take the place of natural products, and new sources of all the important natural mineral and agricultural products are being developed.

Chile, for example, had practically a world monopoly on nitrates, until the process of securing nitrogen from the inexhaustible and completely free source of the air was developed. The experiments with synthetic rubber already have come so near success that it is practically certain that no industrialized country could be deprived of rubber supplies even in time of war. Nitrogen fixation from the air was a direct result of the attempt to deprive Germany of nitrogen supplies during the World War. Synthetic rubber is the result, in part at least, of attempts to exercise monopoly control over sources of supplies. There is every reason to believe that substitutes for other products could and would be developed if similar needs arose. Consequently, political control over natural sources of supply means much less than it formerly did.

It means less, too, because new sources are being brought into production.[32] Without a single exception in the long list of minerals vital to modern industry, the leading producing countries produced a substantially smaller proportion of the world's total in 1933 than they did ten years ago. The United States' share of world iron ore production, for example, dropped from an average of 39.1 percent in 1925-1928 to 19.7 percent in 1933, but France's share increased from 25.8 to

33.0 percent, and Britain's from 5.7 to 8.3 percent.[33] In 1925-1928, the United States produced 50.5 percent of the world's copper; in 1933, 17.0 percent.[34] But Japan's share increased from 4.4 to 6.6 percent; Asia's from 5.1 to 8.6 percent; Europe's from 7.3 to 14.3 percent.

So one might go down the list. The countries which led in the production of the various minerals ten years ago still lead, as a rule. But their leadership is substantially less than it was, and countries which then were producing practically none now are turning out significant amounts. Witness the emergence of Greece and Norway as important suppliers of nickel, for example.

A parallel change has come in agricultural products: cotton, wool, wheat, sugar, rubber, and others of the "replacable" raw materials.[35] Very definitely, the lead of the leaders has been reduced and new sources have been developed.

There is one important non-mineral exception. Japan today takes a distinctly larger share of the world's sea products than she did ten years ago.[36] Her share increased from 29.4 percent in 1925-1929, to 34.5 percent in 1933. Recently, she has been taking more from the sea than all of Europe, while the next three countries, the United States, the United Kingdom, and Norway, have been taking proportionately less than formerly.

In this connection, an interesting point is worth noting, which bears on the question of Japan's much discussed congestion of population and the food supply of the people. As is well known, the Japanese eat a great deal of fish and relatively little meat. But few realize how important a part of the food supply sea products form. The figures show that Japan exports between a fourth and a fifth, by weight, of her takings from the sea. The difference between the catch and the exports is the consumption in Japan. Thus the Japanese people in the past ten years have eaten approximately a fourth of all the fish and other sea products taken by all the nations from all the seas of the world. To get a really accurate picture of the area from which Japanese get their food, therefore, it is necessary to add a large section of the ocean to the dry land of the islands.

This record of the changes in the production of the essential raw materials shows conclusively that if ever political control of sources gave the controlling nations anything like a monopoly advantage, that time has passed. The development of substitutes and of new sources of supply has increased the competition in production to the point where an attempt to maintain monopoly prices for foreigners as against nationals is doomed to failure from the start. Competition will increase, not decrease.

A FORWARD STEP

The older methods of getting and administering colonies proved ruinously costly and led to bitter international jealousies. The present colonial situation is satisfactory to no one. But there is a way out.

It would be no real solution for all the

powers which have colonies simply to withdraw their control. Under present world conditions, it is not practicable to leave any part of the earth without an administration capable of taking a responsible part in the society of nations. The people in some of

[33] Table L-F.
[34] Table L-G.
[35] Tables XLIX-A, XLIX-B, L-A, L-B, and L-C.
[36] Table XLIX-C.

the present colonies probably could set up an administration of their own which would be reasonably satisfactory, if the present control were withdrawn. In many of the colonies, this would be impossible. To remove the present control over these regions would be to leave them in chaos and to make of them simply new centers of conflict. This is particularly true of most of the colonies in Africa and the Pacific.

The alternative to the present system therefore is not the removal of all outside control of the "colonial" areas but the readjustment of the administration of these areas so as to remove the causes of international friction over them. A change in the form and technique of administration will not make these areas any more useful than they have been as population outlets. But the right changes can put an end to the conflicts over colonies which spring from economic causes.

The fundamental requirement is to insure real equality of economic opportunity in the colonies for nationals of all countries; not simply the "most favored nation" equality as between foreigners, but real "free trade" equality as between foreigners and nationals of the controlling country.

The English found free trade decidedly profitable. The Dutch have found it so, in their colonies; and the fact that they have left the doors wide open in their holdings has been one of the principal reasons why no stronger nation has tried to take her colonies from the Netherlands.

If access to the markets and raw materials in colonial territories were made entirely a matter of ordinary business, uncomplicated by distinctions of nationality or politics, the chief cause of the irritation would be removed from the colonial system as it now is. Emotional reactions to talk about "prestige" might continue to be troublesome for a time, but with the economic irritant gone, the emotional inflammation would disappear in due course.

This does not mean that there should be no tariffs or other similar levies in the colonies, to produce revenue for paying the costs of administration. It means simply that whatever such charges are levied should be collected equally from all those doing business in or with the colonial area, without reference to nationality.

The voluntary, unilateral declaration by each of the colony-holding powers that it would put such a completely free-trade policy into effect in its holdings would be a long step in the right direction. But something more than that is needed.

Just as important as the establishment of equality of economic opportunity, perhaps more important, is the assurance that it will be permanent. Governments change, and their policies are altered. The declaration by any government therefore is not sufficient, in itself, to give that assurance of permanence of equality of opportunity which is essential if the danger from the economic motives for taking colonies is to be removed permanently. The single government's declaration must be supplemented and reinforced by some sort of commitment to, or assumption of responsibility by, the society of nations as a whole which will give the necessary assurance that the equality of opportunity will be maintained.

The world already has, in the mandate system, the precedent for the step which needs to be taken. The mandated areas are administered by individual governments, not by an international body. But the administrations are under certain very specific obligations as to what they shall and shall not do. Far from the least important of these is that they shall maintain equality of economic opportunity, in the A and B mandates, as between all the members of the League of Nations, including themselves. The

League, too, has a permanent body to keep watch of the administration of the mandated areas, and while it has no technical authority to enforce obedience to instructions which it may issue relating to this administration, it does have the powerful weapon of publicity.

The powers which received the mandates have taken a long step forward, and established a vital precedent, by pledging themselves to do certain things and to refrain from others, not simply on their own individual assurances but in formal commitments to the society of nations represented by the League. Another step in the same direction needs to be taken.

This next step is for the powers which hold colonies, as a start perhaps those with colonies in Africa, to establish complete equality of economic opportunity within these colonies, *and to give the League the right to insist that that policy be maintained.* To do this would be to go a little, though not much, beyond the requirements of the mandate system. But the mandate system itself is a long step away from the old system which has proved so completely unsatisfactory, and certainly the need is desperate for some real further advance toward a solution of the problem of colonies.

It is not difficult to see what should be done. It will be difficult to get those who speak for the governments to do it. The old and trouble-breeding fallacies still grip the minds of the leaders and people generally. The old sentiment about the "glory" which comes to a nation through having large areas under its flag is still rooted deeply in people's feelings. The old emotions centering around the idea of "independence," and the unwillingness to submit to any outside authority, have been re-aroused by the recent revival of "nationalism." Therefore it will not be easy for those who can act to do so, or for the people to insist that their leaders act sensibly.

Yet the case against the old colonial system is damningly clear. The need for a new method of handling these "colonial" areas is overwhelmingly urgent. Is it too much to hope that people will demand, and that statesmen will show, common sense in dealing with colonies? If they do not, much worse lies ahead than has gone before.

STATISTICAL TABLES
and
OTHER SOURCE MATERIAL

This table gives the figures showing the divisions of the territory of the earth under various political and geographical classifications, and the possessions of the colony-holding countries, and China and Russia, for the years 1878, 1913, and 1933 - i.e., just before the scramble for colonies which started early in the 1880's, just before the World War, and at present. It shows corresponding population figures for 1933 and the density of population. The summary of the figures for the world as a whole is followed by detailed figures for each continent.

These figures show, among other things, that there has been a distinct swing back toward political independence in the world since 1913, though the proportion of independent territory to the total still is less than it was in 1878. In 1878, 66% of the total world area was politically independent; in 1913, 54%; in 1933, 56%. The territory which made up the colonies, dependencies, protectorates, etc., politically controlled from outside (not including the British Dominion areas), on the other hand, were: in 1878, 20%; in 1913, 30%; in 1933, 26%. The non-colony-holding independent countries were: in 1878, 50%; in 1913, 45%; in 1933, 48%.

This down-and-up swing in independence is apparent even in Africa, which politically was much more affected by the pre-war colonial expansion than any other continent. The proportion of Africa which was independent dropped from 57% in 1878 to 3.4% in 1913, but rose again to 6.7% in 1933. Correspondingly, the dependent territory rose from 43% to 84%, then fell to 73% of all Africa, in these same intervals.

The figures for the individual countries show what a small part the "mother country" forms of the principal colonial powers. The United Kingdom, for example, is only 0.8% of the territory under the British flag, while the British dependencies are 31% and the Self-governing British Dominions are 61%. France is 4.5% of French territory; Italy, 11% of Italian; Japan, 19% of Japanese. In 1913, Germany was 14% of the German areas. Every European country which has territory outside of Europe, including Denmark but excepting Spain, is very much smaller than its overseas holdings. The United States' dependencies (including Alaska), on the other hand, are only 19% of all the American territory.

The record of the changes in political status of the various parts of the colonized continents (Africa, the Americas, Asia, and Oceania) is given in the section beginning 111.

TABLE I
POLITICAL STATUS OF WORLD AREAS AND POPULATIONS
Areas in 1,000's Square Kilometers and Square Miles. Populations in 1,000's

	1878 Areas (a)			1913 Areas (a)			1933 Areas (a)				1933 Populations (b)				
	Sq.Kms.	% of World Total	% of Political Group Total	Sq.Kms.	% of World Total	% of Political Group Total	Sq.Kms.	Sq. Miles	% of World Total	% of Political Group Total	Number	% of World Total	% of Political Group Total	Population per Sq.Km.	Population per Sq.Mile
World Totals															
By political control															
Independent	87,634	66.19	100.00	71,035	53.66	100.00	73,564	28,403	55.57	100.00	1,366,391	66.40	100.00	18.6	48.1
Colony holding	21,243	16.05	24.24	11,333	8.56	15.95	10,030	3,873	7.58	13.63	375,762	18.26	27.50	37.5	97.0
Non-colony holding	66,391	50.15	75.76	59,702	45.10	84.05	63,534	24,530	47.99	86.37	990,269	48.14	72.50	15.6	40.4
World Totals	132,390	100.00	....	132,390	100.00	....	132,390	51,116	100.00	....	2,057,800	100.00	....	15.5	40.3
International areas	....	....	....	2,534	1.91	100.00	2,534	978	1.91	100.00	5,869	0.29	100.00	2.3	6.0
Mandates	....	....	....	....	....	....	2,971	1,147	2.24	100.00	18,260	0.89	100.00	6.1	15.9
Dependencies	26,820	20.26	100.00	39,663	29.96	100.00	34,094	13,164	25.75	100.00	636,593	30.94	100.00	18.7	48.4
British self-governing	17,936	13.55	71.84	19,158	14.47	64.98	19,227	7,424	14.52	60.89	30,682	1.49	6.11	1.6	4.1
Holdings of individual countries															
British areas	24,968	18.86	100.00	29,484	22.27	100.00	31,575	12,191	23.86	100.00	501,810	24.39	100.00	15.9	41.2
United Kingdom	313	0.24	1.25	313	0.24	1.06	244	94	0.18	0.77	46,610	2.27	9.29	191.0	495.9
Mandates	....	....	....	....	....	....	2,232	862	1.69	7.07	8,425	0.41	1.68	3.8	9.8
Dependencies	6,719	5.08	26.91	10,013	7.56	33.96	9,872	3,812	7.46	31.27	416,093	20.22	82.92	42.1	109.2
Self-governing	17,936	13.55	71.84	19,158	14.47	64.98	19,227	7,423	14.52	60.89	30,682	1.49	6.11	1.6	4.1
India	4,679	3.53	18.74	4,684	3.54	15.89	4,684	1,808	3.54	14.83	365,100	17.65	72.36	77.5	200.8
French areas	4,934	3.73	100.00	11,493	8.68	100.00	12,371	4,776	9.34	100.00	109,153	5.26	100.00	8.7	22.6
France	551	0.42	11.17	551	0.42	4.79	551	213	0.42	4.45	41,900	2.04	38.74	76.0	196.7
Mandates	....	....	....	....	....	....	682	263	0.52	5.51	6,253	0.30	5.78	9.2	23.8
Dependencies	4,383	3.31	88.83	10,942	8.26	95.21	11,138	4,300	8.41	90.03	60,000	2.92	55.48	5.4	14.0
Italian areas	310	0.23	100.00	2,549	1.93	100.00	2,775	1,071	2.10	100.00	44,671	2.17	100.00	16.1	41.7
Italy	310	0.23	100.00	310	0.23	12.16	310	119	0.23	11.17	42,217	2.05	94.51	136.2	351.8
Dependencies	....	....	....	2,239	1.69	87.84	2,465	952	1.86	88.83	2,454	0.12	5.49	1.0	2.6
Japanese areas (c)	382	0.29	100.00	679	0.51	100.00	1,981	765	1.50	100.00	127,232	6.18	100.00	64.2	166.3
Japan	382	0.29	100.00	382	0.29	56.26	382	147	0.29	19.28	67,500	3.28	53.05	176.7	459.2
Mandates	....	....	....	....	....	....	2	1	0.00	0.10	82	0.00	0.06	41.0	82.0
Dependencies	....	....	....	297	0.22	43.74	1,597	617	1.21	80.62	59,650	2.90	46.88	37.4	96.7
Belgian areas	30	0.02	100.00	2,415	1.82	100.00	2,470	954	1.87	100.00	21,748	1.06	100.00	8.8	22.8
Belgium	30	0.02	100.00	30	0.02	1.24	30	12	0.02	1.21	8,248	0.40	37.93	274.9	687.3
Mandates	....	....	....	....	....	....	55	21	0.04	2.23	3,500	0.17	16.09	63.6	166.7
Dependencies	....	....	....	2,385	1.80	98.76	2,385	921	1.80	96.56	10,000	0.49	45.98	4.2	10.9

(Continued on next page)

TABLE I
POLITICAL STATUS OF WORLD AREAS AND POPULATIONS
(Continued. 1)

	1878 Areas (a)			1913 Areas (a)			1933 Areas (a)				1933 Populations (b)				
	Sq.Kms.	% of World Total	% of Political Group Total	Sq.Kms.	% of World Total	% of Political Group Total	Sq.Kms.	Sq.Miles	% of World Total	% of Political Group Total	Number	% of World Total	% of Political Group Total	Population per Sq.Km.	Population per Sq.Mile
World Totals—Continued															
Chinese areas (c)	11,860	8.96	100.00	11,103	8.39	100.00	9,103	3,515	6.88	100.00	418,200	20.32	100.00	45.9	11.9
China	11,103	8.39	93.62	11,103	8.39	100.00	9,103	3,515	6.88	100.00	418,200	20.32	100.00	45.9	11.9
Dependencies	757	0.57	6.38	...	...	...	...	...	...	...	...	...	...	...	...
Danish areas	357	0.27	100.00	357	0.27	100.00	357	138	0.27	100.00	3,682	0.18	100.00	10.3	26.7
Denmark	44	0.03	12.32	44	0.03	12.32	44	17	0.03	12.32	3,665	0.18	99.54	83.3	215.6
Dependencies	313	0.24	87.68	313	0.24	87.68	313	121	0.24	87.68	17	0.00	0.46	0.1	0.1
German areas (e)	471	0.36	100.00	3,453	2.61	100.00	471	182	0.36	100.00	65,219	3.17	100.00	138.5	358.3
Germany	471	0.36	100.00	471	0.38	13.64	471	182	0.36	100.00	65,219	3.17	100.00	138.5	358.3
Dependencies	...	...	...	2,982	2.25	86.36	...	...	...	...	...	...	...	...	...
Netherlands areas	2,089	1.58	100.00	2,089	1.58	100.00	2,089	806	1.58	100.00	72,030	3.50	100.00	34.5	89.3
Netherlands	34	0.03	1.63	34	0.03	1.63	34	13	0.03	1.63	8,290	0.40	11.51	243.8	637.7
Dependencies	2,055	1.55	98.37	2,055	1.55	98.37	2,055	793	1.55	98.37	63,740	3.10	88.49	31.0	80.4
Portuguese areas	2,184	1.65	100.00	2,184	1.65	100.00	2,184	843	1.65	100.00	15,710	0.76	100.00	7.2	18.6
Portugal	93	0.07	4.26	93	0.07	4.26	93	36	0.07	4.26	7,090	0.34	45.13	76.2	196.9
Dependencies	2,091	1.58	95.74	2,091	1.58	95.74	2,091	807	1.58	95.74	8,620	0.42	54.87	4.1	10.7
Russia	22,700	17.15	100.00	22,700	17.15	100.00	21,177	8,176	16.00	100.00	168,000	8.16	100.00	7.9	20.5
In Asia	15,178	11.46	66.86	15,178	11.46	66.86	15,178	5,860	11.46	71.87	35,500	1.73	21.13	2.3	6.1
In Europe	7,522	5.68	33.14	7,522	5.68	33.14	5,999	2,316	4.53	28.33	132,500	6.44	78.87	22.1	57.2
Spanish areas	954	0.72	100.00	837	0.63	100.00	837	323	0.63	100.00	25,247	1.23	100.00	30.2	78.2
Spain	503	0.38	52.73	503	0.38	60.10	503	194	0.38	60.10	24,242	1.18	96.02	48.2	125.0
Dependencies	451	0.34	47.27	334	0.25	39.90	334	129	0.25	39.90	1,005	0.05	3.98	3.0	7.8
Turkish areas (d)	9,295	7.02	100.00	4,931	3.72	100.00	763	294	0.58	100.00	15,200	0.74	100.00	19.9	51.5
Turkey	763	0.58	8.21	763	0.58	15.47	763	294	0.58	100.00	15,200	0.74	100.00	19.9	51.5
In Asia	739	0.56	7.95	739	0.56	14.99	739	285	0.56	96.85	14,050	0.68	92.43	19.0	49.3
In Europe	24	0.02	0.26	24	0.02	0.49	24	9	0.02	3.15	1,150	0.06	7.57	47.9	127.8
Dependencies	8,532	6.44	91.79	4,168	3.15	84.53	...	...	...	...	...	...	...	...	...
United States areas	9,358	7.07	100.00	9,683	7.31	100.00	9,683	3,739	7.31	100.00	141,014	6.85	100.00	14.6	37.7
United States	7,839	5.92	83.77	7,839	5.92	80.96	7,839	3,027	5.92	80.96	126,000	6.12	89.35	16.1	41.6
Dependencies	1,519	1.15	16.23	1,844	1.39	19.04	1,844	712	1.39	19.04	15,014	0.73	10.65	8.1	21.1

(Continued on next page)

TABLE I
POLITICAL STATUS OF WORLD AREAS AND POPULATIONS
(Continued. 2)

	1878 Areas (a)				1913 Areas (a)				1933 Areas (a)					1933 Populations (b)					
	Sq.Kms.	% of World Total	% of Continental Total	% of Political Group Total	Sq.Kms.	% of World Total	% of Continental Total	% of Political Group Total	Sq.Kms.	Sq.Miles	% of World Total	% of Continental Total	% of Political Group Total	Number	% of World Total	% of Continental Total	% of Political Group Total	Population per Sq.Km.	Population per Sq.Mile
Africa (e)	29,950	22.62	100.00	....	29,950	22.62	100.00	....	29,950	11,564	22.62	100.00	....	144,900	7.04	100.00	....	4.8	12.5
Independent	16,934	12.79	56.54	19.32	1,020	0.77	3.41	1.44	2,020	780	1.53	6.74	2.75	23,210	1.13	16.02	17.0	11.5	29.8
International areas					2,522	1.90	8.42	99.53	2,522	974	1.90	8.42	99.53	5,809	0.28	4.01	98.98	2.3	6.0
Anglo-Egyptian Sudan					2,521	1.90	8.42	99.49	2,521	973	1.90	8.42	99.49	5,729	0.28	3.95	97.64	2.3	5.9
Tangier					1	0.00	0.00	0.04	1	0.4	0.00	0.00	0.04	80	0.00	0.06	1.36	80.0	200.0
Mandates									2,464	951	1.86	8.23	82.94	12,964	0.63	8.95	71.00	5.2	13.3
British									1,927	744	1.46	6.43	6.10	6,411	0.31	4.42	1.28	3.3	8.6
French									482	186	0.36	1.61	3.90	3,053	0.15	2.11	2.82	6.3	16.4
Belgian (e)									55	21	0.04	0.18	2.23	3,500	0.17	2.42	16.09	63.6	166.7
Dependencies	13,016	9.83	43.46	48.53	25,186	19.02	84.09	63.50	21,722	8,387	16.41	72.53	63.71	94,473	4.59	65.20	14.84	4.4	11.3
British (e)	1,536	1.16	5.13	6.15	4,331	3.27	14.46	14.69	4,189	1,617	3.16	13.27	13.27	37,278	1.81	25.73	7.43	8.9	23.1
French (e)	4,020	3.04	13.42	81.48	10,008	7.62	33.68	87.78	10,284	3,971	7.77	34.34	88.72	36,520	1.77	25.20	33.77	3.6	9.2
Italian (e)					2,239	1.69	7.84	87.84	2,462	951	1.86	8.22	96.56	2,320	0.11	1.60	....	0.9	2.4
Belgian					2,385	1.80	7.96	98.76	2,385	921	1.80	7.96	....	10,000	0.49	6.90	45.98	4.2	11.9
German (e)					2,741	2.07	9.15	79.38											
Portuguese	2,068	1.56	6.90	84.69	2,068	1.56	6.90	79.38	2,068	798	1.56	6.90	94.69	7,350	0.36	5.07	46.79	3.6	9.2
Spanish (d)	28	0.02	0.09	2.94	334	0.25	1.12	39.90	334	129	0.25	1.12	39.90	1,005	0.05	0.69	3.98	3.0	7.8
Turkish (d)	5,364	4.05	17.91	57.71	1,000	0.76	3.34	20.28											
British self-governing (Union of S. Africa)					1,222	0.92	4.08	4.14	1,222	472	0.92	4.08	3.87	8,430	0.41	5.82	1.68	6.9	17.9
Total British areas	1,536	1.16	5.13	6.15	5,553	4.19	18.07	18.83	7,338	2,853	5.54	24.50	23.24	52,119	2.53	35.97	10.39	7.1	18.4
Total French areas	4,020	3.04	13.42	81.48	10,088	7.62	33.68	87.78	10,786	4,157	8.13	35.95	87.03	39,573	1.92	27.31	36.59	3.7	9.5
Total Belgian areas					2,385	1.80	7.96	98.76	2,440	942	1.84	8.14	98.79	13,500	0.66	9.32	62.07	6.5	14.3
The Americas	40,555	30.63	100.00	....	40,555	30.63	100.00	....	40,555	15,658	30.63	100.00	....	282,490	12.76	100.00	....	6.5	16.8
North America	19,635	14.83	48.42	....	19,635	14.83	48.42	....	19,635	7,581	14.83	48.42	....	137,130	6.66	52.24	....	7.0	18.1
Independent (United States)	7,839	5.92	19.33	8.95	7,839	5.92	19.33	11.04	7,839	3,027	5.92	19.33	10.66	126,000	6.12	48.24	9.22	16.1	41.6
Dependencies	1,832	1.39	4.52	6.83	1,832	1.39	4.52	4.62	1,832	707	1.39	4.52	5.37	81	0.00	0.03	0.01	0.04	0.1
Greenland (Danish)	313	0.24	0.77	87.68	313	0.24	0.77	87.68	313	121	0.24	0.77	87.68	17	0.00	0.01	0.46	0.05	0.1
Alaska (United States)	1,519	1.15	3.75	16.23	1,519	1.15	3.75	15.00	1,519	586	1.15	3.75	15.69	60	0.00	0.02	0.04	0.04	0.1
French	0.2	0.00	0.00	0.00	0.2	0.00	0.00	0.00	0.2	0.07	0.00	0.00	0.00	4	0.00	0.00	0.00	20.0	57.1
British self-governing	9,964	7.53	24.57	39.91	9,964	7.53	24.57	33.79	9,964	3,874	7.53	24.57	31.56	11,049	0.54	4.21	2.20	1.1	2.9
Canada	9,542	7.21	23.53	38.22	9,542	7.21	23.53	32.36	9,542	3,684	7.21	23.53	30.22	10,760	0.52	4.10	2.14	1.1	2.9
Newfoundland and Labrador	422	0.32	1.04	1.69	422	0.32	1.04	1.43	422	163	0.32	1.04	1.34	289	0.01	0.11	0.06	0.7	1.8
Mexico and the Caribbean	2,765	2.09	6.82	....	2,765	2.09	6.82	....	2,765	1,066	2.09	6.82	....	36,580	1.78	13.94	....	13.2	34.3
Independent	2,581	1.95	6.37	2.95	2,695	2.04	6.65	3.79	2,695	1,041	2.04	6.65	3.66	32,115	1.56	12.23	2.35	11.9	30.9
Dependencies	184	0.14	0.45	0.69	70	0.05	0.18	0.19	70	27	0.05	0.18	0.21	4,465	0.22	1.70	0.70	63.8	165.4
British	55	0.04	0.14	0.22	55	0.04	0.14	0.18	55	21	0.04	0.14	0.17	2,182	0.11	0.83	0.43	39.7	103.9
French	2.8	0.00	0.00	0.06	2.8	0.00	0.00	0.02	2.8	1.1	0.00	0.01	0.02	510	0.02	0.19	0.47	182.1	463.6
Netherlands	2.1	0.00	0.00	0.05	2.1	0.00	0.00	0.05	2.1	0.4	0.00	0.00	0.05	79	0.00	0.03	0.11	79.0	197.5
Spanish	125	0.09	0.31	13.10															
United States					11	0.01	0.03	0.1	11	4	0.01	0.03	0.11	1,694	0.08	0.65	1.20	154.0	423.5
South America	18,155	13.71	44.77	....	18,155	13.71	44.77	....	18,155	7,010	13.71	44.77	....	88,780	4.31	33.82	....	4.9	12.7
Independent	17,668	13.35	43.57	20.16	17,668	13.35	43.57	24.87	17,668	6,822	13.35	43.57	24.02	88,269	4.29	33.63	6.46	5.0	12.9
Dependencies	487	0.37	1.20	1.82	487	0.37	1.20	1.23	487	188	0.37	1.20	1.43	511	0.02	0.19	0.08	1.0	2.7
British	247	0.19	0.61	0.99	247	0.19	0.61	0.84	247	95	0.19	0.61	0.78	324	0.02	0.12	0.06	1.3	3.4
French	90	0.07	0.22	1.83	90	0.07	0.22	0.78	90	35	0.07	0.22	0.73	26	0.00	0.10	0.02	0.3	0.7
Netherlands	150	0.11	0.37	7.18	150	0.11	0.37	7.18	150	58	0.11	0.37	7.18	161	0.01	0.06	0.22	1.1	2.8

(Continued on next page)

TABLE I

POLITICAL STATUS OF WORLD AREAS AND POPULATIONS

(Continued. 3)

	1878 Areas (a)				1913 Areas (a)				1933 Areas (a)					1933 Populations (b)					
	Sq.Kms.	% of World Total	% of Conti-nental Total	% of Politi-cal Group Total	Sq.Kms.	% of World Total	% of Conti-nental Total	% of Politi-cal Group Total	Sq.Kms.	Sq.Miles	% of World Total	% of Conti-nental Total	% of Politi-cal Group Total	Number	% of World Total	% of Conti-nental Total	% of Politi-cal Group Total	Population per Sq.Km.	Population per Sq.Mile
All the Americas	40,555	30.63	100.00		40,555	30.63	100.00		40,555	15,658	30.63	100.00		262,490	12.76	100.00	18.03		
Independent	28,088	21.22	69.29	32.05	28,202	21.30	69.54	39.70	28,202	10,889	21.30	69.54	38.34	246,384	11.97	93.87		8.7	23.5
Dependencies	2,503	1.89	6.17	9.33	2,389	1.80	5.89	6.02	2,389	922	1.80	5.89	7.01	5,057	0.25	1.93	0.79	2.1	5.2
British	302	0.23	0.74	1.21	302	0.23	0.74	1.02	302	117	0.23	0.74	0.96	2,506	0.12	0.95	0.50	8.3	21.4
French	93	0.07	0.23	1.88	93	0.07	0.23	0.81	93	36	0.07	0.23	0.75	540	0.03	0.21	0.50	5.8	15.0
Danish	313	0.24	0.77	87.68	313	0.24	0.77	87.68	313	121	0.24	0.77	87.68	17	0.00	0.01	0.46	0.05	0.1
Netherlands	151	0.11	0.37	7.23	151	0.11	0.37	7.23	151	58	0.11	0.37	7.23	240	0.01	0.09	0.33	1.6	4.1
Spanish	125	0.09	0.31	13.10															
United States	1,519	1.15	3.75	16.23	1,530	1.16	3.77	15.80	1,530	591	1.16	3.77	15.80	1,754	0.09	0.67	1.25	1.1	3.0
British self-governing	9,964	7.53	24.57	39.91	9,964	7.53	24.57	33.79	9,964	3,847	7.53	24.57	31.56	11,049	0.54	4.21	2.20	1.1	2.9
Total British areas	10,266	7.75	25.31	41.12	10,266	7.75	25.31	34.82	10,266	3,964	7.75	25.31	32.51	13,555	0.66	5.16	2.70	1.3	3.4
Total United States areas	9,358	7.08	23.10	100.00	9,369	7.08	23.10	96.76	9,369	3,617	7.08	23.10	96.76	127,754	6.21	48.67	90.60	13.6	35.3
Asia	41,911	31.66	100.00		41,911	31.66	100.00		41,911	16,182	31.66	100.00		1,121,200	54.49	100.00		26.8	69.3
The Far East	30,766	23.24	73.41	31.35	30,766	23.24	73.41	38.26	30,766	11,879	23.24	73.41	35.18	700,151	34.02	62.45	39.14	22.8	58.9
Independent (including Russia)	27,472	20.75	65.55		27,181	20.53	64.86		25,881	9,993	19.55	61.75		534,870	25.99	47.71		20.7	53.5
Dependencies	3,294	2.49	7.86	12.28	3,585	2.71	8.55	9.04	4,885	1,886	3.69	11.66	14.32	165,281	8.03	14.74	25.96	87.6	87.6
British	77	0.06	0.18	0.31	332	0.25	0.79	1.13	332	128	0.25	0.79	1.05	6,061	0.30	0.54	1.21	18.3	47.4
French	246	0.19	0.59	4.99	737	0.56	1.76	6.41	737	285	0.56	1.76	5.96	22,550	1.10	2.01	20.85	30.6	79.1
Japanese (c)					297	0.22	0.71	43.74	1,597	617	1.21	3.81	80.62	59,650	2.90	5.32	46.88	37.4	96.7
Chinese (c)	762	0.57	1.79	6.38															
Netherlands	1,904	1.44	4.54	91.14	1,904	1.44	4.54	91.14	1,904	735	1.44	4.54	91.14	63,500	3.09	5.66	88.16	33.4	86.4
Portuguese	19	0.01	0.05	0.87	19	0.01	0.05	0.87	19	7	0.01	0.05	0.87	670	0.03	0.06	4.26	35.3	95.7
Spanish																			
United States	296	0.22	0.71	31.03	296	0.22	0.71	3.06	296	114	0.22	0.71	3.06	12,850	0.62	1.15	9.11	43.4	112.7
The Middle East	5,595	4.23	13.35		5,595	4.23	13.35		5,595	2,160	4.23	13.35		382,383	18.58	34.10		68.3	177.0
Independent	840	0.63	2.00	0.96	840	0.63	2.00	1.18	840	324	0.63	2.00	1.14	12,850	0.62	1.15	0.94	15.3	39.7
Dependencies	4,755	3.59	11.35	17.73	4,755	3.59	11.35	11.99	4,755	1,836	3.59	11.35	13.95	369,533	17.96	32.96	58.05	77.7	201.3
British	4,745	3.58	11.32	19.00	4,750	3.59	11.33	16.11	4,750	1,834	3.59	11.33	15.04	368,643	17.91	32.88	73.46	77.6	201.0
French					1	0.00	0.00	0.01	1	0.4	0.00	0.00	0.01	290	0.01	0.03	0.27	290.0	725.0
Chinese	5	0.00	0.00	0.02															
Portuguese	4	0.00	0.01	0.18	4	0.00	0.01	0.18	4	2	0.00	0.01	0.18	600	0.03	0.05	3.82	150.0	300.0
India	4,679	3.53	11.16	18.74	4,684	3.54	11.18	15.89	4,684	1,808	3.54	11.18	14.83	363,100	17.65	32.38	72.36	77.5	200.8
The Near East	5,550	4.19	13.24		5,550	4.19	13.24		5,550	2,143	4.19	13.24		38,667	1.88	3.45		7.0	18.0
Independent (d)	2,373	1.79	5.66	2.71	2,369	1.79	5.66	3.33	5,267	2,034	3.98	12.57	7.16	33,350	1.62	2.97	2.44	6.3	16.4
Mandates									266	103	0.20	0.63	8.96	4,640	0.23	0.41	25.41	17.4	45.0
British									66	26	0.05	0.16	0.21	1,440	0.07	0.13	0.29	21.8	57.6
French									200	77	0.15	0.48	1.62	3,200	0.16	0.29	2.96	16.0	41.6
Dependencies	3,177	2.40	7.58	11.85	3,181	2.40	7.59	8.02	17	7	0.01	0.03	0.05	677	0.03	0.06	0.11	39.8	96.7
British	9	0.01	0.02	0.04	13	0.01	0.03	0.04	14	6	0.01	0.03	0.04	543	0.03	0.05	0.11	38.6	108.6
Italian									3	1	0.00	0.01	0.11	134	0.01	0.01	0.30	44.7	134.0
Turkish (d)	3,168	2.39	7.56	34.08	3,168	2.39	7.56	64.25											
All Asia	41,911	31.66	100.00		41,911	31.66	100.00		41,911	16,178	31.66	100.00		1,121,200	54.49	100.00		26.8	69.3
Independent (including Turkey and Russia)	30,685	23.18	73.22	35.01	30,390	22.95	72.51	42.78	31,988	12,351	24.16	76.33	43.48	581,070	28.24	51.83	42.53	18.2	47.0
Mandates									266	103	0.20	0.63	8.96	4,640	0.23	0.41	25.41	17.4	45.0
British									66	25	0.05	0.16	0.21	1,440	0.07	0.13	0.29	21.8	57.6
French									200	77	0.15	0.48	1.62	3,220	0.16	0.29	2.96	16.0	41.6

(Continued on next page)

TABLE I
POLITICAL STATUS OF WORLD AREAS AND POPULATIONS
(Continued. 4)

Area	1878 Sq.Kms.	1878 % World Total	1878 % Conti-nental Total	1878 % Political Group Total	1913 Sq.Kms.	1913 % World Total	1913 % Conti-nental Total	1913 % Political Group Total	1933 Sq.Kms.	1933 Sq.Miles	1933 % World Total	1933 % Conti-nental Total	1933 % Political Group Total	1933 Number	1933 % World Total	1933 % Conti-nental Total	1933 % Political Group Total	Population per Sq.Km.	Population per Sq.Mile
Asia—Continued																			
Dependencies	11,266	8.48	26.79	41.86	11,521	8.70	27.49	29.05	9,657	3,729	7.29	23.04	28.32	535,491	26.02	47.76	84.12	55.5	143.6
British	4,831	3.65	11.53	19.35	5,095	3.85	12.16	17.28	5,096	1,968	3.85	12.16	16.14	375,247	18.24	33.47	74.78	73.7	190.9
French	247	0.19	0.59	5.01	738	0.56	1.76	6.42	738	285	0.56	1.76	5.97	22,840	1.11	2.04	21.12	30.9	80.1
Italian (c)					297	0.22	0.71		3		0.00	0.01	0.11	134	0.01	0.01	0.30	44.7	134.0
Japanese (c)									1,597	617	1.21	3.81	80.62	59,650	2.90	5.32	46.88	37.4	96.7
Chinese (c)	757	0.57	1.81	6.38															
Netherlands	1,904	1.44	4.54	91.14	1,904	1.44	4.54	91.14	1,904	735	1.44	4.54	91.14	63,500	3.09	5.66	88.16	33.4	86.4
Portuguese	23	0.02	0.05	1.05	23	0.02	0.05	1.05	23	9	0.02	0.05	1.05	1,270	0.06	0.11	8.08	55.2	141.1
Spanish	296	0.22	0.71	31.03															
Turkish (d)	3,168	2.39	7.56	34.08	3,168	2.39	7.56	64.25											
United States					296	0.22	0.71	3.06	296	114	0.22	0.71	3.06	12,850	0.62	1.15	9.11	43.4	112.7
India	4,679	3.53	11.16	18.74	4,684	3.54	11.18	15.89	4,684	1,808	3.54	11.18	14.83	363,100	17.65	32.38	72.36	77.5	200.8
Total British areas	4,831	3.65	11.53	19.35	5,095	3.85	12.16	17.28	5,162	1,993	3.90	12.32	16.35	376,687	18.31	33.60	75.06	73.0	189.0
Total French areas	247	0.19	0.59	5.01	738	0.56	1.76	6.42	938	362	0.71	2.24	7.58	26,040	1.27	2.32	24.08	27.8	71.9
Total Japanese areas (c)	382	0.29	0.91	100.00	679	0.51	1.62	100.00	1,979	764	1.49	4.72	99.90	127,150	6.18	11.34	100.00	64.2	166.4
Japan	382	0.29	0.91	100.00	382	0.29	0.91	56.26	382	147	0.29	0.91	19.28	67,500	3.28	6.02	53.05	176.7	459.2
Dependencies					297	0.22	0.71	43.74	1,597	617	1.21	3.81	80.62	59,650	2.90	5.32	46.88	37.4	96.7
Total Chinese areas (c)	11,860	8.96	28.30	100.00	11,103	8.39	26.49	100.00	9,103	3,515	6.88	21.72	100.00	418,200	20.32	37.30	100.00	45.9	119.0
China (including Mongolia, Sinkiang (c), and Tibet)	11,103	8.39	26.49	93.62	11,103	8.39	26.49	100.00	9,103	3,515	6.88	21.72	100.00	418,200	20.32	37.30	100.00	45.9	119.0
Dependencies (under Chinese suzerainty)	757	0.57	1.81	6.38															
Total Turkish areas (d)	3,907	2.95	9.32	42.03	3,907	2.95	9.32	79.23	739	285	0.56	1.76	96.85	14,050	0.68	1.25	92.43	19.0	49.3
Turkey-in-Asia	739	0.56	1.76	7.95	739	0.56	1.76	14.99	739	285	0.56	1.76	96.85	14,050	0.68	1.25	92.43	19.0	49.3
Dependencies	3,168	2.39	7.56	34.08	3,168	2.39	7.56	64.25											
Europe	11,424	8.63	100.00		11,424	8.63	100.00		11,424	4,411	8.63	100.00		519,140	25.23	100.00		45.4	117.7
Independent	11,423	8.63	99.99	13.03	11,423	8.63	99.99	16.08	11,354	4,384	8.59	99.39	15.43	515,727	25.06	99.34	37.74	45.4	117.6
Non-colony holding (including Russia in Europe)	9,861	7.45	86.32	11.25	9,050	6.84	79.22	12.74	9,545	3,685	7.22	83.55	12.98	333,465	16.21	64.23	24.40	34.9	90.5
Colony holding	1,562	1.18	13.67	1.78	2,373	1.79	20.77	3.34	1,809	698	1.37	15.84	2.46	182,262	8.86	35.11	13.34	100.8	261.1
Britain	313	0.24	2.74	1.25	313	0.24	2.74	1.06	244	94	0.18	2.14	0.77	45,610	2.27	8.98	9.29	191.0	495.9
France	551	0.42	4.82	11.17	551	0.42	4.82	4.79	551	213	0.42	4.82	4.45	41,900	2.04	8.07	38.74	76.0	196.7
Italy					310	0.23	2.71	12.16	310	120	0.23	2.71	11.17	42,217	2.05	8.13	94.51	136.2	351.8
Belgium					30	0.02	0.26	1.24	30	12	0.02	0.26	1.21	8,248	0.40	1.59	37.93	274.9	687.3
Denmark	44	0.03	0.39	12.32	44	0.03	0.39	12.32	44	17	0.03	0.39	1.21	3,665	0.18	0.71	9.54	83.3	215.6
Germany					471	0.36	4.12	13.64											
Netherlands	34	0.03	0.30	1.63	34	0.03	0.30	1.63	34	13	0.03	0.30	1.63	8,090	0.40	1.60	11.51	243.8	637.9
Portugal	93	0.07	0.81	4.26	93	0.07	0.81	4.25	93	36	0.07	0.81	4.25	7,090	0.34	1.37	45.13	76.2	196.9
Spain	503	0.38	4.41	52.73	503	0.38	4.40	60.10	503	194	0.38	4.40	60.10	24,242	1.18	4.67	96.02	48.2	125.0
Turkey (in Europe)	24	0.02	0.21	0.26	24	0.02	0.21	0.49	24		0.02	0.21	0.49						
Dependencies: British	1	0.00	0.01	0.00	1	0.00	0.01	0.00	1	0.4	0.00	0.01	0.00	413	0.02	0.08	0.08	413.0	1,032.5
British self-governing (Irish Free State)									69	27	0.05	0.60	0.22	3,000	0.15	0.58	0.60	43.5	111.1
Total British areas	314	0.24	2.75	1.26	314	0.24	2.75	1.06	314	121	0.24	2.75	0.99	50,023	2.44	9.64	9.97	159.3	413.4

(Continued on next page)

TABLE I
POLITICAL STATUS OF WORLD AREAS AND POPULATIONS
(Continued. 5)

	1878 Areas (a) Sq.Kms.	1878 % of World Total	1878 % of Continental Total	1878 % of Political Group Total	1913 Areas (a) Sq.Kms.	1913 % of World Total	1913 % of Continental Total	1913 % of Political Group Total	1933 Areas (a) Sq.Kms.	1933 Areas Sq.Miles	1933 % of World Total	1933 % of Continental Total	1933 % of Political Group Total	1933 Pop. Number	Pop. % of World Total	Pop. % of Continental Total	Pop. % of Political Group Total	Population per Sq.Km.	Population per Sq.Mile
Oceania:	8,550.	6.46	100.00	...	8,550	6.46	100.00	...	8,550	3,301	6.46	100.00	...	10,080	0.49	100.00	...	1.2	3.1
Independent.	504	0.38	5.89	0.58	12	0.01	0.14	0.47	12	5	0.01	0.14	0.47	...	...	...	...	...	...
International area (New Hebrides)	...	...	...	...	...	...	...	...	...	...	...	...	...	60	0.00	0.60	1.02	5.0	12.0
Mandates	...	...	...	...	...	...	...	...	241	93	0.18	2.82	8.11	656	0.03	6.51	3.59	2.7	7.1
British	...	...	...	...	...	...	...	...	239	92	0.18	2.80	0.76	574	0.03	5.70	0.11	2.4	6.2
Japanese	...	...	...	...	...	...	...	...	2	1	0.00	0.02	0.10	82	0.00	0.81	0.06	41.0	82.0
Dependencies.	74	0.06	0.87	0.28	566	0.43	6.62	1.43	325	125	0.25	3.80	0.95	1,159	0.06	11.50	0.18	3.6	9.3
British.	49	0.04	0.56	0.20	284	0.21	3.32	0.96	284	110	0.21	3.32	0.90	649	0.03	6.44	0.13	2.3	5.9
French.	23	0.02	0.27	0.47	23	0.02	0.27	0.20	23	9	0.02	0.27	0.19	100	0.00	1.00	0.09	4.3	11.1
German.	...	...	...	...	241	0.18	2.82	7.59	...	...	...	...	...	...	...	...	...	...	...
Spanish	2	0.00	0.04	0.31	18	0.01	0.21	0.19	...	...	...	...	...	...	...	...	...	...	...
United States	...	...	...	...	18	0.01	0.21	0.19	18	7	0.01	0.21	0.19	410	0.02	4.07	0.29	22.8	58.6
British self-governing.	7,972	6.02	93.24	31.93	7,972	6.02	93.24	27.04	7,972	3,078	6.02	93.24	25.25	8,203	0.40	81.37	1.63	1.0	2.7
Australia.	7,704	5.82	90.11	30.86	7,704	5.82	90.11	26.13	7,704	2,975	5.82	90.11	24.40	6,657	0.32	66.04	1.33	0.9	2.2
New Zealand.	268	0.20	3.13	1.07	268	0.20	3.13	0.91	268	103	0.20	3.13	0.85	1,546	0.08	15.34	0.31	5.8	15.0
Total British areas	8,021	6.06	93.80	32.13	8,256	6.24	96.56	28.00	8,495	3,280	6.42	99.36	26.90	9,426	0.46	93.51	1.88	1.1	2.9

Sources:
Calculated principally from data in: League of Nations, Statistical Year-Book, 1934/35.

Notes:
(a) Area data: Figures given for 1933 are those in the Year-Book, except for the adjustments for China and Japan noted. Areas for 1878 and 1913 are calculated from Year-Book 1933 figures, with suitable adjustments for changes of political status, though the areas of the regions whose political status has changed have been taken as given in the Year-Book. Conversions to square miles from the Year-Book figures, which are in square kilometers, have been made at the rate of: 1 sq. km. = 0.3861 sq. miles.

(b) Population data: Continental totals are as given in the Year-Book. In the Year-Book these totals vary, in some cases, by several units from the sum of the figures given for the individual countries.

(c) For 1933, the following deductions have been made from the area and population figures for China given in the Year-Book:
(1) On account of "Manchukuo": 1,300,000 sq. kms. and 30,800,000 in population. Though Manchukuo nominally is independent, these amounts have been added to Japanese dependencies.
(2) On account of the Mongolian Soviet Republic: 700,000 sq.kms. and 1,000,000 of population. These are included in the independent totals.

(d) For the purposes of these comparisons the Turkish areas are treated as follows:
(1) The area given in the League Year-Book for 1933 (763,000 sq.kms.; 24,000 in Europe and 739,000 in Asia) is treated as "Turkey Proper", this being, roughly, the heart of the former Turkish Empire.
(2) The other parts of the former Turkish Empire in Africa and the Near East are treated as Turkish dependencies in 1878 and 1913. These were: Egypt (1,000,000 sq.kms.), the Anglo-Egyptian Sudan (2,521,000 sq.kms.), Libya (1,842,000 sq.kms.), Arabia (2,600,000 sq.kms.), Iraq (302,000 sq.kms.), and the French and British mandate areas (266,000 sq.kms.). The Anglo-Egyptian Sudan and Libya had passed from Turkish suzerainty in 1913.

(e) Transfers of territory in Africa have been taken into account as follows:
(1) To Italy since 1919, from France: 81,000 sq.kms., from Britian: 142,000 sq.kms. total: 223,000 sq.kms.
(2) To Germany in 1911, from France: 272,000 sq.kms., returned in 1919.

TABLE II
DIVISIONS OF TERRITORIAL HOLDINGS BY WESTERN AND NON-WESTERN CONTROL
Areas in 1,000's of Square Kilometers

The extent to which the Western nations pushed their expansion in the 30 years before the World War and have added slightly to their territory since 1913 is shown in this table. They held only 26% of Africa in 1878, but 93% in 1913 and 1933. More than half of Asia already was under their control in 1878: 54%. In 1913, they held 55% of this continent, and in 1933, 56%. The change from 1913 to 1933 was due primarily to the transfer of certain Turkish dependencies to British and French mandate control. Westerners controlled all the Americas in 1878, as they still do, and all but a small part of Oceania. Now all of Oceania except the 0.02% of the land which Japan holds under mandate, is controlled by Western powers. Of the world as a whole, the Westerners held 66% in 1878, 84% in 1913, and 85% in 1933.

	Africa Area	Africa % of Continental Total	Africa % of Political Total	The Americas Area	Amer. % of Continental Total	Amer. % of Political Total	Asia Area	Asia % of Continental Total	Asia % of Political Total	Europe Area	Europe % of Continental Total	Europe % of Political Total	Oceania Area	Oceania % of Continental Total	Oceania % of Political Total	Total Area	Total % of Continental Total	Total % of Political Total
Independent non-colony holding.																		
Western.																		
1878.	128	0.43	0.28	20,249	49.93	44.59	15,178	36.21	33.42	9,861	86.32	21.71	0	0	...	45,416	34.30	100.00
1913.	0	...	...	20,363	50.21	45.66	15,178	36.21	34.04	9,050	79.22	20.30	0	0	...	44,591	33.68	100.00
1933.	0	...	...	20,363	50.21	45.19	15,178	36.21	33.68	9,521	83.34	21.13	0	0	...	45,062	34.04	100.00
Non-Western.																		
1878.	16,806	56.11	80.12	0	0	...	3,665	8.74	17.48	0	0	...	504	5.89	2.40	20,975	15.84	100.00
1913.	1,020	3.41	6.75	0	...	...	14,091	33.62	93.25	0	...	...	0	0	...	15,111	11.41	100.00
1933.	2,020	6.74	10.94	0	...	...	16,428	39.20	88.93	24	0.21	0.13	0	0	...	18,472	13.95	100.00
Total																		
1878.	16,934	56.54	25.51	20,249	49.93	30.50	18,843	44.96	28.38	9,861	86.32	14.85	504	5.89	0.76	66,391	50.15	100.00
1913.	1,020	3.41	1.71	20,363	50.21	34.11	29,269	69.84	49.03	9,050	79.22	15.16	0	...	...	59,702	45.10	100.00
1933.	2,020	6.74	3.18	20,363	50.21	32.05	31,606	75.41	49.75	9,545	83.55	15.02	0	...	...	63,534	47.99	100.00
Colony holding (including holdings)																		
Western.																		
1878.	7,652	25.55	17.06	20,306	50.07	45.28	7,301	17.42	16.28	1,539	13.47	3.43	8,046	94.11	17.94	44,844	33.87	100.00
1913.	27,930	93.26	41.64	20,192	49.79	30.10	8,056	19.22	12.01	2,350	20.57	3.50	8,550	100.00	12.75	67,078	50.67	100.00
1933.	27,930	93.26	41.76	20,192	49.79	30.19	8,326	19.87	12.45	1,879	16.45	2.81	8,648	99.98	12.78	66,875	50.51	100.00
Non-Western.																		
1878.	5,364	17.91	25.36	0	...	...	15,767	37.62	74.53	24	0.21	0.11	0	0	...	21,155	15.98	100.00
1913.	1,000	3.34	17.83	0	...	...	4,586	10.94	81.75	24	0.21	0.43	0	0	...	5,610	4.24	100.00
1933.	0	...	...	0	...	...	1,979	4.72	99.90	...	...	...	2	0.02	0.10	1,981	1.50	100.00
Total																		
1878.	13,016	43.46	19.72	20,306	50.07	30.77	23,068	55.04	34.95	1,563	13.68	2.37	8,046	94.11	12.19	65,999	49.85	100.00
1913.	28,930	96.59	39.80	20,192	49.79	27.78	12,642	30.17	17.39	2,374	20.78	3.27	8,550	100.00	11.76	72,688	54.90	100.00
1933.	27,930	93.26	40.56	20,192	49.79	29.32	10,305	24.59	14.97	1,879	16.45	2.73	8,550	100.00	12.42	68,856	52.01	100.00
Totals																		
Western.																		
1878.	7,780	25.98	8.62	40,555	100.00	44.93	22,479	53.64	24.90	11,400	99.79	12.63	8,046	94.11	8.91	90,260	68.18	100.00
1913.	27,930	93.26	25.01	40,555	100.00	36.32	23,234	55.44	20.81	11,400	99.79	10.21	8,550	100.00	7.66	111,669	84.35	100.00
1933.	27,930	93.26	24.95	40,555	100.00	36.23	23,504	56.08	21.00	11,400	99.79	10.18	8,548	99.98	7.64	111,937	84.55	100.00
Non-Western.																		
1878.	22,170	74.02	52.62	0	...	...	19,432	46.36	46.12	24	0.21	0.06	504	5.89	1.19	42,130	31.82	100.00
1913.	2,020	6.74	9.75	0	...	...	18,677	44.56	90.14	24	0.21	0.12	2	0.02	0.01	20,721	15.65	100.00
1933.	2,020	6.74	9.88	0	...	...	18,407	43.92	90.00	24	0.21	0.12	...	...	...	20,453	15.45	100.00
Total																		
1878.	29,950	100.00	22.62	40,555	100.00	30.63	41,911	100.00	31.66	11,424	100.00	8.63	8,550	100.00	6.46	132,390	100.00	100.00
1913.	29,950	100.00	22.62	40,555	100.00	30.63	41,911	100.00	31.66	11,424	100.00	8.63	8,550	100.00	6.46	132,390	100.00	100.00
1933.	29,950	100.00	22.62	40,555	100.00	30.63	41,911	100.00	31.66	11,424	100.00	8.63	8,550	100.00	6.46	132,390	100.00	100.00

For sources and other notes see Table I.

TABLE III
CHANGES IN TERRITORIAL HOLDINGS OF THE WESTERN POWERS
Areas in 1,000's of Square Kilometers

In 1878, the British Empire included more territory than that under any other flag. Only between 1878 and 1913, and only in Africa, did any other Western power add more than the British Empire to its territorial holdings in the past six decades. France got more square kilometers in Africa than Britain, in the pre-war rush for colonies: 6,068,000 sq.kms. as against Britain's 4,017,000 sq.kms. But in every other part of the world in the 1878–1913 period, and in Africa also since 1913, the British boundaries have moved outward more than any other. The French additions in Africa in 1878–1913, however, were enough larger than the British, by a small margin, to give France a larger territorial gain than Britain between 1878 and 1933, by 830,000 sq.kms. Britain remains considerably the largest landholder in the world, as the percentage figures in Table I show.

	Total Western Holdings (a)	British	French	Italian	Belgium	German	Netherlands	Portuguese	Spanish	United States	International Areas	Other Western Powers (a)
Africa												
1933 holdings	27,930	7,338	10,766	2,462	2,440	0	...	2,068	334	...	2,522	0
1913 holdings	27,930	5,553	10,088	2,239	2,385	2,741	...	2,068	334	...	2,522	0
1878 holdings	7,780	1,536	4,020	0	0	0	...	2,068	28	...	0	128
Change, 1878–1913	+20,150	+4,017	+6,068	+2,239	+2,385	+2,741	...	0	+306	...	+2,522	−128
With Western powers	0	+128	0	0	0	0	...	0	0	...	0	−128
Increase of Western holdings	+20,150	+3,889	+6,068	+2,239	+2,385	+2,741	...	0	+306	...	+2,522	0
Change, 1931–1933	0	+1,785	+678	+223	+55	−2,741	...	0	0	...	0	0
With Western powers	0	+1,785	+678	+223	+55	−2,741	...	0	0	...	0	0
Increase of Western holdings	0	0	0	0	0	0	...	0	0	...	0	0
Change, 1878–1933	+20,150	+5,802	+6,746	+2,462	+2,440	0	...	0	+306	...	+2,522	−128
With Western powers (b)	0	−14	+33	+109	0	0	...	0	0	...	0	−128
Increase of Western holdings	+20,150	+5,816	+6,713	+2,353	+2,440	0	...	0	+306	...	+2,522	0
Asia												
1933 holdings	23,504	5,162	938	3	...	...	1,904	23	0	296	...	15,178
1913 holdings	23,234	5,095	738	0	...	...	1,904	23	0	296	...	15,178
1878 holdings	22,479	4,831	247	0	...	...	1,904	23	296	0	...	15,178
Change, 1878–1913	+755	+264	+491	...	...	...	0	0	−296	+296	...	0
With Western powers	0	0	0	...	...	...	0	0	−296	+296	...	0
Increase of Western holdings	+755	+264	+491	...	...	...	0	0	0	0	...	0
Change, 1913–1933	+270	+67	+200	+3	...	...	0	0	0	0	...	0
With Western powers	0	0	0	0	...	...	0	0	0	0	...	0
Increase of Western holdings	+270	+67	+200	+3	...	...	0	0	0	0	...	0
Change, 1878–1933	+1,025	+331	+691	+3	...	...	0	0	−296	+296	...	0
With Western powers (b)	0	0	0	0	...	...	0	0	−296	+296	...	0
Increase of Western holdings	+1,025	+331	+691	+3	...	...	0	0	0	0	...	0
Oceania												
1933 holdings	8,548	8,495	23	...	...	0	...	...	...	18	12	...
1913 holdings	8,550	8,256	23	...	...	241	...	...	...	18	12	...
1878 holdings	8,046	8,021	23	...	...	0	...	...	2	0	0	...
Change, 1878–1913	+504	+235	0	...	...	+241	...	...	−2	+18	+12	...
With Western powers	0	0	0	...	...	+2	...	...	−2	0	0	...
Increase of Western holdings	+504	+235	0	...	...	+239	...	...	0	+18	+12	...
Change, 1913–1933	−2	+239	0	...	...	−241	...	...	0	0	0	...
With Western powers	0	+239	0	...	...	−239	...	...	0	0	0	...
Increase of Western holdings	−2	0	0	...	...	−2	...	...	0	0	0	...
Change, 1878–1933	+502	+474	0	...	...	0	...	...	−2	+18	+12	...
With Western powers (b)	0	0	0	...	...	0	...	...	0	0	0	...
Increase of Western holdings	+502	+474	0	...	...	0	...	...	−2	+18	+12	...

(Continued on next page)

TABLE III
CHANGES IN TERRITORIAL HOLDINGS OF THE WESTERN POWERS
Concluded
Areas in 1,000's of Square Kilometers

	Total Western Holdings	British	French	Italian	Belgium	German	Netherlands	Portuguese	Spanish	United States	International Areas	Other Western Powers
Totals (c)												
1933 holdings.	111,937	31,575	12,371	2,775	2,470	471	2,089	2,184	837	9,683	2,534	44,948
1913 holdings.	111,669	29,484	11,493	2,549	2,415	3,453	2,089	2,184	837	9,683	2,534	44,948
1878 holdings.	90,260	24,968	4,934	310	30	471	2,089	2,184	954	9,358	0	44,962
Change, 1878-1913.	+ 21,409	+ 4,516	+ 6,559	+2,239	+2,385	+2,982	0	0	- 117	+ 325	+2,534	- 14
With Western powers	0	+ 128	0	0	0	+ 2	0	0	- 423	+ 307	0	- 14
Increase of Western holdings.	+ 21,409	+ 4,388	+ 6,559	+2,239	+2,385	+2,980	0	0	+ 306	+ 18	+2,534	0
Change, 1913-1933.	+ 268	+ 2,091	+ 878	+ 226	+ 55	-2,982	0	0	0	0	0	0
With Western powers	0	+ 2,024	+ 678	+ 223	+ 55	-2,980	0	0	0	0	0	0
Increase of Western holdings.	+ 268	+ 67	+ 200	+ 3	0	- 2	0	0	0	0	0	0
Change, 1878-1933.	+ 21,677	+ 6,607	+ 7,437	+2,465	+2,440	0	0	0	- 117	+ 325	+2,534	- 14
With Western powers (b) . . .	0	- 14	+ 33	+ 109	0	0	0	0	- 421	+ 307	0	- 14
Increase of Western holdings.	+ 21,677	+ 6,621	+ 7,404	+2,356	+2,440	0	0	0	+ 304	+ 18	+2,534	0

For sources and notes, see Table IV.

Measured in terms of proportions of Western holdings, Belgium, France, and Italy have been the most actively expanding Western powers in the past six decades, for they increased their shares of the total land under Western flags both between 1878 and 1913 and after 1913. Britain's share decreased slightly in the pre-war period of expansion, but the greater part of the former German holdings gave her a larger share in 1913 than she had had either in 1913 or in 1878. The proportions of the Western total held by the Netherlands and Portugal have decreased since 1878, though the amount of territory in their colonies has remained the same. The United States has added a little to its holdings, but proportionately less than the Western countries as a whole, and its share of the whole decreased between 1878 and 1913 and again since 1913.

TABLE IV
PERCENTAGES OF TERRITORIAL HOLDINGS OF THE WESTERN POWERS

	Total Western Holdings		British	French	Italian	Belgian	German	Nether-lands	Portu-guese	Spanish	United States	Inter-national Areas	Other Western Powers (a)
	% of Regional Total (d)	% of Western Holdings	% of Western Holdings	% of Western Holdings	% of Western Holdings	% of Western Holdings	% of Western Holdings	% of Western Holdings	% of Western Holdings	% of Western Holdings	% of Western Holdings	% of Western Holdings	% of Western Holdings
Africa:													
1933 holdings	93.26	100.00	26.27	38.55	8.81	8.74	...	...	7.40	1.20	...	9.03	...
1913 holdings	93.26	100.00	19.88	36.12	8.02	8.54	9.81	...	7.40	1.20	...	9.03	...
1878 holdings	25.98	100.00	19.74	51.67	...	...	...	...	26.58	0.36	...	...	1.65
Asia:													
1933 holdings	56.08	100.00	21.96	3.99	0.01	...	...	8.10	0.10	...	1.26	...	64.58
1913 holdings	55.44	100.00	21.93	3.18	...	...	...	8.19	0.10	...	1.27	...	65.33
1878 holdings	53.64	100.00	21.49	1.10	...	...	...	8.47	0.10	1.32	...	...	67.52
Oceania:													
1933 holdings	99.98	100.00	99.38	0.27	...	...	...	...	...	...	0.21	0.14	...
1913 holdings	100.00	100.00	96.58	0.27	...	...	2.82	...	...	...	0.21	0.14	...
1878 holdings	94.10	100.00	99.69	0.29	...	...	...	...	...	0.02	...	...	...
World Total (c):													
1933 holdings	84.55	100.00	28.21	11.05	2.48	2.21	0.42	1.87	1.95	0.75	8.65	2.26	40.16
1913 holdings	84.35	100.00	26.40	10.29	2.28	2.16	3.09	1.87	1.96	0.75	8.67	2.27	40.25
1878 holdings	68.18	100.00	27.66	5.47	0.34	0.03	0.52	2.31	2.42	1.06	10.37	...	49.81

Sources:
Compiled chiefly from data in the League of Nations, Statistical Year-Book, 1934/35. In making the calculation, it has been assumed that the areas of the different regions have not changed with changes in political status. Transfer of territory in Africa have been taken into account as follows:
(1) to Italy since 1919, from France: 81,000 sq. kms; from Britain: 142,000 sq. kms; total: 223,000 sq. kms.
(2) to Germany in 1911, from France: 277,000 sq. kms; returned to France in 1919, as reported in 118 British and Foreign State Papers 315 and 119 same 433.

Notes:
(a) Includes Russia but not Turkey.
(b) These figures indicate the net transfers of territory from one Western power to another between 1878 and 1933. The German holdings in 1913, transferred by mandate to other Western powers, are treated in the 1878-1933 change record as having been taken over directly from the 1878 holders by the holders in 1933.
(c) Includes areas in Europe and the Americas, all of which regions were controlled by Westerners in 1878, 1913 and 1933.
(d) The percents shown here are of the Western holdings to the continental and world total areas.

TABLE V
DIVISION OF CONTROL OF THE BRITISH AREAS, 1933
Areas in 1,000's Square Kilometers and Square Miles

As a result of the successful assertion by the British Dominions of the right to manage their own affairs, London today actually controls only slightly more than a third of the territory under the British flag: 4.3 million square miles out of a total of 12.2 million; 35% as compared with 65% under Dominion authority. All the British terri-tory in Asia is managed from London, but elsewhere, even in Europe itself now that the Irish Free State has been created, the other members of the league of independent nations which is the British Common-wealth have the larger shares; in the Americas and Oceania well over 95%.

	Controlled from London (a)			Controlled by Self-governing Dominions (b)			Totals		
	Sq.Kms.	Sq.Miles	% of Total	Sq.Kms.	Sq.Miles	% of Total	Sq.Kms.	Sq.Miles	% of Total
In Africa.	5,281	2,039	71.97	2,057	794	28.03	7,338	2,833	23.24
In the Americas.	302	117	2.95	9,964	3,847	97.05	10,266	3,964	32.51
In Asia.	5,162	1,993	100.00	. . .	. . .	. . .	5,162	1,993	16.35
In Europe.	245	94	78.03	69	27	21.97	314	121	0.99
In Oceania	49	17	0.51	8,446	3,263	99.49	8,495	3,280	26.90
Total	11,033	4,260	34.94	20,542	7,931	65.06	31,575	12,191	100.00

Sources:
See Table IV

Notes:
(a) British India and mandates held by London, included in "Controlled from London" figures.
(b) Territory of Canada, Newfoundland, Australia, New Zealand, Union of South Africa, and Irish Free State, together with dependencies administered by these countries and mandates held by them.

TABLE VI
POPULATIONS OF THE COLONIES
A — French

Only quite incomplete figures are available for the populations of the various colonial territories, but such as they are they serve to emphasize how few nationals of the controlling countries are in the overseas holdings -- few compared either with the local population or with the population of the home areas.

In the German territories in Africa, for example, Europeans of all nationalities were only 0.2% of the population, in 1913, while the Germans were only 0.16%. The Europeans of all nationalities and the "assimilated" in French Indo-China today are only 0.2% of the total population there.

The number of Japanese in Korea and Formosa (see Table IV-D) and the proportion of Japanese to the total population are relatively high, though the Japanese still are only a small part of the total. The Japanese figures show an increase in the Japanese population in these areas which is relatively large, compared to increases in the European population of the European colonies in recent years: 82,000 (49%) in Formosa, and 176,000 (50%) in Korea, from 1920 to 1932. Part of this increase, of course, is due to excess of births over deaths in the Japanese population. Calculating at approximately the rate which has prevailed in Japan Proper (15 per 1,000 per year) the addi-tions from this source to the Japanese population in these colonies in this period were: Formosa, 35,500; Korea, 74,400. This leaves roughly 148,000 as the net migration from Japan to these colonies in these 13 years. Japanese Saghalin contained only a very few people when Japan took it from Russia in 1905. Today it is as completely Japanese in population as Japan Proper. The Japanese in the Pacific mandate territories have increased more than the non-Japanese there since Japan secured control. Even so, the total number of Japanese going to this area has been, and can be, only a very small fraction of the increase in Japan's home population.

	Algeria	Tunis	Morocco	West Africa	Equatorial Africa	Total (a) Africa	Indo-China	Oceania	Americas	Total (a)
1911 – Total	5,564,000	1,957,000	5,000,000	11,344,000	(b)	36,948,000	16,900,000	81,000	429,000	54,781,000
1931										
French.	(c)	91,427	128,151	14,408	3,806	(c)	(c)	(c)	530,148	(c)
Europeans and Assimilated (c) . . .	920,788	103,866	44,304	8,730	881	1,548,428	42,000	19,513	4,753	2,182,789
Total	6,553,000	2,411,000	5,057,000	14,576,000	3,197,000	38,728,000	21,452,000	153,000	535,000	63,539,000
Percent of Europeans and assimilated, including French	14.05	8.10	3.41	0.16	0.15	4.00	0.20	12.75	99.98	3.44
Change 1911–1931										
Total population	+989,000	+454,000	+50,000	+3,232,000	. . . .	+1,780,000	+4,552,000	+72,000	+106,000	+8,808,000
Percent of change	+ 17.77	+ 22.20	+10.00	+ 28.49	. . . .	+ 4.82	+ 26.93	+88.89	+ 24.71	+ 16.09

Source:
Annuaire statistique de la republique francaise, 1911 and 1931.

Notes:
(a) Includes areas not separately listed.
(b) No figures given.
(c) Including French where there are not listed separately.

TABLE VI
POPULATIONS OF THE COLONIES
B — German

	Togo	Kamerun	S.W. Africa	East Africa	Total Africa	South Seas	Kiaochao	Total
1896								
Germans	83	161	932	507	1,683	120	. . . .	1,803
Europeans	91	236	2,025	1,000	3,352	229	. . . .	3,581
Military and police								
Germans	4	18	749	171	942	2	. . . .	944
Natives	150	227	(a)	1,632	2,009	50	. . . .	2,059
1913								
Germans	320	1,643	12,292	4,107	18,362	1,334	4,256	23,952
Europeans	368	1,871	14,830	5,336	22,405	1,971	4,470	28,846
Total population . . .	1,032,000	2,649,000	81,000	7,646,000	11,408,000	635,000	187,000	12,230,000
Percent of Europeans . . .	.04	.07	18.31	0.07	0.20	0.31	2.39	0.24
Military and police								
Germans	9	252	2,583	327	3,171	34	2,659	5,864
Natives	560	3,100	959	4,612	9,231	984	100	10,315
1934								
Germans	100	230	13,000	3,000	16,330	444	200	16,974
Europeans	700	2,500	32,000	6,000	41,200	4,700	(a)	45,900

Source:
Statistische Jahrbuch für das Deutsche Reich, for 1896 and 1913 figures; Jacob, Deutsche Kolonialkunde, for 1934 figures.

Note:
(a) Data not given in Jahrbuch.

TABLE VI
POPULATIONS OF THE COLONIES
C — Italian

	Libya	Eritrea	Somaliland	Aegean Islands	Total
1913					
Italians and foreigners.	(b)	(b)	(b)	. . . . .	. . . . . .
Natives.	(b)	(b)	(b)		
Total population	900,000–1,000,000 (a)	300,000	500,000	. . . . .	1,800,000
1931					
Italians and foreigners.	49,607	4,565	1,671	13,598	69,441
Natives.	659,806	593,897	1,014,600	117,257	2,380,560
Total population	704,413	598,462	1,016,271	130,855	2,450,001
% Italian and foreign.	7.04	0.76	0.16	10.39	2.89

Source:
Annuario Statistico, annual volumes.

Notes:
(a) As given.
(b) Not given.

TABLE VI
POPULATIONS OF THE COLONIES
D — Japanese

	Formosa	Korea	Kwantung Leased Territory	Japanese Saghalin	South Seas Mandate	Total Number as given
1910						
Japanese.	(a)	(a)	(a)	(a)	. . . . .	
Total Population.	3,106,223	15,128,780	687,316	(a)	. . . . .	18,922,319
% Japanese.					. . . . .	. . . . .
1920						
Japanese.	166,621	347,850	241,248	89,257	(a)	844,976
Total population.	3,757,878	17,288,989	1,089,678	91,136	52,222	22,279,903
% Japanese.	4.45	2.01	22.14	97.94		3.79
1932						
Japanese.	248,539	523,452	272,482	290,950	28,291	1,363,714
Total population.	4,932,455	20,599,876	1,323,666	293,172	78,457	27,227,616
% Japanese.	5.04	2.54	20.58	99.24	36.06	5.01
Change, 1920–1932						
Number:						
Japanese.	+ 81,918	+ 175,602	+ 31,234	+201,693	+28,291	+ 518,738
Total population.	+1,174,567	+ 3,310,887	+ 233,988	+202,036	+26,235	+ 4,947,713
Percent of 1920						
Japanese.	+ 49.16	+ 50.48	+ 12.95	+225.97	. . . . .	+ 61.40
Total population.	+ 46.45	+ 19.15	+ 21.47	+221.69	+50.24	+ 22.21

Source:
Financial and Economic Annual of Japan, annual volumes.

Note:
(a) Not given.

Spending 1,002 million marks more than the local receipts in her colonies, between 1894 and 1913, Germany nevertheless did a total trade with them of only 972 million marks - including trade with Kiaochao, though not including any of the heavy expenses which the acquisition, fortification, and administration of that port involved. And Germany's share of her colonies' trade decreased between the first and second of these two decades - from 35% in 1894-1903 to 28% in 1904-1913 - though her share of world trade was increasing in this same period. The trade of the colonies increased 404%, while Germany's trade with them grew 280%.

TABLE VII
TRADE AND FINANCES OF THE GERMAN COLONIES
Merchandise—Special (Net) Trade. Value in 1,000's of Marks

| | TRADE | | | | | | | | FINANCES (b) | | | | | | | |
| | Imports | | Exports | | Total Trade | | Balance (c) | | Local Receipts | | | Expenditures | | Balance | | |
	Value	% of Total Import by Colonies	Value	% of Total Exports from Colonies	Value	% of Total Trade of Colonies	Value	% of Total Trade of Each Region	Amount	% of Total Receipts of Colonies	% of Expenditures of Each Region	Amount	% of Total Expenditures of Colonies	Amount	% of Expenditures of Each Region	% of Trade of Each Region
Prior to 1894																
African Colonies	43,586	100.00	39,890	100.00	83,476	100.00	- 3,696	4.43	6,624	100.00	32.36	20,472	100.00	- 13,848	67.64	16.59
All Colonies (b)	43,586	100.00	39,890	100.00	83,476	100.00	- 3,696	4.43	6,624	100.00	32.36	20,472	100.00	- 13,848	67.64	16.59
1894-1903																
African Colonies	280,494	72.69	137,988	73.07	418,482	72.81	- 142,506	34.05	59,942	96.86	28.17	212,769	96.72	- 152,827	71.83	36.52
South Seas Colonies	31,309	8.11	21,898	11.60	53,207	9.26	- 9,411	17.69	1,943	3.14	26.91	7,221	3.28	- 5,278	73.09	9.92
Kiaochao	74,078	19.20	28,947	15.33	103,025	17.93	- 45,131	43.81	. . .	. . .	. . .	. . .	. . .	. . .	. . .	. . .
All Colonies (b)	385,881	100.00	188,833	100.00	574,714	100.00	- 197,048	34.29	61,885	100.00	28.13	219,990	100.00	- 158,105	71.87	33.52
Total with Germany (a)	147,170	38.14	55,273	29.27	202,443	35.22	- 91,897	45.39	. . .	. . .	. . .	. . .	. . .	. . .	. . .	. . .
1904-1913																
African Colonies	967,092	55.28	613,808	53.63	1,580,900	54.63	- 353,284	22.35	278,930	93.80	25.12	1110,260	97.25	- 83,330	74.88	52.59
South Seas Colonies	90,363	5.17	96,596	8.44	186,959	6.46	+ 6,233	3.33	18,440	6.20	58.71	31,410	2.75	- 12,970	41.29	6.94
Kiaochao	691,872	39.55	434,064	37.93	1,125,956	38.91	- 257,788	22.90	. . .	. . .	. . .	. . .	. . .	. . .	. . .	. . .
All Colonies (b)	1,749,327	100.00	1,144,488	100.00	2,893,815	100.00	- 604,839	20.90	297,370	100.00	26.05	1141,670	100.00	- 844,300	73.95	47.76
Total with Germany (a)	446,742	25.54	322,716	28.20	769,458	26.59	- 124,026	16.12	. . .	. . .	. . .	. . .	. . .	. . .	. . .	. . .
1894-1913																
African Colonies	1,247,586	58.43	751,796	56.38	1,999,382	57.64	- 495,790	24.80	338,872	94.33	25.61	1323,029	97.16	- 984,157	74.39	49.22
South Seas Colonies	121,672	5.70	118,494	8.89	240,166	6.93	- 3,178	1.32	20,383	5.67	52.76	38,631	2.84	- 18,248	47.24	7.60
Kiaochao	765,950	35.87	463,031	34.73	1,228,981	35.43	- 302,919	24.65	. . .	. . .	. . .	. . .	. . .	. . .	. . .	. . .
All Colonies (b)	2,135,208	100.00	1,333,321	100.00	3,468,529	100.00	- 801,887	23.12	359,255	100.00	26.38	1361,660	100.00	- 1,002,405	73.62	44.76
Total with Germany (a)	593,912	27.82	377,989	28.35	971,901	28.02	- 215,923	22.22	. . .	. . .	. . .	. . .	. . .	. . .	. . .	. . .
From begining through 1913																
African Colonies	1,291,172	59.26	791,686	57.65	2,082,858	58.64	- 499,486	23.98	345,496	94.43	25.72	1343,501	97.20	- 998,005	74.28	47.92
South Seas Colonies	121,672	5.58	118,494	8.63	240,166	6.76	- 3,178	1.32	20,383	5.57	52.76	38,631	2.80	- 18,248	47.24	7.60
Kiaochao	765,950	35.16	463,031	33.72	1,228,981	34.60	- 302,919	24.65	. . .	. . .	. . .	. . .	. . .	. . .	. . .	. . .
All Colonies (b)	2,178,794	100.00	1,373,211	100.00	3,552,005	100.00	- 805,583	22.68	365,879	100.00	26.47	1382,132	100.00	- 1,016,253	73.53	43.75

Sources:
Statistische Jahrbuch fur das Deutsche Reich, annual volumes, for trade figures. Zimmerman:Geschichte der Deutschen Kolonien, for finance figures.

Accounts begin in following years; for trade, calendar years; for finances, fiscal years:
East Africa: trade, 1892; finances 1892-93. Southwest Africa: trade, 1893; finances 1884-85. Kamerun: trade,1891; finances 1885-86. Togo: trade, 1888; finances, 1885-86. New Guinea; Caroline Islands, Marshall Islands, Papua, etc.: trade, 1896; finances, 1899-1900. Samoa: trade, 1899; finances, 1899-1900.
Kiaochao: trade, 1901 (and end in 1912); finances, none available.

Figures for New Guinea, Marshall Islands, Caroline Islands, and Papua are not available for this year. South Seas totals include Samoa only for this year.

Notes:
(a) Based on records of German trade with the colonies, i.e., the amounts given here as imports are the German exports to the colonies.
(b) Finance figures cover African and South Seas colonies only; Kiaochao not included.
(c) + and - indicate excess of exports and imports, respectively.

Calculated in marks at the current exchange, the areas which were German colonies in Africa did an external trade in 1933 only a little more than half as valuable as these same areas did in 1913. But in 1929 their trade was not much less than twice the 1913 figure. In other words, the shift from German to mandate control apparently has not materially affected the development of the total trade of these areas, since these changes in trade values roughly correspond to the fluctuations in world trade generally.

While the trade balance under German control changed from an import excess of 19.9 million marks in 1904 to an export surplus of 2.1 million marks in 1913, the balance was "unfavorable" again by the equivalent of 7.2 million marks in 1933. Both in 1929 and in 1933, however, the British mandate areas showed substantial export surpluses (equivalents of 7.6 and 17.3 million marks) while the French and Belgian mandate regions had import excesses (equivalents of 14.8 and 7.4 million marks). The British areas thus have served since the War more as sources of raw materials than as markets, while the French and Belgian mandates in Africa have been markets more than sources of supplies.

TABLE VIII
EXTERNAL TRADE OF THE GERMAN COLONIAL AREAS IN AFRICA
Merchandise—Gross Trade. Value in 1,000's of the Currencies Indicated

	IMPORTS — Value			EXPORTS — Value			TOTAL TRADE — Value			BALANCE (b) — Value		
	In 1000's Currency Used	In 1000's of Marks at Current Exchange (a)	% of Total for These Areas	In 1000's Currency Used	In 1000's of Marks at Current Exchange (a)	% of Total for These Areas	In 1000's Currency Used	In 1000's of Marks at Current Exchange (a)	% of Total for These Areas	In 1000's Currency Used	In 1000's of Marks at Current Exchange (a)	% of Total for These Areas
East Africa: divided between Tanganyika (British Mandate) and Ruanda Urundi (Belgian Mandate) after 1920.												
1904 (in 1,000's marks)	14,339	14,339	35.26	8,951	8,951	42.99	23,290	23,290	37.87	− 5,388	− 5,388	23.13
1913 (in 1,000's marks)	53,358	53,358	37.57	35,550	35,550	24.66	88,908	88,908	31.07	− 17,808	− 17,808	20.03
1929												
Belgian area (in 1,000's francs)	58,476	9,637	4.46	14,554	2,398	1.15	73,030	12,035	2.83	− 43,924	− 7,239	60.15
British area (in £ 1,000's)	4,286	87,469	40.52	3,988	81,387	39.00	8,274	168,856	39.77	− 298	− 6,082	3.60
Total		97,106	44.98		83,785	40.15		180,891	42.60		− 13,321	7.36
1933												
Belgian area (in 1,000's francs)	27,559	4,550	6.56	15,646	2,583	3.26	43,205	7,133	4.80	− 11,913	− 1,963	27.52
British area (in £ 1,000's)	1,947	25,745	37.13	2,726	36,046	45.48	4,673	61,791	41.58	+ 779	+ 10,301	16.67
Total		30,295	43.69		38,629	48.74		68,924	46.38		+ 8,338	12.10
Southwest Africa: under Union of South Africa Mandate after 1920.												
1904 (in 1,000's marks)	10,057	10,057	24.73	299	299	1.44	10,356	10,356	16.84	− 9,758	− 9,758	94.23
1913 (in 1,000's marks)	43,426	43,426	30.58	70,302	70,302	48.77	113,728	113,728	39.74	+ 26,876	+ 26,876	23.63
1929 (in £ 1,000's)	3,185	64,999	30.11	3,599	73,448	35.20	6,784	138,447	32.61	+ 414	+ 8,449	6.10
1933 (in £ 1,000's)	1,073	14,188	20.46	1,475	19,504	24.61	2,548	33,692	22.57	+ 402	+ 5,316	15.78
Togo: divided between French and British Mandates after 1920.												
1904 (in 1,000's marks)	6,898	6,898	16.96	3,551	3,551	17.05	10,449	10,449	16.99	− 3,347	− 3,347	32.03
1913 (in 1,000's marks)	10,631	10,631	7.48	9,138	9,138	6.34	19,769	19,769	6.91	− 1,493	− 1,493	7.55
1929												
French area (in 1,000's francs)	102,416	16,878	7.82	80,131	13,206	6.33	182,547	30,084	7.09	− 22,285	− 3,672	12.21
British area (in £ 1,000's)	50	1,020	0.47	191	3,898	1.87	241	4,918	1.16	+ 141	+ 2,878	58.52
Total		17,898	8.29		17,104	8.20		35,002	8.24		− 794	2.27
1933												
French area (in 1,000's francs)	64,486	10,647	15.35	29,238	4,827	6.09	93,724	15,474	10.41	− 35,248	− 5,820	37.61
British area (in £ 1,000's)	18	238	0.34	96	1,269	1.60	114	1,507	1.01	+ 78	+ 1,031	68.41
Total		10,885	15.70		6,096	7.69		16,981	11.43		− 4,789	28.20

(Continued on next page)

TABLE VIII

EXTERNAL TRADE OF THE GERMAN COLONIAL AREAS IN AFRICA
(Concluded)

	IMPORTS			EXPORTS			TOTAL TRADE			BALANCE (b)		
	Value			Value			Value			Value		
	In 1000's Currency Used	In 1000's of Marks at Current Exchange (a)	% of Total for These Areas	In 1000's Currency Used	In 1000's of Marks at Current Exchange (a)	% of Total for These Areas	In 1000's Currency Used	In 1000's of Marks at Current Exchange (a)	% of Total for These Areas	In 1000's Currency Used	In 1000's of Marks at Current Exchange (a)	% of Total for These Areas
Kamerun: divided between French and British Mandates after 1920.												
1904 (in 1,000's marks)	9,378	9,378	23.06	8,021	8,021	38.52	17,399	17,399	28.29	− 1,357	− 1,357	7.80
1913 (in 1,000's marks)	34,616	34,616	24.37	29,151	29,151	20.22	63,767	63,767	22.28	− 5,465	− 5,465	8.57
1929												
French areas (in 1,000's francs)	193,618	31,908	14.78	170,275	28,061	13.45	363,893	59,969	14.12	− 23,343	− 3,847	6.41
British area (in £1,000's)	195	3,980	1.84	308	6,286	3.01	503	10,266	2.42	+ 113	+ 2,306	22.46
Total		35,888	16.62		34,347	16.46		70,235	16.54		+ 1,541	2.19
1933												
French area (in 1,000's francs)	75,263	12,426	17.92	77,562	12,805	16.16	152,825	25,231	16.98	+ 2,299	+ 379	22.32
British area (in £1,000's)	117	1,547	2.23	168	2,221	2.80	285	3,768	2.54	+ 51	+ 674	17.89
Total		13,973	20.15		15,026	18.96		28,999	19.52		+ 1,053	3.63
Total African regions formerly held by Germany.												
1904	40,672	40,672	100.00	20,822	20,822	100.00	61,494	61,494	100.00	− 19,850	− 19,850	32.28
1913	142,031	142,031	100.00	144,141	144,141	100.00	286,172	286,172	100.00	+ 2,110	+ 2,110	0.74
1929												
In 1,000's francs	354,510	58,423	27.06	264,960	43,665	20.92	619,470	102,088	24.04	− 89,552	− 14,758	14.46
In £1,000's	7,716	157,468	72.94	8,086	165,019	79.08	15,802	322,487	75.96	+ 370	+ 7,551	2.34
Total		215,891	100.00		208,684	100.00		424,575	100.00		− 7,207	1.70
1933												
In 1,000's francs	167,308	27,623	39.84	122,446	20,215	25.51	289,754	47,838	32.19	− 44,862	− 7,404	15.48
In £1,000's	3,155	41,718	60.16	4,465	59,040	74.49	7,620	100,758	67.81	+ 1,310	+ 17,322	17.19
Total		69,341	100.00		79,255	100.00		148,596	100.00		+ 9,918	6.67

Sources:
Compiled from data in the Statistische Jahrbuch für das Deutsche Reich, annual volumes, for 1904 and 1913, and official reports on the mandated areas to the League of Nations Mandates Commission, for 1929 and 1933.

Notes:
(a) Exchange rates used: calculated from Statistical Year-Book of the League of Nations, 1934/35, Pp.224-26.
    1929: 1/0/0 - Marks 20.408   Frs. 1.00 - 0.1648
    1933: 1/0/0 - Marks 13.223   Frs. 1.00 - 0.1651

(b) Balance percents are of corresponding total trade. + and − indicate exports and imports surplus, respectively.

The relatively meager data which are available on the trade of the Italian colonies show that regularly they have bought more than they sold, by a substantial margin, in their total trade and in their trade with Italy.

Italy's share of the trade of her African colonies has increased somewhat in recent years, but the imports from Italy by both Eritrea and Libya have increased proportionately less than the exports to Italy, indicating that these regions are becoming less important than they have been to Italy as markets and more important as sources of supplies. The trend in Italian Somaliland is in the other direction.

TABLE IX
EXTERNAL TRADE OF THE ITALIAN COLONIES
Merchandise—Special Trade. Value in 1,000's of Lire

	Libya (Total of Tripolitania and Cyrenaica in 1913)			Eritrea			Somaliland			Aegean Islands			Total		
	Value	% with Italy	% of All Colonies	Value	% with Italy	% of All Colonies	Value	% with Italy	% of All Colonies	Value	% with Italy	% of All Colonies	Value	% with Italy	% of All Colonies
1913															
Imports, total	(a)	…	…	20,454	…	72.38	7,804	…	27.62	…	…	…	28,258	…	100.00
From Italy	(a)	…	…	9,557	46.72	…	1,801	…	13.45	…	…	…	9,557	…	…
Exports, total	(a)	…	…	11,590	…	86.55	1,801	…	13.45	…	…	…	13,391	…	100.00
To Italy	(a)	…	…	4,161	35.90	…	…	…	…	…	…	…	4,161	…	…
Total Trade	(a)	…	…	32,044	…	76.94	9,605	…	23.06	…	…	…	41,649	…	100.00
With Italy	(a)	…	…	13,718	42.81	…	…	…	…	…	…	…	13,718	…	…
Balance (b), total	(a)	…	…	− 8,864	…	27.66	− 6,003	…	40.38	…	…	…	− 14,867	…	35.70
With Italy	(a)	…	…	− 4,604	19.41	…	…	…	…	…	…	…	− 5,396	…	…
1929															
Imports, total	387,961	…	47.63	207,504	…	25.47	143,907	…	17.67	75,200	…	9.23	814,572	…	100.00
From Italy	258,039	66.51	…	122,557	59.06	…	37,436	26.01	…	(a)	…	…	418,032	51.32	…
Exports, total	56,692	…	29.01	72,499	…	37.10	49,981	…	25.58	16,240	…	8.31	195,412	…	100.00
To Italy	25,589	45.14	…	44,048	60.76	…	29,088	58.20	…	(a)	…	…	98,725	50.52	…
Total Trade	444,653	…	44.03	280,003	…	27.72	193,888	…	19.20	91,440	…	9.05	1,009,984	…	100.00
With Italy	283,628	63.79	…	166,605	59.50	…	66,524	34.31	…	…	…	…	516,757	51.16	…
Balance (b), total	− 331,269	…	74.50	− 135,005	…	48.22	− 93,926	…	48.44	− 58,960	…	9.52	− 619,160	…	61.30
With Italy	− 232,450	81.96	72.80	− 78,509	47.12	24.59	− 8,348	12.55	2.61	…	64.48	− 319,307	61.79	…
1933															
Imports, total	278,112	…	44.82	176,566	…	28.46	117,376	…	18.92	48,427	…	7.80	620,481	…	100.00
From Italy	194,663	69.99	48.22	96,475	54.64	23.90	96,475	82.19	23.90	16,099	33.24	3.99	403,712	65.06	…
Exports, total	42,794	…	17.41	62,490	…	25.42	125,658	…	51.11	14,892	…	6.06	245,834	…	100.00
To Italy	26,216	61.26	21.99	42,306	67.70	35.33	41,945	33.38	35.03	9,281	62.32	7.75	119,748	48.71	…
Total Trade	320,906	…	37.04	239,056	…	27.59	243,034	…	28.05	63,319	…	7.31	866,315	…	100.00
With Italy	220,879	68.83	42.20	138,781	58.05	26.51	138,420	56.95	26.44	25,380	40.08	4.85	523,460	60.42	…
Balance (b), total	− 235,318	…	73.33	− 114,076	…	47.72	+ 8,282	…	3.41	− 33,535	…	52.96	− 374,647	…	43.25
With Italy	− 168,447	76.26	59.32	− 54,169	39.03	19.08	− 54,530	39.39	19.20	− 6,818	26.86	2.40	− 283,964	54.25	…

Source:
Compiled from data in the Annuario Statistico Italiano, annual volumes.

Notes:
(a) Data not available.
(b) Balance percents are of the corresponding total trade. + and − indicate export and import surplus respectively.

Just before the World War, Formosa and Korea did 73% and 64% of their trade with Japan. In 1934 the proportions were 88% and 86%. But in both cases, the increase in the proportion of total exports going to Japan was substantially larger than that in the pro- portion of total imports which Japan supplied. In the year 1913, in 1929-1933, and in 1934, the share of their imports which these colonies got from Japan was smaller than the share of their exports which went to Japan. Korea still has a comparatively small "un- favorable" balance in her trade with Japan, but Formosa has developed a good-sized "favorable" balance with the "home country". Both colonies buy substantially more from the non-Japanese countries than they sell to them.

TABLE X
EXTERNAL TRADE OF THE JAPANESE COLONIES
Merchandise—Gross Trade. Value in 1,000's of Yen

| | IMPORTS | | | | EXPORTS | | | | TOTAL TRADE | | | | BALANCES (c) | | | |
| | Total | | From Japan | | Total | | To Japan | | Total | | With Japan | | Total | | With Japan | |
	Value	% of Total Imports by Colonies	Value	% of Total Exports for Region	Value	% of Total Imports by Colonies	Value	% of Total Exports for Region	Value	% of Total Trade of Colonies	Value	% of Total Trade of Regions	Value	% of Total Trade of Region	Value	% of Total Trade of Region with Japan
1913																
Formosa	60,853	37.39	42,830	70.38	53,378	46.22	40,436	75.75	114,231	41.07	83,266	72.89	− 7,475	6.54	− 2,394	2.88
Korea	72,047	44.27	40,429	56.11	31,235	27.05	25,314	81.04	103,282	37.12	65,743	63.65	− 40,812	39.52	− 15,115	22.99
Kwantung (a)	29,836	18.33	29,836	100.00	30,878	26.74	30,878	100.00	60,714	21.82	60,714	100.00	+ 1,042	1.72	+ 1,042	1.72
Total (b)	162,736	100.00	113,095	69.50	115,491	100.00	96,628	83.67	278,227	100.00	209,723	75.38	− 47,245	16.98	− 16,467	7.85
Average per year 1929-1933																
Formosa	173,736	26.55	132,326	76.16	244,669	37.62	222,438	90.91	418,405	32.06	354,764	84.79	+ 70,933	16.95	+ 90,112	25.40
Korea (a)	357,030	54.55	281,935	78.98	310,798	47.78	279,522	89.94	667,828	51.18	561,477	84.08	− 46,232	6.92	+ 2,433	0.43
Kwantung (a)	123,697	18.90	123,697	100.00	94,954	14.60	94,954	100.00	218,651	16.76	218,651	100.00	− 28,743	13.15	− 28,743	13.15
Total (b)	654,463	100.00	537,978	82.20	650,421	100.00	596,914	91.77	1,304,884	100.00	1,134,892	86.97	− 4,042	0.31	+ 58,936	5.19
1934																
Formosa	215,021	20.88	176,991	82.31	305,927	38.31	279,410	91.33	520,948	28.49	456,401	87.61	+ 90,906	17.45	+ 102,419	22.44
Korea	519,150	50.40	439,623	84.68	465,367	58.28	407,694	87.61	984,517	53.84	847,317	86.06	− 53,783	5.46	− 31,929	3.77
Kwantung (a)	295,868	28.72	295,868	100.00	27,223	3.41	27,223	100.00	323,091	17.67	323,091	100.00	− 268,645	83.15	− 268,645	83.15
Total (b)	1,030,039	100.00	912,482	88.59	798,517	100.00	714,327	89.46	1,828,556	100.00	1,626,809	88.97	− 231,522	12.66	− 198,155	12.18

Source:
Financial and Economic Annual of Japan, annual volumes.

Notes:
(a) Kwantung is listed as a foreign country in the Japanese trade returns, and records of the external trade of the Kwantung Leased Territory as such are not available. The figures used here are those from Japanese sources of Japanese trade with Kwantung, the exports and imports being appropriately reversed.
(b) The total is the sum of the figures listed. Japanese Saghalin (Karafuto) trade is included with that of Japan Proper in the Japanese trade returns.
(c) + and − indicate export surplus and import surplus respectively. The balance percents are of the corresponding total trade.

Not one of Japan's colonies has been able to pay its local costs out of local revenues, including borrowings and debt repayments in the revenues and expenses, but not including contributions from Tokyo. The deficits in millions of yen since Japan took control have been: Formosa, 134.5; Korea, 498.0; Kwantung Leased Territory, 121.5; Saghalin, 79.2, making a total of 833.2 million yen. The net deficit, after deducting Tokyo's contributions of 616.3 million yen, is 216.9 million yen. The costs do not include anything for military expenses, but they do cover 663.0 million yen for public works and various other "special undertakings" of the colonial governments - an amount which, it will be observed, is slightly more than Tokyo's contributions.

TABLE XI
FINANCES OF THE JAPANESE COLONIES
Amounts in 1,000's of Yen

	REVENUE					EXPENDITURES					DEBT TRANSACTIONS		BALANCES			
	Local Non-borrowed Revenues		Contributions from Tokyo government		Total non-borrowed working revenue (a)	Public works and "special undertakings of the government."		Subsidies		Total non-debt working expenditures (b)	Borrowings	Payments on debts	Balance on working revenue and expenditures (d)	Balance on debt transactions (e)	Net Balance	Net balance excluding Tokyo contributions.
	Amount	% of Revenue	Amount	% of Revenue	Amount	Amount	% of Expenditures	Amount	% of Expenditures	Amount	Amount	Amount	Amount	Amount	Amount	Amount
1894–1903																
Formosa	103,638	100.00	...	...	103,638	10,115	8.90	4,661	4.10	113,666	13,673	2,718	− 10,028	− 10,955	− 20,983	− 20,983
All Colonies	103,638	100.00	...	...	103,638	10,115	8.90	4,661	4.10	113,666	13,673	2,718	− 10,028	− 10,955	− 20,983	− 20,983
1904–1913																
Formosa	321,166	100.00	...	...	321,166	39,470	13.27	8,864	2.97	297,344	17,368	32,372	+ 23,822	+ 15,004	+ 38,826	+ 38,826
Korea	86,180	71.29	34,700	28.71	120,880	13,047	8.97	6,612	4.54	145,491	36,003	5,916	+ 24,611	+ 30,087	+ 54,698	+ 89,398
Kwantung (f)	12,331	36.72	21,251	63.68	33,582	9,295	37.01	...	...	25,116	...	960	+ 8,466	+ 960	+ 9,426	+ 11,825
Saghalin (f)	9,130	69.19	4,065	30.81	13,195	7,135	52.53	...	3.21	13,582	...	210	+ 387	+ 210	+ 177	− 4,242
All Colonies	428,807	87.72	60,016	12.28	488,823	68,947	14.32	15,476		481,533	53,371	39,458	+ 7,290	+ 13,913	+ 6,623	− 66,639
1914–1918																
Formosa	233,518	100.00	...	...	233,518	26,638	13.08	5,970	2.93	203,645	12,038	26,490	+ 29,873	+ 14,452	+ 44,325	+ 44,325
Korea	245,296	88.46	32,000	11.54	277,296	16,806	6.55	16,470	6.42	256,631	33,880	28,137	+ 20,665	+ 5,743	+ 14,922	+ 17,078
Kwantung (f)	12,220	54.18	10,335	45.82	22,555	5,482	22.97	...	...	23,867	...	640	+ 1,312	+ 640	+ 672	+ 11,007
Saghalin (f)	10,413	89.16	1,266	10.84	11,679	6,996	53.21	...	...	13,147	1,203	210	− 1,468	+ 993	+ 2,461	+ 3,727
All Colonies	501,447	92.00	43,601	8.00	545,048	55,922	11.25	22,440	4.51	497,290	47,121	55,477	+ 47,758	+ 8,356	+ 56,114	+ 12,513
1919–1928																
Formosa	678,222	76.79	204,987c	23.21	883,209	133,058	15.07	47,231	5.35	882,917	53,519	40,562	+ 292	+ 12,957	+ 12,665	+ 217,652
Korea	1,236,635	89.97	137,851	10.03	1,374,486	57,632	3.94	103,571	7.08	1,463,780	198,058	124,350	− 89,294	+ 73,708	− 163,002	− 300,853
Kwantung (f)	103,597	74.05	36,300	25.95	139,897	29,645	19.65	1,589	1.05	150,903	4,044	11,006	− 11,006	+ 2,354	− 13,360	− 49,660
Saghalin (f)	124,682	91.47	11,626	8.53	136,308	84,517	52.81	...	...	160,047	29,127	10,014	− 23,739	+ 19,113	− 42,852	− 54,478
All Colonies (f)	2,143,136	84.58	390,764	15.42	2,533,900	304,852	11.47	152,391	5.73	2,657,647	284,748	176,616	− 123,747	+ 108,132	− 231,879	− 622,643
1929–1934																
Formosa (f)	600,229	100.00	...	...	600,229	85,422	14.14	37,733	6.25	604,044	13,662	38,503	+ 3,815	+ 24,841	+ 21,026	+ 21,026
Korea (f)	1,110,296	92.89	84,964	7.11	1,195,260	50,058	4.15	102,744	8.51	1,207,454	132,482	138,907	− 12,194	+ 6,425	− 5,769	− 90,733
Kwantung (f)	95,802	78.65	26,000	21.35	121,802	15,278	11.04	10,180	7.36	138,378	8,931	2,507	+ 16,576	+ 6,424	+ 23,000	+ 49,000
Saghalin (f)	133,463	92.39	11,000	7.61	144,463	72,383	48.02	14,632	9.71	150,726	11,212	11,700	+ 6,263	+ 488	+ 5,775	+ 16,775
All Colonies (f)	1,939,790	94.08	121,964	5.92	2,061,754	223,141	10.62	165,289	7.87	2,100,602	166,287	191,617	− 38,848	+ 25,330	− 13,518	− 135,482
1894–1934																
Formosa (f)	1,936,773	90.43	204,987c	9.57	2,141,760	294,703	14.02	104,459	4.97	2,101,616	110,260	140,645	+ 40,144	+ 30,385	+ 70,529	+ 134,458
Korea (f)	2,678,407	90.25	289,515	9.75	2,967,922	137,543	4.48	229,397	7.46	3,073,356	400,423	297,310	− 105,434	− 103,113	− 208,547	− 498,062
Kwantung (f)	223,950	70.46	93,886	29.54	317,836	59,700	17.65	11,769	3.48	338,264	12,975	5,797	− 20,428	− 7,178	− 27,606	− 121,492
Saghalin (f)	277,688	90.85	27,957	9.15	305,645	171,031	50.68	14,632	4.34	337,502	41,542	22,134	− 31,857	+ 19,408	− 51,265	− 79,222
All Colonies (f)	5,116,818	89.25	616,345	10.75	5,733,163	662,977	11.33	360,257	6.34	5,850,738	565,200	465,886	− 117,575	+ 99,314	− 216,889	− 833,234

Source:
Calculated from data in the Financial and Economic Annual of Japan, annual volumes. Fiscal years beginning April 1, throughout.
Records begin as follows: For Formosa,1897; for Kwantung and Japanese Saghalin (Karafuto),1907; for Korea, 1911.

Notes:
(a) Total revenue is the total as shown in the Financial and Economic Annual less the nominal surplus brought forward each year.
(b) Total expenditures are the total as shown in the Financial and Economic Annual less the payments on debts. In these latter are included payments into the Consolidated Loan Fund.

(c) Special relief grant made in 1927. (Cf. Moulton: Japan. p.227).
(d) + and − indicate excess of revenue and of expenditures, respectively.
(e) + and − indicate excess of repayments and of borrowings, respectively.
(f) Budget figures for Kwantung Leased Territory and Saghalin, throughout, and for all colonies for 1933 and 1934.

France has increased the share of her trade which is with her colonies from 10% in 1894-1903 to 20% in 1929-1934, while the proportions of her total expenditures which went directly into the colonies decreased from 2.9% in 1894 to 1.3% in 1929-1934. If the old gold value of the franc (roughly five times that of the present franc) be used, the record shows an increase in trade with the colonies on the average per year, between these two periods, of 5,616.2 million old francs (667%), while the increase in total trade was 35,943.6 million old francs (447%). Her colonial expenditures, calculated in the same way, increased on the average per year 30.2 million old francs (29%) while her total expenditures grew 7,012.4 million old francs (196%) and her defense expenditures rose 1,558.6 old francs (160%). The ratio of defense expenditures to total trade increased from 12% to 18%, but that to total expenditures decreased from 27% to 24%.

TABLE XII
EXTERNAL TRADE AND DEFENSE AND COLONIAL EXPENDITURES OF FRANCE
Values and Amounts in 1,000,000's of Francs

EXTERNAL TRADE (a)

	Total Trade Value	With Colonies Value	With Colonies % of Total	With Foreign Countries Value	With Foreign Countries % of Total
1894-1903.	80,318	8,425	10.49	71,893	89.51
1904-1913.	121,761	14,039	11.52	107,722	88.47
1914-1917 (d). . .	86,666	8,058	9.30	78,608	90.71
1922-1928 (d). . .	615,867	81,302	13.20	534,565	86.81
1929-1934.	413,650	81,637	19.74	332,013	80.26
1894-1917 and 1922-1934. . .	1,318,262	193,461	14.68	1,124,801	85.32

EXPENDITURES (b)

	Total Expenditures Amount	Total Expenditures % of Total Trade	Defense Expenditures Amount	Defense Expenditures % of Total Expenditures	Defense Expenditures % of Total Trade	Distribution of Defense Expenditures (c) On Account of Colonial Trade Amount	Distribution of Defense Expenditures (c) On Account of Foreign Trade Amount	Expenditures for Colonies Amount	Expenditures for Colonies % of Total Expenditures
1894-1903.	35,779	44.55	9,776	27.31	12.17	1,026	8,750	1,033	2.89
1904-1913.	38,694	31.78	12,927	33.41	10.62	1,490	11,437	987	2.55
1914-1917 (d). . .	94,424	108.95	72,446	76.72	83.60	6,737	65,715	591	0.63
1922-1928 (d). . .	238,089	38.66	47,660	20.02	7.74	6,291	41,373	2,199	0.92
1929-1934.	317,716	76.81	76,087	23.95	18.39	15,020	61,067	4,004	1.26
1894-1917 and 1922-1934. . .	724,722	54.98	218,896	30.20	16.60	32,134	186,762	8,814	1.22

Sources:
Calculated from the following:
For Trade: Tableau général du commerce (et de la navigation) extérieur, annual volumes, 1894-1932; Statistique mensuelle du commerce, Dec. 1934, for 1933 and 1934.
For Expenditures: Statistique générale, Vol. 1933, summary table, 1894-1928. Subsequent volumes for 1929-1934.

Notes:
(a) Special (net) trade.
(b) Fiscal years, corresponding to calendar years, except in 1932. Figures for 1934 are budget appropriations. The available French sources give no government expenditure data for the years 1918-1921.
(c) Total defense expenditures distributed between colonial and foreign columns in the same proportions as the trade.
(d) No financial data available for the years 1918-1921 inclusive.

TABLE XIII
EXTERNAL TRADE AND DEFENSE AND COLONIAL EXPENDITURES OF GERMANY
Values and Amounts in 1,000,000's of Marks

Records of the Berlin government show direct expenses of the colonies as less than the amount of deficits in the colonial accounts – 875 million marks, from 1894-1913, instead of 1,002 million marks (Table VII). Even so, the proportion of colonial expenses to total governmental expenses was almost five times that of trade with the colonies to total external trade. The colonial trade was 0.38% of the total, 1894-1913, but the colonial expenses, using the Berlin figure of 875 million marks, were 1.83% of the government costs. If the colonial figures of the colonial costs be used (1,002 million marks), the proportion was 2.10%. Germany's trade with her colonies increased, 1894-1903 compared with 1904-1913, 281%, while the colonial expenses as recorded at Berlin grew 430%.

	Total Trade	With Colonies		With Foreign Countries		Total Expenditures		Defense Expenditures			Distribution of Defense Expenditures (c)		Direct Expenditures For Colonies (d)	
	Value	Value	% of Total	Value	% of Total	Amount	% of Total Trade	Amount	% of Total Expenditures	% of Total Trade	On Account of Colonial Trade Amount	On Account of Foreign Trade Amount	Amount	% of Total Expenditures
1894-1903	94,663	202	0.21	94,461	99.79	19,984	21.11	8,079	40.43	...	17	8,062	139	0.70
1904-1913	159,340	770	0.48	158,570	99.52	27,749	17.41	12,041	43.39	...	49	10,192	736	2.65
1894-1913	254,003	972	0.38	253,031	99.62	47,733	18.79	20,120	42.15	...	76	20,044	875	1.83
1914-1918	...	...	...	...	...	163,891	...	...	...	...	...	...	...	...
Ordinary defense	...	...	...	...	...	...	...	1,111	0.68	...	...	1,111	...	...
Special defense	...	...	...	...	...	...	...	131,700	80.36	...	...	131,700	...	...
Total defense	...	...	...	...	...	...	...	132,811	81.04	...	...	132,811	...	...
1919-1922	...	...	...	...	...	8,792,520	...	...	...	...	...	...	...	...
Ordinary defense	...	...	...	...	...	...	...	16,134	0.18	...	...	16,134	...	...
Special defense in 1919	...	...	...	...	...	...	...	28,209	0.32	...	...	28,209	...	...
Total defense	...	...	...	...	...	...	...	44,343	0.50	...	...	44,343	...	...
1914-1922 (e) (h)	...	...	...	...	...	8,956,411	...	...	...	...	...	...	...	...
Ordinary defense	...	...	...	...	...	...	...	17,245	0.19	...	...	17,245	...	...
Special defense in 1919	...	...	...	...	...	...	...	159,909	1.79	...	...	159,909	...	...
Total defense	...	...	...	...	...	...	...	177,154	1.98	...	...	177,154	...	...
1924-1928	109,010	...	...	109,010	100.00	24,602 (f)	22.57	4,570 (f)(g)	18.58	...	...	4,570	...	...
1919-22 and 1924-28	...	...	...	...	...	8,817,122 (f)	...	...	...	...	...	...	...	...
Ordinary defense	...	...	...	...	...	...	...	10,602 (g)	0.12	...	...	10,602	...	...
Special defense in 1919	...	...	...	...	...	...	...	28,209	0.32	...	...	28,209	...	...
Total defense	...	...	...	...	...	...	...	38,811 (f)	0.44	...	...	38,811	...	...
1929-1933 (h)	85,167	...	...	85,167	100.00	31,566 (f)	37.05	4,712 (f)(g)	14.93	...	...	4,712	...	...
1894-1913 and 1924-33 (h)	448,180	...	...	448,180	100.00	103,891	23.18	29,402 (g)	28.30	...	...	29,402	...	...
1894-1922 and 1924-33 (h)	...	...	...	...	...	9,060,302 (f)	...	...	...	...	...	...	...	...
Ordinary defense	...	...	...	...	...	...	...	46,647 (g)	0.51	...	...	46,647	...	...
Special defense	...	...	...	...	...	...	...	159,909 (f)	1.76	...	...	159,909	...	...
Total defense	...	...	...	...	...	...	...	206,556 (f)	2.28	...	...	206,556	...	...

Source:
Calculated from data in the Statische Jahrbuch für das Deutsche Reich, annual volumes.

Notes:
(a) Special (net) trade.
(b) Fiscal years beginning April 1st. Budget figures for 1933.
(c) Total defense expenditures distributed between colonial and foreign columns in the same proportions as the trade.
(d) Expenses for colonies not listed separately prior to 1896.
(e) No trade date available for 1914-1922.
(f) 1924-1933 totals do not include payments abroad on war accounts.
(g) 1924-1933 figures are the total for "Staats-und-Reichsicherheit" and are larger than the sum of the amounts for the army, navy and air expenses. The figures as given in the Jahrbuch are: defense expenditures are fantastically large.
(h) 1923 expenditure figures omitted because the inflation of the mark made the totals fantastically large. The figures as given in the Jahrbuch are: defense expenditures, marks 33,116,858,000; total expenditures, marks 48,725,711,142,000,000. The inflation also affected the expenditure figures in 1921 and 1922, making the 1919-1922 totals sum abnormally large.

TABLE XIV
EXTERNAL TRADE AND DEFENSE AND COLONIAL EXPENDITURES OF ITALY
Values and Amounts in 1,000,000's of Lire

Financially, Italy has much the most devastating record of the unprofitableness of colonies, with recorded direct colonial expenses in the 20 years 1913–1932 amounting to 6,856 million lire and with the total trade with all the colonies in the four decades 1894–1932 being worth only 5,561 million lire. And the colonial share of Italy's external trade has been extremely small – 0.97% for 1894–1932, although it has reached 1.4% in 1929–1932 when the holdings were complete and consolidated. Italy's defense expenditures have been an increasing burden, compared to her trade as well as to her total expenditures; they were 14% of the total trade and 22% of the total expenditures in 1894–1903, but 20% and 24% in 1929–1934.

| | EXTERNAL TRADE (a) | | | | | EXPENDITURES (b) | | | | | Distribution Of Defense Expenditures (c) | | Direct Expenditures For Colonies (d) | |
| | Total Trade | With Colonies | | With Foreign Countries | | Total Expenditures | | Defense Expenditures | | | On Account of Colonial Trade | On Account of Foreign Trade | | |
	Value	Value	% of Total	Value	% of Total	Amount	% of Total Trade	Amount	% of Total Expenditures	% of Total Trade	Amount	Amount	Amount	% of Total Expenditures
1894-1903	27,022	43	0.16	26,979	99.83	16,558	61.28	3,654	22.07	13.52	6	3,648	....	....
1904-1913	49,219	371	0.75	48,848	99.24	21,781	44.25	5,677	26.06	11.53	43	5,634	51 (f)	0.23
1914-1918	60,521	586	0.97	59,935	99.03	91,366	150.97						872	1.44
Ordinary defense								6,265	6.86	10.35	61	6,204		
Special defense								59,909	65.57	98.99	581	59,328		
Total defense								66,174	72.43	109.34	642	65,532		
1919-1928	334,829	3,143	0.94	331,686	99.06	238,447	71.21	50,909 (e)	21.35	15.20	479	50,430	3,994	1.19
1929-1932	102,586	1,417	1.38	101,169	98.62	85,516	83.36	20,251	23.68	19.74	279	19,972	1,939	1.89
1894-1932	574,177	5,561	0.97	568,616	99.03	453,668	79.01						6,856	1.19
Ordinary defense								86,756	19.12	15.11	842	85,914		
Special defense								59,909	13.21	10.43	581	59,328		
Total defense								146,665	32.33	25.54	1,423	145,242		

Source:
Calculated from data in the Annuario statistico Italiano, annual volumes.

Notes:
(a) Special (net) trade.
(b) Fiscal years beginning July 1.
(c) Total defense expenditures distributed between colonial and foreign countries in the same proportions as the trade.
(d) Independent Ministry of the Colonies records beginning 1913.
(e) Air Figures begin 1924.
(f) Figure for 1913 only.

TABLE XV
EXTERNAL TRADE AND DEFENSE EXPENDITURES OF JAPAN
Values and Amounts in 1,000,000's of Yen

Japan's published financial statements do not show, as part of the Tokyo government records, the direct expenditures on colonies, so the costs of these territories have to be calculated from the colonial side. (See Table XI.) But the Tokyo accounts do show that Japan's external trade has been increasing proportionately faster than either her defense or her total expenditures, as the percentages of defense expenditures to total trade in this table indicate.

	EXTERNAL TRADE (a)					EXPENDITURES (b)					Distribution of Defense Expenditures (c)	
	Total Trade	Trade with Colonies (d)		With Foreign Countries		Total Expenditures		Defense Expenditures			On Account of Colonial Trade	On Account of Colonial Trade
	Value	Value	% of Total	Value	% of Total	Amount	% of Total Trade	Amount	% of Total Expenditures	% of Total Trade	Amount	Amount
1868-1893.	2,010	...	...	2,010	100.00	1,672	83.18	389	23.27	19.35	...	389
1894-1903.	4,275	92	2.15	4,183	97.85	2,128	49.78	1,059	49.77	24.77	23	1,036
1904-1913.	10,014	731	7.30	9,283	92.70	5,255	52.48	3,076	58.53	30.72	225	2,851
1914-1918.	12,885	1,304	10.12	11,581	89.88	3,575	27.75	2,100	58.74	16.30	213	1,887
1919-1928.	47,222	7,540	15.97	39,682	84.03	15,279	32.36	5,363	35.10	11.36	856	4,507
1929-1934.	26,723	5,885	22.02	20,838	77.98	11,184	41.85	3,868	34.59	14.47	852	3,016
1894-1934.	101,118	15,551	15.38	85,567	84.62	37,421	37.01	15,467	41.33	15.30	2,379	13,088
1868-1934.	103,129	15,551	15.08	87,578	84.92	39,062	37.88	15,851	40.58	15.37	2,390	13,461

Source:
Calculated from data in the Financial and Economic Annual of Japan, annual volumes.

Notes:
(a) Gross trade. Calendar years.
(b) Fiscal years beginning April 1 since 1875, prior to that the fiscal years varied somewhat. 1933 and 1934 budget figures.
(c) Total military expenditures distributed between colonial and foreign columns in same proportion as the trade.
(d) Korea, Formosa and Kwantung Leased Territory. Formosa records begin in 1897; Leased Territory (Kwantung), in 1907; Korea, in 1911. In the Japanese records, the Kwantung Leased Territory is counted as colonial trade. For the purposes of this comparison, Japan's trade with Kwantung is counted as a foreign country.

TABLE XVI
EXTERNAL TRADE AND DEFENSE EXPENDITURES OF THE UNITED KINGDOM
Values and Amounts in £1,000,000's

Relatively to its trade, the World War was considerably more expensive for Britain than for any other of the principal countries. The special war expenditures of the United Kingdom, in the years 1914-18, were £711 millions more than all of her exports plus all her imports on that same period, these special expenses being 109% of the trade. If the ordinary defense expenses be added, the military and naval costs were 112% of the trade. Italy's special war costs were 99% of her trade and her total defense expenditures in the four years were 109% of the imports and exports (Table XIV). All of Japan's defense expenditures in these years were only 16% of her trade (Table XV). For the years 1914-1917 (1918 finance figures are not available) France spent her defense purposes 84% of the value of her trade (Table XII).

The direct costs of the overseas British territories to Britain cannot be calculated at all accurately from the available records. The Dominions now cost her nothing in direct grants; they are, in fact, beginning to help bear the heavy costs of maintaining the British navy which is so large a part of the defense equipment of the British Commonwealth of Nations. Most of this expense, however, still is carried by the taxpayers of the United Kingdom. A division of Britain's defense expenditures in the same proportions as her trade is divided between foreign and British countries - about two-thirds and one-third for the last 40 years - serves to give a rough idea of the minimum rather than the maximum amount which the overseas territories have cost Britain. For the years 1894-1933 the "colonial" shares of the defense expenditures, calculated in this way have been: of ordinary defense costs, £1,295 million; of special war costs £2,593 million; of total defense costs £3,888 million. These amounts are 7%, 14%, and 22% of the total British trade with the other British Countries.

		EXTERNAL TRADE (a)						EXPENDITURES (b)			Distribution of Defense Expenditures (c)	
	Total Trade Value	With British Countries Value	% of Total Trade	With Foreign Countries Value	% of Total Trade	Total Expenditures Amount	% of Total Trade	Defense Expenditures Amount	% of Total Expenditures	% of Total Trade	On Account of Colonial Trade Amount	On Account of Foreign Trade Amount
1894-1903.	7,975	1,988	24.92	5,987	75.08	1,368	17.15	684	50.00	8.58	170	514
1904-1913.	11,468	3,066	26.73	8,402	73.27	1,651	14.40	756	45.79	6.59	202	554
1914-1918.	7,620	2,453	32.20	5,167	67.80	9,593	125.89					
Ordinary defense. . .								206	2.15	2.70	66	140
Special defense. . .								8,331	86.84	109.33	2,683	5,648
Total defense . . .								8,537	88.99	112.03	2,749	5,788
1919-1928.	22,360	7,482	33.46	14,878	66.54	9,663	43.22	1,971	20.40	8.81	659	1,312
1929-1933.	8,466	3,030	35.79	5,436	64.21	4,199	49.60	542	12.91	15.25	194	348
1894-1933.	57,889	18,018	31.13	39,871	68.87	26,474	45.73					
Ordinary defense. . .								4,159	15.71	7.18	1,295	2,864
Special defense. . .								8,331	31.47	14.39	2,593	5,738
Total defense . . .								12,490	47.18	21.58	3,888	8,602

Sources:
Calculated from data in the Statistical Abstract of the United Kingdom, annual volumes.

Notes:
(a) Gross trade in merchandise.
(b) Budget figures for 1933. Fiscal years beginning April 1.
(c) Total defense expenditures distributed between British and foreign colonies, in the same proportions as total trade.

TABLE XVII
CONTINENTAL AND INTERCONTINENTAL MIGRATION
Nationals and Aliens, 1886-1933

The figures in the migration tables which follow show strikingly how necessary it is to take into account the returning as well as the departing migrants in order to form an accurate picture of what the actual movement of people has been. The movement of aliens as well as nationals also must be considered, and the migration within the continent as well as between continents. Yet only for three countries, Belgium, Sweden and the United Kingdom are complete figures for practically all of the past 50 years available.

In the years 1886-1933 (1891-1933 for the United Kingdom), for example, the records for these three countries show a total outward flow, continental and intercontinental, aliens and nationals, of nearly 53 million people; an average of nearly a million and a quarter a year. But 49 million people entered these same countries in these years, so that the net emigration was only 3.9 million, or 7.4% of the total emigration. Belgium showed a net inward movement of 195,000. The migration within the continent of Europe

gave a net immigration for these three countries of 2.5 millions — all of whom and 3.9 millions more were drained off by net emigration overseas. The British ports were by far the most important trans-shipping centers for this migration, with a new inward movement, 1891-1933, of 2.3 millions from the continent and a net outward movement overseas of 5.8 millions, leaving a total net emigration of only 3.5 millions (81,300 per year on the average) or 6.9% of those entering British ports.

	Period Covered	Continental					Intercontinental					Total			
		Number	Average per Year	% of Total	% of Outs		Number	Average per Year	% of Total	% of Outs		Number	Average per Year	% of Outs
Belgium.	1886-1933													
Out		1,076,629	22,429	86.3	100.00		170,276	3,548	13.7	100.0		1,246,905	25,977	100.00
In.		1,371,541	28,574	95.2	127.4		70,095	1,460	4.8	41.2		1,441,636	30,034	115.6
Balance (b)		+ 294,912	6,145		27.4		− 100,181	2,088		58.8		+ 194,731	4,057	15.6
Italy.	1886-1933													
Out		7,521,160	156,691	44.5	100.00		9,391,290	195,652	55.5	100.00		16,912,450	352,343	
In.		(a)					4,276,936	89,103		45.5				
Balance (b)							− 5,114,354	106,549		54.5				
Sweden.	1886-1933													
Out		157,364	3,278	16.4	100.0		803,813	16,746	83.6	100.0		961,177	20,024	100.0
In.		149,723	3,119	43.8	95.1		192,123	4,003	56.2	23.9		341,846	7,122	35.6
Balance (b)		− 7,641	159		4.9		− 611,690	12,743		76.1		619,331	12,902	64.4
United Kingdom (c)	1891-1933													
Out		35,424,773	823,832	69.9	100.0		15,243,476	354,498	30.1	100.0		50,668,249	1,178,330	100.0
In.		37,684,241	876,378	79.9	106.4		9,489,536	220,687	20.1	62.3		47,173,777	1,097,065	93.1
Balance (b)		+ 2,259,468	52,546		6.4		− 5,753,940	133,811		37.7		− 3,494,472	81,265	6.9
Total "Outs" four countries.	1886-1933	44,170,926	996,230	63.3			25,608,855	570,444	36.7			69,788,781	1,576,674	
Total "Outs" except Italy.	1886-1933	36,658,766	849,539	69.3	100.0		16,217,565	374,792	30.7	100.0		52,876,331	1,224,331	100.0
Total "Ins" except Italy.	1886-1933	39,205,505	908,071	80.1	106.9		9,751,754	226,150	19.9	60.1		48,957,259	1,134,221	92.6
Balance except Italy.	1886-1933	+ 2,546,739	58,532		6.9		− 6,465,811	148,642		39.9		− 3,919,072	90,110	7.4

Source:
Calculated from data in:
Ferenczi, International Migrations.
  For 1886-1924, International Labor Office, Migration Movements, 1925-1927.
  For 1925-1927, International Labor Office, Year Book, 1934-35.
  For 1928-1933, Comparable data for other countires are not available.

Notes:
(a) Data not available.
(b) On balance + and − indicate excess of immigration and emigration, respectively.
(c) Includes Northern Ireland after establishment of Irish Free State; Ireland excluded before that.

Except for the Netherlands, more of their nationals left the principal European countries than returned from overseas in the years from 1886 to 1930, inclusive, for which records are available. But more Hollanders went home than left - in spite of the congested population of the Netherlands. The net Japanese and Indian movement also was outward. In the years beginning with 1931, however, the net overseas movement has been definitely and relatively heavily back home for all eight of the European countries for which records are available, and for Japan and India.

This change is due in part, but perhaps not primarily, to the tightening up of immigration restrictions in the Americas and Australia and New Zealand. The number returning home, on the average per year, has been substantially larger, except in Italy's case, since 1930 than in the preceding period.

TABLE XVIII
INTERCONTINENTAL MIGRATION OF NATIONALS
1886-1934

	Period Covered	Up to 1931			1931 and after			Total Covered		
		Number	Average per Year	% of Outs	Number	Average per Year	% of Outs	Number	Average per Year	% of Outs
Belgium.	1886-1933									
Out		144,371	3,208	100.0	4,054	1,351	100.0	148,425	3,092	100.0
In		30,002	667	20.8	7,213	2,404	177.9	37,215	775	25.1
Balance (a)		- 114,369	2,541	79.2	+ 3,159	1,053	77.9	- 111,210	2,317	74.9
Germany.										
Out	1886-1934	1,938,978	43,084	100.0	50,354	12,589	100.0	1,989,512	40,602	100.0
Out	1926-1934	267,068	53,414	...	50,354	12,589	...	317,422	35,269	...
In	1926-1934	164,906	32,981	61.8	168,098	42,025	333.8	333,004	37,000	104.9
Balance (a)	1926-1934	- 102,162	20,432	38.2	+ 117,744	29,436	233.8	+ 15,582	1,731	4.9
Ireland.										
Out	1886-1934	1,343,358	29,849	100.0	4,210	1,052	100.0	1,347,568	27,501	100.0
Out	1926-1934	118,648	23,730	...	4,210	1,052	...	122,858	13,651	...
In (e)	1926-1934	9,794	1,959	8.2	11,840	2,960	281.2	21,634	2,403	17.6
Balance (a)	1926-1934	- 108,854	21,771	91.8	+ 7,630	1,908	181.2	- 101,234	11,248	82.4
Italy.	1886-1934									
Out		9,302,378	206,699	100.0	114,037	28,509	100.0	9,416,415	192,172	100.0
In		4,173,750	92,741	44.9	124,256	31,064	109.0	4,298,006	87,714	45.6
Balance (a)		- 5,128,628	113,958	55.1	+ 10,219	2,555	9.0	- 5,118,409	104,458	54.4
Netherlands.	1886-1924									
Out		115,158	2,559	100.0	(b)			115,158	2,559	100.0
In (a)		174,463	3,877	151.4	(b)			174,463	3,877	151.4
Balance (a)		+ 59,305	1,318	51.4	(b)			+ 59,305	1,318	51.4
Spain.	1886-1932									
Out		4,187,776	93,052	100.0	25,007	12,504	100.0	4,212,783	89,634	100.0
In		2,030,447	45,117	48.5	105,563	52,782	422.3	2,136,010	45,447	50.7
Balance (a)		- 2,157,329	47,935	51.5	+ 80,556	40,278	322.3	- 2,076,773	44,187	49.3
Sweden	1886-1933									
Out		801,108	17,801	100.0	2,705	1,353	100.0	803,813	16,746	100.0
In (a)		175,057	3,890	21.8	17,066	8,533	630.9	192,123	4,003	23.9
Balance (a)		- 626,051	13,911	78.2	+ 14,361	7,180	530.9	- 611,690	12,743	76.1
United Kingdom (c)	1886-1933									
Out		10,976,331	243,894	100.0	492,770	164,257	100.0	11,469,101	238,939	100.0
In (a)		5,962,047	132,477	54.3	605,764	201,921	122.9	6,567,811	136,829	57.3
Balance (a)		- 5,014,284	111,417	45.7	+ 112,994	37,664	22.9	- 4,901,290	102,110	42.7
British India.	1886-1932									
Out		457,359	10,163	100.0	1,249	625	100.0	458,608	9,758	100.0
In (a)		289,642	6,436	63.4	9,330	4,665	747.0	298,972	6,361	65.2
Balance (a)		- 167,717	3,727	36.6	+ 8,081	4,040	647.0	- 159,636	3,397	34.8
Japan (d).	1906-1932									
Out		350,520	14,021	100.0	22,885	11,443	100.0	373,405	13,830	100.0
In (a)		268,355	10,734	76.6	25,366	12,683	110.9	293,721	10,879	78.7
Balance (a)		- 82,165	3,287	23.4	+ 2,481	1,240	10.9	- 79,684	2,951	21.3

Sources:
Calculated from data in: For years 1886-1924, Ferenczi, International Migrations, Vol.I. For years 1925ff: International Labor Office documents.

Notes:
(a) On balances, + and - indicate immigration and emigration surplus, respectively. (b) Data not available.
(c) Includes northern Ireland after establishment of Irish Free State in 1923. Ireland excluded for earlier years. (d) Japanese migration outside of Asia.

TABLE XIX

INTERCONTINENTAL EMIGRATION OF NATIONALS, 1886-1927

A—By Countries of Future Residence

Records for 1886-1927 are available for 12 European countries, showing where their nationals went overseas. The total gross, not net, migration was 28.2 millions, which is about three-quarters of all the gross emigration from Europe in the past 50 years. The distribution by destinations of these emigrants thus furnishes a reasonably good basis for judging where all the emigrants went.

The Americas, Australia, and New Zealand got over nine-tenths of the 28.2 million, and 48% of the total went to the United States. The Spanish and Portuguese movement was chiefly to Central and South America; the Italian, a little under two-fifths to South America and nearly three-fifths to the United States and Canada. Migration from North Europe, including the British Isles, was chiefly to North America: Denmark, Norway, and Sweden sent 94% of their emigrants to the United States, and 99% to North America, for example.

Africa was the destination of 1.7 millions of those who left Europe in these years, or 6.1% of the gross emigration. But the proportion of the net emigration was only about 1.6%, as other records show that not more than 300,000 Europeans have gone permanently to Africa in the past 50 years.

	Total		To All American Countries		To the United States		To British North America		To Other American Countries		To Asia		To Oceania		To Africa		To Other Countries and Unknown	
	Number	%	Number	%	Number	%	Number	%	Number	%	Number	%	Number	%	Number	%	Number	%
From Belgium (a)	87,010	100.0	76,728	88.1	54,680	62.8	(b)		22,048	25.3	1,284	1.5	334	0.4	6,511	7.5	2,153	2.5
From Denmark	261,218	100.0	256,930	98.4	220,313	84.4	21,896	8.4	14,721	5.6	763	0.3	2,393	0.9	1,122	0.4	10	0.0
From Germany	1,796,168	100.0	1,747,953	97.4	1,532,105	85.4	30,433	1.7	185,415	10.3	2,717	0.1	8,175	0.4	17,651	1.0	19,672	1.1
From Ireland	1,300,976	100.0	1,246,385	95.8	1,165,130	89.6	81,255	6.2	(b)		(b)		42,776	3.3	3,734	0.3	8,081	0.6
From Italy	9,120,601	100.0	8,783,643	96.4	4,988,905	54.8	185,113	2.0	3,609,625	39.6	11,418	0.1	46,571	0.5	265,675	2.9	13,294	0.1
From the Netherlands	121,468	100.0	116,386	95.8	105,861	87.1	(b)		10,525	8.7	7	0.0	541	0.5	385	0.3	4,149	3.4
From Norway	494,295	100.0	492,400	99.7	458,939	93.0	32,743	6.6	718	0.1	188	0.0	593	0.1	1,114	0.2	....	...
From Portugal	1,303,664	100.0	1,258,942	96.5	(b)		(b)		1,258,942	96.5	191	0.0	5,403	0.5	39,128	3.0	....	...
From Spain	4,094,879	100.0	3,275,563	79.9	41,881	1.0	(b)		3,233,682	78.9	2,043	0.1	63,600	1.6	753,204	18.4	469	0.0
From Sweden	775,919	100.0	771,072	99.4	752,118	97.0	(b)		18,954	2.4	....	...	....	...	....	...	4,847(c)	0.6
From Switzerland	209,332	100.0	199,700	95.5	162,827	77.9	6,554	3.1	30,319	14.5	2,491	1.2	2,298	1.0	4,843	2.3	....	...
From the United Kingdom	8,632,652	100.0	6,228,559	72.2	3,992,888	46.3	2,235,671	25.9	(b)		98,697	1.1	1,130,555(f)	13.1	608,487	7.0	566,354	6.6
Total, of above	28,198,182	100.0	24,454,261	86.7	13,475,647	47.8	2,593,665	9.2	8,384,949	29.7	119,799	0.4	1,303,239	4.6	1,701,854	6.1	619,029	2.2
From British India (d)	454,701	100.0	201,590	44.3	....		....		201,590	44.3	....		54,213	11.9	188,178	41.4	10,720	2.4
From Japan (e)	456,350	100.0	216,077	47.4	87,476	19.2	30,129	6.6	98,472	21.6	44,094	9.7	185,412	40.6	6	0.0	10,761	2.3

Sources:
Calculated from data in:
For 1886-1924, Ferenczi, International Migrations, Vol. I, Table II.
For 1925-1927, and supplementing Ferenczi for 1920-1924, International Labor Office, Migration Movements, 1920-1924 and 1925-1927.

Notes:
(a) No Belgian data for 1914-1918, inclusive.
(b) Not recorded separately; included in "Other Countries".
(c) Listed as to Asia, Oceania and Africa.
(d) 1886-1924 only.
(e) Emigration outside of Asia. Emigrants, not total passengers.
(f) All passengers, 1886-1910. Emigrants only, thereafter.

TABLE XIX

INTERCONTINENTAL EMIGRATION OF NATIONALS, 1886-1927

B—By Certain Countries and Destinations

	From All the Countries Covered (a)		From the United Kingdom			From Portugal and Spain			From Italy, Portugal, and Spain			From Italy, Portugal, Spain, and the United Kingdom			From Denmark, Norway, and Sweden		
	Number	% by Regions	Number	% of Regional Total	% by Regions	Number	% of Regional Total	% by Regions	Number	% of Regional Total	% by Regions	Number	% of Regional Total	% by Regions	Number	% of Regional Total	% by Regions
To all Continents	28,198,182	100.0	8,632,652	30.6	100.0	5,398,543	19.1	100.0	14,519,144	51.5	100.0	23,151,796	82.1	100.0	1,531,432	5.4	100.0
Total less these countries			19,565,530	69.4	100.0	22,799,639	80.9	100.0	13,679,038	48.5	100.0	5,046,386	17.9	100.0	26,666,750	94.6	100.0
To the Americas	24,454,261	86.7	6,228,559	25.5	72.2	4,534,505	18.5	84.0	13,318,148	54.5	91.7	19,546,707	79.9	84.4	1,520,402	6.2	99.3
Total less these countries			18,225,702	74.5	93.1	19,919,756	81.5	87.4	11,136,113	45.5	81.4	4,907,554	20.1	97.2	22,933,859	93.8	86.0
To the United States	13,475,647	47.8	3,992,888	29.6	46.3	41,881	0.3	0.8	5,030,786	37.3	34.6	9,023,674	67.0	39.0	1,431,370	10.6	93.5
Total less these countries			9,482,759	70.4	48.5	13,433,766	99.7	58.9	8,444,861	62.7	61.7	4,451,973	33.0	88.2	12,044,277	89.4	45.2
To British North America	2,593,665	9.2	2,235,671	86.2	25.9	(b)	0.0	0.0	185,113	7.2	1.3	2,420,784	93.3	10.5	54,639	2.1	3.6
Total less these countries			357,994	13.8	1.8	2,593,665	100.0	11.4	2,408,552	92.8	17.6	172,881	6.7	3.4	2,539,026	97.9	9.5
To other American countries	8,384,949	29.7	(b)	100.0		4,492,624	53.6	83.2	8,102,249	96.6	55.8	8,102,249	96.6	35.0	34,393	0.4	2.2
Total less these countries			8,384,949		42.8	3,892,325	46.4	17.1	282,700	3.4	2.1	282,700	3.4	5.6	8,350,556	99.6	31.3
To Africa	1,701,854	6.1	608,487	35.8	7.0	792,332	46.6	14.7	1,058,007	62.2	7.3	1,666,494	97.9	7.2	2,236	0.1	0.1
Total less these countries			1,093,367	64.2	5.6	909,522	53.4	4.0	643,847	37.8	4.7	35,360	2.1	0.7	1,699,618	99.9	6.4
To Oceania	1,303,239	4.6	1,130,555	86.7	13.1	69,003	5.3	1.3	115,574	8.9	0.8	1,246,129	95.6	5.4	2,986	0.2	0.2
Total less these countries			172,684	13.3	0.9	1,234,236	94.7	5.4	1,187,665	91.1	8.7	57,110	4.4	1.1	1,300,253	99.8	4.9
To Asia	119,799	0.4	98,697	82.4	1.1	2,234	1.9	0.0	13,652	11.4	0.1	112,349	93.8	0.5	951	0.8	0.1
Total less these countries			21,102	17.6	0.1	117,565	98.1	0.5	106,147	88.6	0.8	7,450	6.2	0.2	118,948	99.2	0.4
Others and Unknown	619,029	2.2	566,354	91.5	6.6	469	0.1	0.0	13,763	2.2	0.1	580,117	93.7	2.5	4,857	0.8	0.3
Total less these countries			52,675	8.5	0.3	618,560	99.9	2.7	605,266	97.8	4.4	38,912	6.3	0.8	614,172	99.2	2.3

Sources:
See Table XIX A.

Notes:
(a) For complete list of countries covered, see Table XIXA. Only a few Portuguese to North America or British to Latin America.
(b) Not recorded separately, but included in all American countries.

The 15 years before the World War saw a heavy migration from Italy to other countries in Europe as well as overseas, but the movement was large both before and after this period. From 1886 to 1933, in fact, 7.5 million aliens and nationals (chiefly nationals) left Italy for other European countries as compared with 9.4 millions who went overseas (Table XVII). Since the War, the continental movement has been larger than the overseas. A relatively large share of the Italian continental emigrants are seasonal laborers. The net emigration to other countries on the continent therefore is proportionately smaller than the net overseas emigration. Nevertheless, something over a million Italians have settled in France since the War, as French records show.

The relative importance of Switzerland as a destination for Italian emigrants all through the years 1886 to 1927, but especially between 1900 and 1915, is worthy of notice. Since the War France has been preferred by the Italians as a place to go almost as preponderantly as by the Belgians.

TABLE XX
CONTINENTAL EMIGRATION OF NATIONALS
1887-1927

	1886-1890	1891-1895	1896-1900	1901-1905	1906-1910	1911-1915	1916-1920	1921-1925	1926-1927	1886-1927
Numbers:										
From Belgium (a)										
To Austria-Hungary	54	119	268	125	157	140	31	··	··	894
France	37,111	44,217	41,563	39,900	57,836	37,606	55,385	81,979	26,742	422,339
Germany	2,299	2,752	4,542	4,867	5,532	2,957	2,949	2,457	792	29,147
Switzerland	96	185	167	235	343	347	239	296	134	2,042
Other Countries	6,931	8,084	11,976	11,230	13,508	8,211	10,081	7,979	4,447	82,447
Total	46,491	55,357	58,516	56,357	77,376	49,261	68,685	92,711	32,115	536,869
From Italy										
To Austria-Hungary	170,589	181,724	231,335	272,268	185,694	159,416	5,071	17,978	2,136	1,226,211
France	151,570	134,484	124,799	271,493	301,123	325,317	339,170	750,332	168,035	2,546,323
Germany	51,758	76,228	154,703	280,045	310,999	280,906	4,167	7,054	1,508	1,167,368
Switzerland	36,014	60,829	128,233	269,141	386,527	357,977	75,525	54,122	31,767	1,400,135
Other Countries	28,780	78,157	84,642	74,284	59,917	58,215	28,214	92,064	17,201	521,474
Total	438,711	531,422	723,712	1,167,231	1,244,260	1,181,831	452,147	901,550	220,647	6,861,511
Percentages:										
From Belgium (a)										
To Austria-Hungary	0.1	0.2	0.5	0.2	0.2	0.3	0.1	··	··	0.2
France	79.9	79.9	71.0	70.8	74.8	76.3	80.6	88.5	83.2	78.7
Germany	4.9	5.0	7.8	8.6	7.1	6.0	4.3	2.6	2.5	5.4
Switzerland	0.2	0.3	0.3	0.4	0.4	0.7	0.3	0.3	0.4	0.4
Other Countries	15.0	14.6	20.4	20.0	17.5	16.7	14.7	8.6	13.9	15.3
Total	100.0	100.0	100.0	100.0	100.0	100.0	100.0	100.0	100.0	100.0
From Italy										
To Austria-Hungary	38.9	34.2	32.0	23.3	14.9	13.5	1.1	2.0	0.9	17.9
France	34.5	25.3	17.2	23.3	24.2	27.5	75.0	81.0	76.2	37.1
Germany	11.8	14.3	21.4	24.0	25.0	23.8	0.9	0.8	0.7	17.0
Switzerland	8.2	11.4	17.0	23.1	31.1	30.3	16.7	6.0	14.4	20.4
Other Countries	6.6	14.8	11.7	6.3	4.8	4.9	6.3	10.2	7.8	7.6
Total	100.0	100.0	100.0	100.0	100.0	100.0	100.0	100.0	100.0	100.0

Sources:
Calculated from data as follows:
1886-1924, Ferenczi, International Migrations, Vol. I.
1925-1927, International Labor Office, Migration Movements, 1925-1927.

Note:
(a) No data available for 1914-1918 inclusive for Belgium.

Only about one-eighth of the net overseas migration from North European countries for which records are available for the years 1886-1933 were others than British nationals (Table XVIII). But for the 118 years 1815-1933, somewhat more than a third of those who sailed from British ports were aliens. The distribution of this migration from British ports therefore can be taken as indicating roughly where the migrants from Europe have gone in the past century, though the proportions do not hold well for the Iberian and Italian migration. The general applicability of the geographical distribution of this British-ports emigration, given in this table and the next two, is further confirmed by the fact that it shows 89% of the total as having gone to North America, Australia, and New Zealand, while the record of nationals departing overseas, from all Europe, 1886-1933, shows 91% as choosing these same areas as their destinations (Table XIX).

In these 118 years, 28.0 million people sailed from British ports (gross, not net, emigration). The areas which have become the British Dominions got 10.1 millions (36%) of these, while 16.0 millions (57%) went to the United States. The movement to the United States grew steadily and rapidly from 1841 to 1895. Thereafter the Dominions' share increased and that of the United States fell off.

TABLE XXI
OVERSEAS PASSENGERS FROM BRITISH PORTS, 1815-1933
A—Totals
Nationals and Aliens

	Total		Nationals (a)		Aliens and Nationality Unknown (a)		British North America		Australia and New Zealand (b)		South Africa (c)		British East Indies (d)		Other British Areas (c)		Total British Areas		United States		Other Countries	
	Number	% of Total	Number	% of Total	Number	% of Total	Number	% of Total	Number	% of Total	Number	% of Total	Number	% of Total	Number	% of Total	Number	% of Total	Number	% of Total	Number	% of Total
1815-1840	1,076,488	100.0	.....	..	1,076,488	100.0	532,192	49.4	76,817	7.2	.....	..	.....	..	.....	..	609,009	56.6	458,407	42.6	9,072	0.8
1841-1865	4,827,500	100.0	2,030,479	42.1	2,797,021	57.9	740,573	15.3	830,746	17.2	34,458	0.8	28,582	0.6	21,069	0.4	1,655,428	34.3	3,139,382	65.0	32,690	0.7
1866-1885	5,111,768	100.0	3,825,261	74.8	1,286,507	25.2	552,792	10.8	618,791	12.1	97,216	1.9	62,113	1.2	33,875	0.7	1,364,787	26.7	3,650,461	71.4	96,520	1.9
1886-1895	3,246,582	100.0	2,244,800	69.1	1,001,782	30.9	365,576	11.3	230,894	7.1	127,009	3.9	53,657	1.7	22,457	0.7	799,593	24.7	2,357,803	72.6	89,186	2.7
1896-1905	3,251,559	100.0	1,935,055	59.5	1,316,504	40.5	566,304	17.4	134,817	4.1	341,364	10.5	60,689	1.9	57,290	1.8	1,160,464	35.7	2,006,343	61.7	84,752	2.6
1906-1915	5,232,230	100.0	3,460,581	66.1	1,771,649	33.9	1,538,270	29.4	485,173	9.3	260,010	5.0	95,365	1.8	96,866	1.8	2,475,484	47.3	2,559,392	48.9	197,354	3.8
1916-1920	783,967	100.0	647,419	82.6	136,548	17.4	269,002	34.3	79,886	10.2	55,509	7.1	38,247	4.9	41,069	5.2	483,513	61.7	258,115	32.9	42,339	5.4
1921-1925	1,910,645	100.0	1,367,907	71.6	542,738	28.4	566,756	29.7	276,354	14.5	128,103	6.7	.....	..	139,501	7.3	1,110,714	58.2	701,972	36.7	97,959	5.1
1926-1930	1,941,189	100.0	1,333,789	68.7	607,400	31.3	613,966	31.6	229,770	11.8	137,176	7.1	.....	..	151,560	7.8	1,132,472	58.3	688,121	35.4	120,596	6.3
1931-1933	661,704	100.0	492,770	74.5	168,934	25.5	116,817	17.7	36,572	5.5	60,396	9.1	.....	..	82,556	12.5	296,341	44.8	207,158	31.3	158,205	23.9
1886-1933	17,027,876	100.0	11,482,321	67.4	5,545,555	32.6	4,036,691	23.7	1,473,266	8.6	1,109,567	6.5	247,958	1.5	591,099	3.5	7,458,581	43.8	8,778,904	51.6	790,391	4.6
1815-1933	28,043,632	100.0	17,338,061	61.8	10,705,571	38.2	5,862,248	20.9	2,999,620	10.7	1,241,241	4.4	336,653	1.2	646,043	2.3	11,087,805	39.5	16,027,154	57.2	928,673	3.3
1815-1885	11,015,756	100.0	5,855,740	53.2	5,160,016	46.8	1,825,557	16.6	1,526,354	13.8	131,674	1.2	90,695	0.8	54,944	0.5	3,629,224	32.9	7,248,250	65.8	138,282	1.3
1886-1915	11,730,371	100.0	7,640,436	65.1	4,089,935	34.9	2,470,150	21.0	850,884	7.3	728,383	6.2	209,711	1.8	176,413	1.5	4,435,541	37.8	6,923,538	59.0	371,292	3.2
1921-1933	4,513,538	100.0	3,194,466	70.8	1,319,072	29.2	1,297,539	28.8	542,696	12.0	325,675	7.2	.....	..	373,617	8.3	2,539,527	56.3	1,597,251	35.4	376,760	8.3

Sources:
Calculated from data in Ferenczi, International Migrations, Vol.I.
British Board of Trade Journal, March 11,1926, March 22,1928, March 6,1930, March 3,1932, March 8,1934.

Notes:
(a) Nationals and aliens recorded separately, beginning in 1853.
(b) Separate records begin with 1821.
(c) Separate records begin with 1841.
(d) Separate records begin with 1843. Included with "Other British Areas" after 1920.

TABLE XXI
OVERSEAS PASSENGERS FROM BRITISH PORTS, 1815-1933
B—Yearly Averages
Nationals and Aliens

	Total		Nationals		Aliens and Nationality Unknown (a)		British North America		Australia and New Zealand (b)		South Africa (c)		British East Indies (d)		Other British Areas (c)		Total British Areas		United States		Other Countries	
	Number	% of Total	Number	% of Total	Number	% of Total	Number	% of Total	Number	% of Total	Number	% of Total	Number	% of Total	Number	% of Total	Number	% of Total	Number	% of Total	Number	% of Total
Average 1815-1840	41,403	100.0	....	....	41,403	100.0	20,469	49.4	2,954	7.2	....	....			....	....	23,423	56.6	17,631	42.6	349	0.8
Average 1841-1865	193,100	100.0	81,219	42.1	111,881	57.9	29,623	15.3	33,230	17.2	1,378	0.8	1,143	0.6	843	0.4	66,217	34.3	125,575	65.0	1,308	0.7
Average 1866-1885	255,588	100.0	191,263	74.8	64,325	25.2	27,639	10.8	30,939	12.1	4,861	1.9	3,106	1.2	1,694	0.7	68,239	26.7	182,523	71.4	4,826	1.9
Average 1886-1895	324,658	100.0	224,480	69.1	100,178	30.9	36,557	11.3	23,089	7.1	12,701	3.9	5,366	1.7	2,246	0.7	79,959	24.7	235,780	72.6	8,919	2.7
Average 1896-1905	325,156	100.0	193,506	59.5	131,650	40.5	56,630	17.4	13,482	4.1	34,137	10.5	6,069	1.9	5,729	1.8	116,047	35.7	200,634	61.7	8,475	2.6
Average 1906-1915	523,223	100.0	346,058	66.1	177,165	33.9	153,827	29.4	48,517	9.3	26,001	5.0	9,537	1.8	9,667	1.8	247,549	47.3	255,939	48.9	19,735	3.8
Average 1916-1920	156,793	100.0	129,484	82.6	27,309	17.4	53,800	34.3	15,937	10.2	11,102	7.1	7,649	4.9	8,214	5.2	96,702	61.7	51,623	32.9	8,468	5.4
Average 1921-1925	382,129	100.0	273,581	71.6	108,548	28.4	113,351	29.7	55,271	14.5	25,621	6.7	....	....	27,900	7.3	222,143	58.2	140,394	36.7	19,592	5.1
Average 1926-1930	388,238	100.0	266,758	68.7	121,480	31.3	122,794	31.6	45,954	11.8	27,435	7.1	....	....	30,312	7.8	226,495	58.3	137,624	35.4	24,119	6.3
Average 1931-1933	220,568	100.0	164,257	74.5	56,311	25.5	38,939	17.7	12,191	5.5	20,132	9.1	....	....	27,518	12.5	98,780	44.8	69,053	31.3	52,735	23.9
Average 1886-1933	293,584	100.0	197,971	67.4	95,613	32.6	69,598	23.7	25,402	8.6	19,130	6.5	4,275	1.5	10,191	3.5	128,596	43.8	151,360	51.6	13,628	4.6
Average 1815-1933	235,661	100.0	145,698	61.8	89,963	38.2	49,263	20.9	25,207	10.7	10,430	4.4	2,846	1.2	5,429	2.3	93,175	39.5	134,682	57.2	7,804	3.3
Average 1815-1885	155,151	100.0	82,475	53.2	72,676	46.8	25,712	16.6	21,498	13.8	1,855	1.2	1,277	0.8	774	0.5	51,116	32.9	102,088	65.8	1,948	1.3
Average 1886-1915	391,012	100.0	254,681	65.1	136,331	34.9	82,338	21.0	28,363	7.3	24,279	6.2	6,990	1.8	5,881	1.5	147,851	37.8	230,785	59.0	12,376	3.2
Average 1921-1933	347,195	100.0	245,728	70.8	101,467	29.2	99,810	28.8	41,746	12.0	25,052	7.2	....	....	28,740	8.3	195,348	56.3	122,865	35.4	28,982	8.3

Source:
Calculated from data in Ferenczi, International Migrations, Vol.I.
British Board of Trade Journal, March 11,1926, March 22,1928, March 6,1930, March 3,1932, March 8,1934.

Notes:
(a) Nationals and aliens recorded separately beginning in 1853.
(b) Separate records begin with 1821.
(c) Separate records begin with 1841.
(d) Separate records begin with 1843. Included with "Other British Areas" after 1920.

TABLE XXI
OVERSEAS PASSENGERS FROM BRITISH PORTS, 1815-1933
C—Certain Percentages

	To British N. America	To Australia and New Zealand	To South Africa	To These Dominion Areas	To Other British Areas	To All British Areas	To the United States	To Dominions and United States	To Other Countries	To All Countries
	%	%	%	%	%	%	%	%	%	%
1815-1385 - Total.	16.6	13.8	1.2	31.6	1.3	32.9	65.8	97.4	1.3	100.0
British areas	50.3	42.1	3.6	96.0	4.0	100.0	. . . .	. . . .	. . . .	. . . .
Dominions and U.S	17.0	14.2	1.3	32.5	. . . .	. . . .	67.5	100.0	. . . .	. . . .
1886-1915 - Total.	21.0	7.3	6.2	34.5	3.3	37.8	59.0	93.5	3.2	100.0
British areas	55.7	19.2	16.4	91.3	8.7	100.0	. . . .	. . . .	. . . .	. . . .
Dominions and U.S	22.5	7.8	6.6	36.9	. . . .	. . . .	63.1	100.0	. . . .	. . . .
1921-1933 - Total.	28.8	12.0	7.2	48.0	8.3	56.3	35.4	83.4	8.3	100.0
British areas	51.1	21.4	12.8	85.3	14.7	100.0	. . . .	. . . .	. . . .	. . . .
Dominions and U.S	34.5	14.4	8.7	57.6	. . . .	. . . .	42.4	100.0	. . . .	. . . .
1886-1933 - Total.	23.7	8.6	6.5	38.8	5.0	43.8	51.6	90.4	4.6	100.0
British areas	54.1	19.8	14.9	88.8	11.2	100.0	. . . .	. . . .	. . . .	. . . .
Dominions and U.S	26.2	9.6	7.2	43.0	. . . .	. . . .	57.0	100.0	. . . .	. . . .
1815-1933 - Total.	20.9	10.7	4.4	36.0	3.5	39.5	57.2	93.2	3.3	100.0
British areas	52.9	27.0	11.2	91.1	8.9	100.0	. . . .	. . . .	. . . .	. . . .
Dominions and U.S	22.4	11.5	4.8	38.7	. . . .	. . . .	61.3	100.0	. . . .	. . . .

For sources, see Table XXI-B.

TABLE XXII
MIGRATION INTO AND OUT OF BELGIUM, 1841-1933
Nationals and Aliens

Belgium has kept extraordinarily complete migration records, running back to 1841, showing movement in and out, and subdividing the record by nationals and aliens since 1884. For the 70 years 1864-1933, these records show a total net inward movement of aliens and nationals together of 303,000 or an average of 4,300 a year. In the 50 years 1884-1933 there was a net outward movement of nationals to the number of 317,900, but 570,100 aliens more came into the country than left it, so that the total migration added 252,000 people to Belgium's population in this period. The obvious and inescapable conclusion from this record is that other factors than the relative congestion of population in a country determine the movement of migration in and out. The Netherlands' record of a net inward movement even confirms this conclusion (Table XXIV).

	OUT			IN				BALANCE (A)		
	Number	Average per Year	% of Total	Number	Average per Year	% of Total	% of Outs	Number	Average per Year	% of Outs
1841-1863: Total . . .	162,891	7,082	100.00	120,577	5,242	100.00	74.02	-42,314	-1,890	25.98
1864-1883: Total . . .	237,563	11,878	100.00	287,995	14,400	100.00	121.23	+50,432	+2,522	21.23
1884-1893: Total . . .	193,335	19,333	100.00	202,953	20,295	100.00	104.97	+ 9,618	+ 962	4.97
Nationals	117,191	11,719	60.62	50,742	5,074	25.00	43.30	-66,449	-6,645	56.70
Aliens.	76,144	7,614	39.38	152,211	15,221	75.00	199.90	+76,067	+7,607	99.90
1894-1903: Total . . .	217,201	21,720	100.00	275,296	27,530	100.00	126.75	+58,095	+5,810	26.75
Nationals	120,028	12,003	55.26	78,173	7,817	28.40	65.13	-41,855	-4,186	34.87
Aliens.	97,173	9,717	44.74	197,123	19,712	71.60	202.86	+99,950	+9,995	102.86
1904-1913: Total . . .	336,917	33,692	100.00	400,979	40,098	100.00	119.01	+64,062	+6,406	19.01
Nationals	183,340	18,334	54.42	92,844	9,284	23.15	50.64	-90,496	-9,050	49.36
Aliens.	153,577	15,358	45.58	308,135	30,814	76.85	200.64	+154,558	+15,456	100.64
1919-1923: Total . . .	202,202	40,440	100.00	184,090	36,818	100.00	91.04	-18,112	-3,622	8.96
Nationals	140,267	28,053	69.37	67,325	13,465	36.57	48.00	-72,942	-14,588	52.00
Aliens.	61,935	12,387	30.63	116,765	23,353	63.43	188.53	+54,830	+10,966	88.53
1924-1933: Total . . .	275,040	27,504	100.00	413,546	41,355	100.00	150.36	+138,506	+13,851	50.36
Nationals	142,842	14,284	51.93	96,688	9,669	23.38	67.69	-46,154	-4,615	32.31
Aliens.	132,198	13,220	48.07	316,858	31,686	76.62	239.68	+184,660	+18,466	139.68
1884-1933: Total reported	1,224,695	24,494	100.00	1,476,864	29,537	100.00	120.59	+252,169	+5,043	20.59
Nationals	703,668	14,073	57.46	385,772	7,715	26.12	54.82	-317,896	-6,358	45.18
Aliens.	521,027	10,421	42.54	1,091,092	21,822	73.88	209.41	+570,065	+11,401	109.41
1864-1933-Total reported	1,462,258	20,889	100.00	1,764,859	25,212	100.00	120.69	+302,601	+4,323	20.69
1841-1933-Total reported	1,625,149	17,475	100.00	1,885,436	20,274	100.00	116.02	+260,287	+2,799	16.02

Sources:
For 1841-1924, Ferenczi, International Migrations, Vol.I.
For 1925-1933, League of Nations publications.

Note:
(a) + and - indicate excess of immigration and emigration, respectively.

TABLE XXIII
FRENCH MIGRATION, 1920-1933

The French are peculiarly disinclined to migrate, as the total gross intercontinental migration of only 33,000 in 1920-1933 shows. But France has been attractive as a prospective home for others, as is indicated by the net immigration of aliens in the same post-war years of 1,164,000. Most of these are Italians, chiefly laborers, but the migration from Belgium also is substantial (Table XX).

	NATIONALS INTERCONTINENTAL	ALIENS - CONTINENTAL				
	Out	Out	In		Balance (a)	
	Number	Number	Number	% of Outs	Number	% of Outs
1920.	4,010	12,151	129,803	1,068.2	+ 117,652	968.2
1921 - 1925	8,253	275,819	868,595	314.9	+ 592,776	214.9
1926 - 1930	17,310	267,574	725,116	271.0	+ 457,542	171.0
1931 - 1933	3,432	250,476	246,394	98.4	– 4,082	1.6
1920 - 1933	33,005	806,020	1,969,908	244.4	+1,163,888	144.4

Sources:
Calculated from data in International Labor Office, Migration Movements, 1920 – 1924; Migration Movements, 1925 - 1927; Year-Book, 1934/35.

Note:
(a) + and – indicate excess of immigration and emigration, respectively.

TABLE XXIV
NETHERLANDS MIGRATION, 1865-1924
Nationals

In connection with all the talk about colonies as outlets for population, it is interesting to observe that from 1865 to 1924 the net movement of Hollanders was from the colonies to the homeland, to the number of 17,000. The relatively large net inward movement from foreign countries, continental and inter-continental, in 1916-1924 probably was due in part to war conditions, but it will be observed that the net outward movement to these foreign lands had decreased steadily in the successive decades from 1865 to 1915 - though the Netherlands' own population was growing rapidly.

	Dutch Colonies			Foreign Countries			Total Number		
	Number	% of Outs	% of Total	Number	% of Outs	% of Total	Number	% of Outs	% of Total
1865-1885									
Out.	31,267	100.0	12.3	223,555	100.0	87.7	254,822	100.0	100.0
In	47,692	152.5	22.0	168,685	75.5	78.0	216,377	84.9	100.0
Balance (a).	+16,425	52.5	....	- 54,870	24.5	....	- 38,445	15.1	....
1886-1895									
Out.	36,332	100.0	18.4	161,435	100.0	81.6	197,767	100.0	100.0
In	29,069	80.0	19.8	117,769	73.0	80.2	146,838	74.2	100.0
Balance (a).	- 7,263	20.0	....	- 43,666	27.0	....	- 50,929	25.8	....
1896-1905									
Out.	39,381	100.0	15.3	217,376	100.0	84.7	256,757	100.0	100.0
In	42,145	107.0	18.8	182,334	83.9	81.2	224,479	87.4	100.0
Balance (a).	+ 2,764	7.0	....	- 35,042	16.1	....	- 32,278	12.6	....
1906-1915									
Out.	48,927	100.0	14.4	291,948	100.0	85.6	340,875	100.0	100.0
In	48,019	98.1	14.1	292,732	100.3	85.9	340,751	100.0	100.0
Balance (a).	- 908	1.9	....	+ 784	0.3	....	- 124	0.0	....
1916-1924									
Out.	49,095	100.0	18.3	218,477	100.0	81.7	267,572	100.0	100.0
In	55,230	112.5	15.2	308,369	141.1	84.8	363,599	135.9	100.0
Balance (a).	+ 6,135	12.5	....	+ 89,892	41.1	....	+ 96,027	35.9	....
1865-1924									
Out.	205,002	100.0	15.6	1,112,791	100.0	84.4	1,317,793	100.0	100.0
In	222,155	108.4	17.2	1,069,889	96.1	82.8	1,292,044	98.0	100.0
Balance (a).	+17,153	8.4	....	- 42,902	3.9	....	- 25,749	2.0	....

Source:
Calculated from data in Ferenczi, International Migrations, Vol.I.

Note:
(a) + and - indicate excess of immigration and emigration, respectively.

TABLE XXV
ALGERIAN MIGRATION
1893-1924
Passengers by Sea

Algerian records of arrivals and departures by sea, 1893-1924, offer a fairly good basis for judging what the net migration from Europe to North Africa has been. They show that the number of those who remain out of those who **arrive** is exceedingly small - 0.7% for all arrivals, and 2.1% of the arrivals from England, France, Italy, and Spain.

The figures of gross emigration from Europe to North Africa need to be reduced in some such proportions as these to get the net emigration. 3,433,000 people reached Algeria from France, for example, but 3,400,000 left for France, leaving a net inward movement of only 33,000, or 0.97% of the arrivals.

	OUT		IN		BALANCE (a)		
	Number	% of Total	Number	% of Total	Number	% of Outs	% of Ins
Country of Origin and Destination England.	5,499	0.1	8,012	0.2	+ 2,513	45.7	31.4
France	3,399,640	74.6	3,432,965	74.8	+ 33,325	1.0	1.0
Italy.	31,256	0.7	32,100	0.7	+ 844	2.7	2.5
Morocco.	467,620	10.3	396,196	8.6	− 71,424	15.3	18.0
Spain.	554,257	12.2	604,868	13.2	+ 50,611	9.1	8.4
Tunis.	35,501	0.8	35,227	0.8	− 274	0.8	0.8
Other countries.	64,431	1.4	78,816	1.7	+ 14,385	22.3	18.3
Total	4,558,204	100.0	4,538,184	100.0	+ 29,980	0.7	0.7
Total of England, France, Italy, and Spain	3,990,652	87.5	4,077,945	88.9	+ 87,293	2.2	2.1

Source:
Calculated from data in Ferenczi, International Migrations, Vol. I.

Note:
(a) + and − indicate excess of immigration and emigration, respectively.

TABLE XXVI
TOTAL MIGRATION OF AUSTRALIA AND NEW ZEALAND
1886-1933

The very large preponderance of Britishers in Australian migration is indicated in the 1921-1930 figures for migration by nationalties. And it is interesting to observe that Britishers have formed a larger proportion of those who arrived (89%) than of those who left (84%). The large proportion of the Italian arrivals who stayed (66%) is striking. Italians still are a much smaller part of the net immigration than Britishers, but they are increasing in numbers.

	Australia			New Zealand			Total	
	Number	% of Total	% of Ins	Number	% of Total	% of Ins	Number	% of Ins
Out								
1886 - 1900	(a)	...	...	253,610	...	93.6	....	...
1901 - 1920	1,576,443	75.3	86.4	517,663	24.7	79.1	2,094,106	84.5
1921 - 1930	634,932	67.1	67.0	311,453	32.9	81.5	946,385	71.1
1931 - 1933	142,946	69.1	109.8	64,061	30.9	112.5	207,007	110.6
1901 - 1933	2,354,321	72.5	81.1	893,177	27.5	81.7	3,247,498	81.3
1886 - 1933	(a)	...	...	1,146,787	...	84.1	....	...
In								
1886 - 1900	(a)	...	...	270,866	...	100.0	....	...
1901 - 1920	1,824,499	73.6	100.0	654,490	26.4	100.0	2,478,989	100.0
1921 - 1930	948,532	71.3	100.0	382,101	28.7	100.0	1,330,633	100.0
1931 - 1933	130,202	69.6	100.0	56,930	30.4	100.0	187,132	100.0
1901 - 1933	2,903,233	72.6	100.0	1,093,521	27.4	100.0	3,996,754	100.0
1886 - 1933	(a)	...	...	1,364,387	...	100.0		
Balance (b)								
1886 - 1900	+ 183,580(c)	91.4	...	+ 17,256	8.6	6.4	+ 200,836	...
1901 - 1920	+ 248,056	64.4	13.6	+ 136,827	35.6	20.9	+ 384,883	15.5
1921 - 1930	+ 313,600	81.6	33.0	+ 70,648	18.4	18.5	+ 384,248	28.9
1931 - 1933	- 12,744	64.1	9.8	- 7,131	35.9	12.5	- 19,875	10.6
1901 - 1933	+ 548,912	73.3	18.9	+ 200,344	26.7	18.3	+ 749,256	18.7
1886 - 1933	+ 732,492(c)	77.1	...	+ 217,600	22.9	15.9	+ 950,092	...

Sources:
Calculated from data in Ferenczi, International Migrations, Vol. I.
Official Year-Book of the Commonwealth of Australia, 1934.
New Zealand Official Year-Book, 1934.

Notes:
(a) Data not available.
(b) + and - indicate excess of arrivals and departures, respectively.
(c) The available records for these years give balances, but not total arrivals and departures.

TABLE XXVII
AUSTRALIAN INTERCONTINENTAL MIGRATION
A—Nationals and Aliens, 1901-1933

A total immigration for Australia and New Zealand in the years 1901-1933 of just under 4 millions, looks as though these regions had been decidedly useful as population outlets. But more than four fifths as many left as arrived; the net immigration was 19% of the gross, and amounted to only 749,000, including the movement between these two Dominions. Incomplete earlier records suggest that a larger proportion than this of the arrivals stayed in earlier years, but it seems quite safe to conclude that not over a fourth of those who immigrated to these regions have remained. On this basis, the net migration to Australia and New Zealand from the British ports, 1815-1933, would be well under 800,000, instead of the 3 millions shown as the gross emigration (Table XXI).

The reversal of the migration movement since 1930 which is so noticeable in Europe shows also in the net emigration from Australia and New Zealand.

	Out (a)			In			Balance (b)		
	Number	Average per Year	% of Ins	Number	Average per Year	Number	Average per Year	% of Ins
1901 - 1905	297,953	59,591	106.0	281,160	56,232	− 16,793	− 3,359	6.0
1906 - 1910	313,756	62,711	84.6	371,034	74,207	+ 57,278	+ 11,436	15.4
1911 - 1915	495,958	99,192	78.4	632,820	126,564	+ 136,862	+ 27,372	21.6
1916 - 1920	468,776	93,755	86.9	539,485	107,897	+ 70,709	+ 14,142	13.1
1921 - 1925	294,509	58,902	61.6	478,052	95,610	+ 183,543	+ 36,708	38.4
1926 - 1930	340,423	68,085	72.4	470,480	94,096	+ 130,057	+ 26,011	27.6
1931 - 1933	142,941	47,649	109.8	130,202	43,401	− 12,744	− 4,248	9.8
1901 - 1930	2,211,375	73,713	79.7	2,773,031	92,434	+ 561,656	+ 18,721	20.3
1901 - 1933	2,354,321	71,343	81.1	2,903,233	87,977	+ 548,912	+ 16,634	18.9

Source:
Calculated from data in the Official Yearbook of the Commonwealth of Australia, 1933, p. 779.

Notes:
(a) There is a small discrepancy between the 1921-1930 total here and that shown in the immigration by nationalities. This appears in the original figures; it is reflected here in the discrepancy in the balances.
(b) + and − indicate excess of arrivals and departures, respectively.

TABLE XXVII
AUSTRALIAN INTERCONTINENTAL MIGRATION
B — By Nationalities, 1921-1930

	Out (a)				In				Balance (b)	
	Number	% of Western and non-Western	% of Grand Total	% of Ins	Number	% of Western and non-Western	% of Grand Total	Number	% of Ins
Grand Total	644,214	. . . . .	100.0	67.9	948,532	. . . . .	100.0	+ 304,318	32.1
Total Westerners.	589,266	100.0	91.5	65.8	895,349	100.0	94.4	+ 306,083	34.2
British.	538,282	91.3	83.6	68.0	791,461	88.4	83.4	+ 253,179	32.0
Italian.	12,234	2.1	1.9	33.7	36,262	4.0	3.8	+ 24,028	66.3
United States.	12,368	2.1	1.9	78.3	15,791	1.8	1.7	+ 3,423	21.7
Others	26,382	4.5	4.1	50.9	51,835	5.8	5.5	+ 25,453	49.1
Total Non-Western	54,948	100.0	8.5	103.3	53,183	100.0	5.6	− 1,765	3.3
Chinese.	36,294	66.1	5.6	110.7	32,782	61.6	3.5	− 3,512	10.7
Others	18,654	33.9	2.9	91.4	20,401	38.4	2.1	+ 1,747	8.6

Source:
Calculated from data in the Official Yearbook of the Commonwealth of Australia, 1933, pp. 780-781.

Notes:
(a) There is a slight discrepancy between the total here and the 1921-1930 total in the table of migrations for 1901-1932. This appears in the original figures.
(b) + and − indicate excess of arrivals and departures, respectively.

TABLE XXVIII
SOUTH AFRICAN MIGRATION
1900-1927
Nationals and Aliens

The net immigration into the Union of South Africa in the 18 years 1910-1927 averaged exactly 507 a year. If figures were available for the years since then, they probably would show a net outward movement, especially of East Indians. But even if the record be carried back to 1900, it shows that the region has not been useful to an important extent as a population outlet - not with an average net annual immigration, 1900-1927, of only 5,420 people.

	Out		In		Balance (a)	
	Number	% of Ins	Number	% of Ins	Number	% of Ins
1900 - 1909	562,959	79.8	705,532	100.00	+ 142,573	20.2
Natal.	258,506	76.9	336,094	100.00	+ 77,588	23.1
Cape of Good Hope.	304,453	82.4	369,438	100.00	+ 64,985	17.6
1910 - 1927	449,008	98.0	458,135	100.00	+ 9,127	2.0
Union of South Africa						
1900 - 1927	1,011,967	87.0	1,163,667	100.00	+ 151,700	13.0
(Total of above)						

Sources:
Calculated from data in Ferenczi, International Migrations, Vol. I.
International Labor Office, Migration Movements, 1920 - 1924; Migration Movements, 1925 - 1927.

Note:
(a) + and - indicate excess of immigration and emigration, respectively.

TABLE XXIX
WORLD TRADE OF THE WESTERN AND NON-WESTERN COUNTRIES
Average per Year 1929-1933. Values in 1,000's of Old U.S.A. Gold Dollars

The Western countries' share of world trade is substantially larger than the proportion of the earth's surface which they control. In 1933 their territory (Table II) was 85% of the total. For the years 1929-1933 they did 93% of the world's total importing and exporting. The British Commonwealth alone contains more territory (Table I) and does more business than all the non-Western countries, by a large margin. Incidentally, it is interesting to observe how nearly the British area and trade proportions come to a fourth of the total. In 1933, British areas were 24% and non-Western areas 15% of the earth's surface. British imports, 1929-1933, were 29% of the world total; non-Western, 7.4%. British exports, 26%; non-Western exports, 7.1%. The United States and France also do more foreign trade than all the non-Western world. Their shares of world imports, 1929-1933, were 11.2% and 9.9%; of world exports, 14.3% and 8.1%.

A great deal has been said about Japan's competition in world trade, but in terms of old U.S. gold dollars she did a distinctly smaller share of the world's importing and exporting, 1929-1933, than the Netherlands, and only a slightly larger share than Belgium.

	Imports				Exports			
	$1,000's	% of World Total	% of Regional Total	% of Country	$1,000's	% of World Total	% of Regional Total	% of Country
World Total	22,382.4	100.00	100.00		20,609.4	100.00	100.00	
Africa	1,176.4	5.26	100.00		1,072.6	5.20	100.00	
The Americas	4,647.2	20.76	100.00		5,484.5	26.61	100.00	
North America	3,143.2	14.04	67.64		3,606.7	17.50	65.76	
Central America	498.5	2.23	10.73		587.1	2.85	10.70	
South America	1,005.5	4.49	21.63		1,290.7	6.26	23.54	
Asia	2,911.0	13.01	100.00		2,934.6	14.24	100.00	
Europe	13,146.4	58.74	100.00		10,551.6	51.20	100.00	
Oceania.	501.4	2.24	100.00		566.1	2.75	100.00	
Total home countries trade. . . .	18,082.7	80.79	100.00		16,177.7	78.50	100.00	
Western.	16,642.0	74.35	92.03		14,925.6	72.42	92.26	
Non-Western.	1,440.7	6.44	7.97		1,252.1	6.08	7.74	
Total Colonial trade.	4,299.7	19.21	100.00		4,431.7	21.50	100.00	
Western.	4,094.1	18.29	95.22		4,217.9	20.47	95.18	
Non-Western.	205.6	0.92	4.78		213.8	1.03	4.82	
Total Western trade	20,736.1	92.64	100.00		19,143.5	92.89	100.00	
Home countries trade	16,642.0	74.35	80.26		14,925.6	72.42	77.97	
Colonial trade	4,094.1	18.29	19.74		4,217.9	20.47	22.03	
Total Non-Western trade	1,646.3	7.36	100.00		1,465.9	7.11	100.00	
Home countries trade	1,440.7	6.44	87.51		1,252.1	6.08	85.42	
Colonial trade	205.6	0.92	12.49		213.8	1.03	14.58	
British trade: Total.	6,538.2	29.21	. . . .	100.00	5,279.5	25.62	. . . .	100.00
Africa	455.9	2.04	38.75	6.97	563.4	2.73	52.53	10.67
The Americas	802.9	3.59	17.28	12.28	823.2	3.99	15.01	15.59
Asia	965.0	4.31	33.15	14.76	1,066.6	5.18	36.35	20.20
Europe	3,824.1	17.08	29.09	58.49	2,272.3	11.03	21.54	43.04
Oceania.	490.4	2.19	97.81	7.50	554.0	2.69	97.86	10.50
Dominions: Total	1,694.8	75.7	100.00	25.92	1,816.0	8.81	100.00	34.40
Australia and New Zealand. . . .	479.9	2.14	28.32	7.34	539.9	2.62	29.73	10.23
Canada and Newfoundland.	737.0	3.29	43.49	11.27	762.1	3.70	41.97	14.44
Irish Free State	210.2	0.94	12.40	3.21	152.4	0.74	8.39	2.89
Union of South Africa.	267.7	1.20	15.80	4.09	361.6	1.75	19.91	6.85
India, Ceylon, and Malaya: Total.	898.8	4.02	100.00	13.75	1,026.7	4.98	100.00	19.45
India.	537.0	2.40	59.75	8.21	669.8	3.25	65.24	12.69
Ceylon	75.8	0.34	8.43	1.16	80.5	0.39	7.84	1.52
British Malaya	286.0	1.28	31.82	4.37	276.4	1.34	26.92	5.24
United Kingdom.	3,599.3	16.08	27.38	55.05	2,119.6	10.28	20.85	40.15
Total colonies and Dominions. . .	2,938.9	13.13	. . . .	44.95	3,159.9	15.33	. . . .	59.85
French trade: Total	2,217.9	9.91	. . . .	100.00	1,658.9	8.05	. . . .	100.00
Africa	436.9	1.95	37.14	19.70	292.2	1.42	27.24	17.61
The Americas	16.2	0.07	0.35	0.73	15.8	0.08	0.27	0.95
Asia	103.3	0.46	3.55	4.65	79.8	0.39	2.72	4.81
Europe (France).	1,656.1	7.40	12.60	74.67	1,267.2	6.15	12.01	76.39
Oceania.	5.4	0.02	1.08	0.24	3.9	0.02	0.69	0.24
Total colonies.	561.8	2.51	. . . .	25.33	391.7	1.90	. . . .	23.61
Italian trade: Total.	729.1	3.26	. . . .	100.00	538.0	2.61	. . . .	100.00
Africa	35.1	0.16	2.98	4.81	11.7	0.06	1.09	2.17
Europe (Italy)	694.0	3.10	5.28	95.19	526.3	2.55	4.99	97.83

(Continued on next page)

TABLE XXIX
WORLD TRADE OF THE WESTERN AND NON-WESTERN COUNTRIES
Concluded

	Imports				Exports			
	$1,000's	% of World Total	% of Regional Total	% of Country	$1,000's	% of World Total	% of Regional Total	% of Country
Belgian trade: Total.	701.8	3.14	. . . . .	100.00	640.4	3.11	. . . .	100.00
Africa	27.7	0.12	2.35	3.95	29.9	0.15	2.79	4.67
Europe (Belgium)	674.1	3.01	5.13	96.05	610.5	2.96	5.78	95.33
Danish trade (Europe)	328.9	1.47	2.50	100.00	306.9	1.49	2.91	100.00
Netherlands trade: Total.	1,143.2	5.11	. . . . .	100.00	1,000.3	4.85	. . . .	100.00
The Americas	107.8	0.48	2.32	9.43	118.8	0.58	2.17	11.88
Asia	265.5	1.19	9.12	23.22	351.4	1.71	11.97	35.13
Europe (Netherlands)	769.9	3.44	5.85	67.35	530.1	2.57	5.02	52.99
Total colonies.	373.3	1.67	. . . .	32.65	470.2	2.28	. . . .	47.01
Portuguese trade: Total	107.4	0.48	. . . . .	100.00	52.2	0.25	. . . . .	100.00
Africa	26.5	0.12	2.25	24.67	17.4	0.08	1.62	33.33
Europe (Portugal).	80.9	0.36	0.62	75.33	34.8	0.17	0.33	66.67
Russian trade (Europe).	421.6	1.88	3.21	100.00	396.6	1.92	3.76	100.00
Spanish trade: Total.	324.2	1.45	. . . . .	100.00	263.7	1.28	. . . . .	100.00
Africa	8.8	0.04	0.75	2.71	2.2	0.01	0.21	0.83
Europe (Spain)	315.4	1.41	2.40	97.29	261.5	1.27	2.48	99.17
United States trade: Total. . . .	2,497.9	11.16	. . . .	100.00	2,953.5	14.33	. . . .	100.00
The Americas (United States) . . .	2,397.0	10.71	51.58	95.96	2,834.4	13.75	51.68	95.97
Asia (Philippines)	100.9	0.45	3.47	4.04	119.1	0.58	4.06	4.03
Other Western trade	5,725.9	25.58	. . . .	100.00	6,053.5	29.37	. . . .	100.00
Africa	18.0	0.08	1.53	0.31	12.0	0.06	1.12	0.20
The Americas	1,323.3	5.91	28.48	23.11	1,692.3	8.21	30.86	27.96
Europe	4,381.5	19.58	33.33	76.52	4,345.4	21.08	41.18	71.78
Oceania.	3.1	0.01	0.62	0.06	3.8	0.02	0.67	0.06
Total Western trade	20,736.1	92.64	. . . .	100.00	19,143.5	92.89	92.89	100.00
Africa	1,008.9	4.51	85.76	4.87	928.8	4.51	86.59	4.85
The Americas	4,647.2	20.76	100.00	22.41	5,484.5	26.61	100.00	28.65
Asia	1,434.7	6.41	49.29	6.92	1,616.9	7.85	55.10	8.45
Europe	13,146.4	58.74	100.00	63.40	10,551.6	51.20	100.00	55.12
Oceania.	498.9	2.23	99.50	2.40	561.7	2.73	99.22	2.93
Chinese trade: Asia	439.8	1.97	15.11	100.00	229.3	1.11	7.81	100.00
Egyptian trade: Africa.	164.0	0.73	13.94	100.00	142.4	0.69	13.28	100.00
Iranian trade: Asia	44.7	0.20	1.54	100.00	94.5	0.46	3.22	100.00
Iraq trade: Asia.	24.2	0.11	0.83	100.00	5.9	0.03	0.20	100.00
Japanese trade: Total	826.1	3.69	. . . .	100.00	804.4	3.90	. . . .	100.00
Asia	823.6	3.68	28.29	99.70	800.0	3.88	27.26	99.45
Japan Proper.	620.5	2.77	21.32	75.11	590.6	2.86	20.13	73.42
Colonies.	203.1	0.91	6.98	24.59	209.4	1.02	7.13	26.03
Oceania.	2.5	0.01	0.50	0.30	4.4	0.02	0.78	0.55
Total colonies.	205.6	0.92	. . . .	24.89	213.8	1.04	. . . .	26.58
Manchurian trade: Asia.	88.4	0.39	3.04	100.00	124.6	0.60	4.25	100.00
Siamese trade: Asia	49.2	0.22	1.69	100.00	58.3	0.28	1.99	100.00
Other non-Western trade: Total. . .	9.9	0.04	. . . .	100.00	6.5	0.03	. . . .	100.00
Africa	3.5	0.02	0.30	35.35	1.4	0.01	0.13	21.54
Asia	6.4	0.03	0.22	64.65	5.1	0.02	0.17	78.46
Total non-Western trade	1,646.3	7.36	. . . .	100.00	1,465.9	7.11	. . . .	100.00
Africa	167.5	0.75	14.24	10.17	143.8	0.70	13.41	9.81
Asia	1,476.3	6.60	50.71	89.67	1,317.7	6.39	44.90	89.89
Oceania.	2.5	0.01	0.50	0.16	4.4	0.02	0.78	0.30

Source:
Calculated from data in League of Nations, Statistical Year-Book, 1934/35.

Consistently since 1934, France has sold more to her colonies than she has bought from them, though the balance has been comparatively small except during the World War years. On the other hand, her foreign trade has shown a fairly heavy import surplus, with this "unfavorable" balance rising, in 1914-1918, to more than twice the value of all the exports to foreign countries. The proportion of French colonial trade to total was a little more than a tenth of the total external trade in the 20 years before the World War and the ten years beginning with 1919. Since then, it has risen to nearly 20% of the total, and in 1934 it was 28% (Table XXXI).

TABLE XXX
EXTERNAL TRADE OF FRANCE, 1894-1934
Merchandise—Special (Net) Trade. Value in 1,000,000's of Francs

	1894-1903		1904-1913		1914-1918		1919-1928		1929-1934		1894-1934	
	Value	% of Total	Value	% of Total	Value	% of Total	Value	% of Total	Value	% of Total	Value	% of Total
Imports:												
From foreign countries	38,379	90.14	58,041	89.42	81,343	92.50	371,585	89.20	195,760	83.57	745,108	88.05
From colonies	4,199	9.86	6,868	10.58	6,596	7.50	44,991	10.80	38,478	16.43	101,132	11.95
Total imports	42,578	100.00	64,909	100.00	87,939	100.00	416,576	100.00	234,238	100.00	846,240	100.00
Exports:												
To foreign countries	33,514	88.80	49,681	87.39	21,955	85.24	311,687	85.09	136,253	75.94	553,090	83.04
To colonies	4,226	11.20	7,171	12.61	3,802	14.76	54,611	14.91	43,159	24.06	112,969	16.96
Total exports	37,740	100.00	56,852	100.00	25,757	100.00	366,298	100.00	179,412	100.00	666,059	100.00
Total Trade:												
With foreign countries	71,893	89.51	107,722	88.47	103,298	90.85	683,272	87.28	332,013	80.26	1,298,198	85.84
With colonies	8,425	10.49	14,039	11.53	10,398	9.15	99,602	12.72	81,637	19.74	214,101	14.16
Total trade	80,318	100.00	121,761	100.00	113,696	100.00	782,874	100.00	413,650	100.00	1,512,299	100.00
Balance (a):												
With foreign countries	− 4,865	6.77	− 8,360	7.76	− 59,388	57.49	− 59,898	8.77	− 59,507	17.92	− 192,018	14.79
With colonies	+ 27	0.32	− 303	2.16	− 2,794	26.87	+ 9,620	9.66	+ 4,681	5.73	+ 11,837	5.53
Total balance	− 4,838	6.02	− 8,057	6.62	− 62,182	54.69	− 50,278	6.42	− 54,826	13.25	− 180,181	11.91

Source:
Calculated from data in the Tableau général du commerce (et de la navigation), annual volumes, for 1894-1932.
Calculated from data in the Statistique mensuelle du commerce, for 1933 and 1934.

Note:
(a) + and − indicate export and import surplus, respectively. Balance percents are of corresponding total trade.

Algeria is far and away France's most important colony, from the trade point of view. In 1932, 1933, and 1934, France did more business with Algeria alone than with any foreign country, and regularly, since well before the War, Algeria has been more important than all the other colonies combined as a market for exports, though not quite as important as a source of supplies.

The decrease in the share of France's external trade which is with foreign countries has been fairly evenly distributed among the principal countries, though Britain definitely has ceased to hold the leadership which had been hers by a good margin before the War. Both in 1929-1933 and in 1934, as a matter of fact, France did more trade with Germany than with any other foreign country, though she sold more to both Britain and Belgium in 1929-1933 than to Germany, and more to Belgium in 1934 also.

TABLE XXXI
EXTERNAL TRADE OF FRANCE, WITH CERTAIN COUNTRIES
Merchandise—Special (Net) Trade. Value in 1,000,000's of Francs

	Total Trade		Trade with Foreign Countries		Trade with Colonies		Trade with Algeria		Trade with Germany		Trade with Italy		Trade with the United Kingdom		Trade with the United States		Trade with Belgium and Luxemburg	
	Value	% of Total	Value	% of Corresponding Total	Value	% of Corresponding Total	Value	% of Corresponding Total	Value	% of Corresponding Total	Value	% of Corresponding Total	Value	% of Corresponding Total	Value	% of Corresponding Total	Value	% of Corresponding Total
1904																		
Imports	4,502	100.00	4,015	89.18	487	10.82	234	5.20	429	9.53	151	3.35	524	11.64	423	9.40	306	6.80
Exports	4,451	100.00	3,893	87.46	558	12.54	315	7.08	555	12.47	190	4.27	1,214	27.27	251	5.64	678	15.23
Total trade	8,953	100.00	7,908	88.33	1,045	11.67	549	6.13	984	10.99	341	3.81	1,738	19.41	734	8.20	984	10.99
Balance (a)	− 51	0.57	− 122	1.54	+ 71	6.79	+ 81	14.75	+ 126	12.80	+ 39	11.44	+ 690	39.70	− 172	23.43	+ 372	37.80
balance % of Total		100.00		239.22		139.22		158.82		247.06		76.47		1,352.94		337.25		729.41
1913																		
Imports	8,421	100.00	7,624	90.35	797	9.46	331	3.93	1,069	12.69	241	2.86	1,115	13.24	895	10.63	556	6.60
Exports	6,880	100.00	5,985	86.99	895	13.01	552	8.02	867	12.60	306	4.45	1,454	21.13	422	6.13	1,109	16.12
Total trade	15,301	100.00	13,609	88.95	1,692	11.06	883	5.77	1,936	12.65	547	3.58	2,569	16.79	1,317	8.61	1,665	10.88
Balance (a)	− 1,541	10.07	− 1,639	11.99	+ 98	5.79	+ 221	25.03	− 202	10.43	+ 65	11.88	+ 339	13.20	− 473	35.91	+ 543	32.61
balance % of Total		100.00		106.36		6.36		14.34		13.11		4.22		22.00		30.69		35.24
Average per year 1929-1933																		
Imports	42,235	100.00	35,702	84.53	6,533	15.47	3,374	7.99	5,447	12.90	1,147	2.72	3,873	9.17	4,588	10.86	3,200	7.58
Exports	32,318	100.00	24,787	76.69	7,531	23.30	3,924	12.14	3,065	9.48	1,195	3.70	4,536	14.03	1,828	5.66	4,526	14.00
Total trade	74,553	100.00	60,489	81.14	14,064	18.87	7,298	9.79	8,512	11.42	2,342	3.14	8,409	11.28	6,416	8.61	7,726	10.36
Balance (a)	− 9,917	13.30	− 10,915	18.04	+ 998	7.10	+ 550	7.54	− 2,381	27.97	+ 48	2.05	+ 663	7.88	− 2,760	43.02	+ 1,326	17.16
balance % of Total		100.00		110.06		10.06		5.55		13.93		0.48		6.67		27.83		13.37
1934																		
Imports	23,061	100.00	17,248	74.80	5,813	25.21	2,786	12.08	2,218	9.62	483	2.09	1,636	7.09	2,216	9.61	1,470	6.37
Exports	17,822	100.00	12,319	69.12	5,502	30.87	3,073	17.24	1,714	9.62	553	3.10	1,536	8.62	839	4.71	1,977	11.09
Total trade	40,883	100.00	29,567	72.32	11,315	27.68	5,859	14.33	3,932	9.62	1,036	2.53	3,172	7.76	3,055	7.47	3,447	8.43
Balance (a)	− 5,239	12.81	− 4,929	16.67	− 311	2.75	+ 287	4.90	− 504	12.50	+ 70	6.76	− 100	3.15	− 1,377	45.07	+ 507	14.71
balance % of Total		100.00		94.08		5.94		5.48		9.62		1.34		1.91		26.28		9.68

Source:
Calculated from data in the Tableau général du commerce extérieur, annual volumes for 1894-1932.
Calculated from data in the Statistique mensuelle du commerce extérieur, for 1933 and 1934.

Note:
(a) Balance percents are of corresponding totals. + and − indicate export and import surplus, respectively.

As either markets or sources of supplies, the German colonies were negligible for Germany, from 1894 to 1913. Imports from them were only 0.3% and exports only 0.5% of Germany's total external imports and exports in these years. But such as it was, this small trade showed an export surplus of a little more than a fifth of the value of exports plus imports. Germany's foreign trade in 1894-1913 and 1924-1933 showed an "unfavorable" balance, though a comparatively small one.

TABLE XXXII
EXTERNAL TRADE OF GERMANY, 1894-1933
Merchandise—Special (Net) Trade. Value in 1,000,000's of Marks.

	1894-1903 Value	% of Total	1904-1913 (a) Value	% of Total	1894-1913 Value	% of Total	1924-1928 (b) Value	% of Total	1929-1933 Value	% of Total	1894-1913 and 1924-1933 (b) Value	% of Total
Imports:												
From foreign countries	53,004	99.90	87,027	99.63	140,031	99.73	59,676	100.00	39,437	100.00	239,144	100.00
From colonies	55	0.10	323	0.37	378	0.27	..	..	..	..	..	..
Total	53,059	100.00	87,350	100.00	140,409	100.00	59,676	100.00	39,437	100.00	239,144	100.00
Exports:												
To foreign countries	41,457	99.65	71,543	99.38	113,000	99.48	49,334	100.00	45,730	100.00	208,064	100.00
To colonies	147	0.35	447	0.62	594	0.52	..	..	..	..	..	..
Total	41,604	100.00	71,990	100.00	113,594	100.00	49,334	100.00	45,730	100.00	208,064	100.00
Total Trade:												
With foreign countries	94,461	99.79	158,570	99.52	253,031	99.62	109,010	100.00	85,167	100.00	447,208	100.00
With colonies	202	0.21	770	0.48	972	0.38	..	..	..	..	..	..
Total	94,663	100.00	159,340	100.00	254,003	100.00	109,010	100.00	85,167	100.00	447,208	100.00
Balance (c):												
With foreign countries	− 11,547	12.22	− 15,484	9.76	− 27,031	10.68	− 10,342	9.49	+ 6,293	7.39	− 31,080	6.95
With colonies	+ 92	45.54	+ 124	16.10	+ 216	22.22	..	..	..	..	..	..
Total	− 11,455	12.10	− 15,360	9.64	− 26,815	10.56	− 10,342	9.49	− 6,293	7.39	− 31,080	6.95

Source:
Calculated from data in Statistische Jahrbuch für das Deutsche Reich, annual volumes.

Notes:
(a) Beginning in 1906, the figures are for the German Reich only. Prior to that, parts of the Zollverein were included in the German trade returns.
(b) No records available for the years 1914-1922, inclusive. 1923 figures omitted because of upset due to inflation of the Mark.
(c) + and − indicate export and import surplus, respectively. Balance percents are of the corresponding total trade.

TABLE XXXIII
EXTERNAL TRADE OF ITALY, 1894-1932
Merchandise—Special (Net) Trade. Value in 1,000,000's of Lire

Italy has had an export surplus on her colonial trade, considerably larger proportionately than France's (Table XXX) or Germany's (Table XXXII). The ratio of her trade with the colonies to her total external trade has been only slightly larger than Germany's and much smaller than that of France: 0.97%, for 1894-1932. But the relative importance of the colonial trade has increased slightly in recent years: from 0.94% in 1919-1928 to 1.38% in 1929-1932. Italy's "unfavorable" foreign trade balance has been an exceptionally high proportion of her total foreign trade, especially since the World War.

	1894-1903		1904-1913		1914-1918		1919-1928		1929-1932		1894-1932	
	Value	% of Total	Value	% of Total	Value	% of Total	Value	% of Total	Value	% of Total	Value	% of Total
Imports:												
From foreign countries	14,523	99.95	29,236	99.78	45,867	99.63	206,063	99.50	58,232	99.44	353,921	99.56
From colonies (a)	6	0.04	61	0.21	169	0.37	1,017	0.49	329	0.56	1,582	0.44
Total trade	14,529	100.00	29,297	100.00	46,036	100.00	207,080	100.00	58,561	100.00	355,503	100.00
Exports:												
To foreign countries	12,456	99.70	19,612	98.45	14,068	97.12	125,623	98.34	42,937	97.53	214,696	98.17
To colonies (a)	37	0.30	310	1.55	417	2.88	2,126	1.66	1,088	2.47	3,978	1.82
Total trade	12,493	100.00	19,922	100.00	14,485	100.00	127,749	100.00	44,025	100.00	218,674	100.00
Total Trade:												
With foreign countries	26,979	99.83	48,848	99.24	59,935	99.03	331,686	99.06	101,169	98.61	568,617	99.03
With colonies (a)	43	0.16	371	0.75	586	0.97	3,143	0.94	1,417	1.38	5,560	0.97
Total trade	27,022	100.00	49,219	100.00	60,521	100.00	334,829	100.00	102,586	100.00	574,177	100.00
Balance (b):												
With foreign countries	– 2,067	7.65	– 9,624	19.55	– 31,799	52.54	– 80,440	24.02	– 15,295	14.91	– 139,225	24.25
With colonies (a)	+ 31	70.47	+ 249	67.27	+ 248	46.06	+ 1,109	35.29	+ 759	53.57	+ 2,396	43.50
Total balance	– 2,036	7.53	– 9,375	19.05	– 31,551	52.13	– 79,331	23.69	– 14,536	14.17	– 136,829	23.83

Source:
Calculated from data in the *Movimento commerciale del Regno d'Italia*, annual volumes.

Notes:
(a) Records begin: For Libya and Eritrea, in 1895; for Somaliland in 1904; for the Aegean Islands, in 1925.
(b) + and – indicate excess of exports and imports, respectively. Balance percents are of the corresponding totals.

For the whole period, 1894-1934, Japan has done with her colonies slightly better than 15% of her external trade. This is very close to the proportions of French colonial trade to total French trade (Table XXX). It also is approximately the share of her total trade that the United Kingdom did in the same period with the overseas territories which she controlled - i.e., with the British countries other than the Dominions (Table XXXIX). But since 1929, the colonies have become relatively more important to Japan in trade than to these other countries. For 1929-1934, colonial trade was 22% of Japan's total trade and 20% of France's, while the United Kingdom's proportion of trade with the territories she controls was 16%. Japan's balance of trade with her colonies, unlike France's, Germany's, and Italy's, but like Britain's, has been "unfavorable." From 1894-1913, the exports to the colonies were more than the imports from them, but the turn came in the War years, and the "unfavorable" balance since then has considerably more than eaten up the earlier small "favorable" balance. Japan regularly has had an "unfavorable" balance on her foreign trade also, over periods of years running back to 1868, though the balance was the other way in the four War years. Over the whole period of modern Japan, 1868-1934, however, the imports have exceeded the foreign exports by only a small margin: 1,622 million yen, or 1.9% of the total foreign trade of 87,578 million yen. Of the colonial trade, the "unfavorable" balance has been 12% of the total.

TABLE XXXIV
EXTERNAL TRADE OF JAPAN PROPER, 1868-1934
Merchandise—Gross Trade. Value in 1,000's of Yen

	1868-1893 Value	% of Total	1894-1903 Value	% of Total	1904-1913 Value	% of Total	1914-1918 Value	% of Total	1919-1928 Value	% of Total	1929-1934 Value	% of Total	1894-1934 Value	% of Total	1868-1934 Value	% of Total
Imports																
From foreign countries	1,009,064	100.00	2,267,561	98.34	4,930,065	93.15	4,588,565	86.56	21,175,335	82.71	10,629,194	76.88	43,590,720	83.30	44,599,784	83.62
From Korea (a)	…	…	…	…	54,022	1.02	314,381	5.93	2,632,539	10.28	1,805,305	13.05	4,806,247	9.18	4,806,247	9.01
From Formosa (b)	…	…	38,251	1.66	308,613	5.83	398,174	7.51	1,793,992	7.01	1,391,602	10.07	3,930,632	7.52	3,930,632	7.37
From colonies	…	…	38,251	1.66	362,635	6.85	712,555	13.44	4,426,531	17.29	3,196,907	23.12	8,736,879	16.70	8,736,879	16.38
Total	1,009,064	100.00	2,305,812	100.00	5,292,700	100.00	5,301,120	100.00	25,601,866	100.00	13,826,101	100.00	52,327,599	100.00	53,336,663	100.00
Exports																
To foreign countries	1,001,234	100.00	1,915,600	97.28	4,353,618	92.20	6,991,980	92.20	18,506,926	85.60	10,206,412	79.16	41,976,536	86.03	42,977,770	86.31
To Korea (a)	…	…	…	…	115,243	2.44	323,009	4.26	2,072,206	9.58	1,849,400	14.34	4,359,858	8.94	4,359,858	8.76
To Formosa (b)	…	…	53,650	2.72	252,924	5.36	268,556	3.54	1,040,691	4.82	838,597	6.50	2,454,418	5.03	2,454,418	4.93
To colonies	…	…	53,650	2.72	368,167	7.80	591,565	7.80	3,112,897	14.40	2,687,997	20.84	6,814,276	13.97	6,814,276	13.69
Total	1,001,234	100.00	1,969,250	100.00	4,721,785	100.00	7,583,545	100.00	21,619,823	100.00	12,896,409	100.00	48,790,812	100.00	49,792,046	100.00
Total Trade																
With foreign countries	2,010,298	100.00	4,183,161	97.85	9,283,683	92.70	11,580,545	89.88	39,682,261	84.03	20,837,606	77.98	85,567,256	84.62	87,577,554	84.92
With Korea (a)	…	…	…	…	169,265	1.69	637,390	4.95	4,704,745	9.97	3,654,705	13.68	9,166,105	9.06	9,166,105	8.89
With Formosa (b)	…	…	91,901	2.15	561,537	5.61	666,730	5.17	2,834,683	6.00	2,230,199	8.34	6,385,050	6.32	6,385,050	6.19
With colonies	…	…	91,901	2.15	730,802	7.30	1,304,120	10.12	7,539,428	15.97	5,884,904	22.02	15,551,155	15.38	15,551,155	15.08
Total	2,010,298	100.00	4,276,062	100.00	10,014,485	100.00	12,884,665	100.00	47,221,689	100.00	26,722,510	100.00	101,118,411	100.00	103,128,709	100.00
Balance (c)																
With foreign countries	- 7,830	0.39	- 351,961	8.41	+ 576,447	6.21	+ 2,403,415	20.75	- 2,668,409	6.72	+ 420,782	2.02	- 1,614,184	1.89	- 1,622,014	1.85
With Korea (a)	…	…	…	…	+ 61,221	36.17	+ 8,628	1.35	- 560,333	11.91	+ 44,095	1.21	+ 446,389	4.87	+ 446,389	4.87
With Formosa (b)	…	…	+ 15,399	16.76	- 55,689	9.92	- 129,618	19.44	- 753,301	26.57	- 553,005	24.80	- 1,476,214	23.12	- 1,476,214	23.12
With colonies	…	…	+ 15,399	16.76	+ 5,532	0.76	- 121,990	9.28	- 1,313,634	17.42	- 508,910	8.65	- 1,922,603	12.36	- 1,922,603	12.36
Total	- 7,830	0.39	- 336,562	7.87	+ 570,915	5.70	+ 2,282,425	17.71	- 3,982,043	8.43	- 929,692	3.48	- 3,536,787	3.50	- 3,544,617	3.44

Source:
Calculated from data in the Financial and Economic Annual of Japan, annual volumes.

Notes:
(a) Records begin in 1911.
(b) Records begin in 1897.
(c) + and - indicate export and import surplus respectively.
Balance percents are of the corresponding total trade.

The proportion of her foreign trade which Japan did with the rest of Asia increased somewhat between 1894 and 1904, but since then it has remained nearly constant, a falling off of the share with China being made up by an increase in the shares with other Asiatic countries. The share with British India and Ceylon has changed but little since 1904. In recent years, the trade with Asia has shown a substantial export surplus contrasting with an "unfavorable" balance before 1914. Total trade with the United States has run fairly close to a fourth of Japan's total, with some increase in recent years. When silk prices were high, Japan showed an export surplus in her trade with the United States, and the reverse when silk was down in value. In 1894 and 1904, the United Kingdom supplied a much larger part of Japan's imports than the United States, though she took a much smaller share of her exports. Since 1929, Britain's share in both the imports and the exports has been quite small; Japan's total trade with her, in fact, was less than with Australia in 1929–1934.

TABLE XXXV
FOREIGN TRADE OF JAPAN PROPER BY COUNTRIES AND CONTINENTAL AREAS
Merchandise—Gross Trade. Value in 1,000's of Yen

	Total Trade Value	Total Trade % of Total	Trade with Asia Amount	Asia % of Corr. Total	Trade with the Americas Value	Americas % of Corr. Total	Trade with China (b) Value	China % of Corr. Total	Trade with British India and Ceylon (c) Value	Brit. India % of Corr. Total	Trade with Netherlands Indies Value	Neth. Indies % of Corr. Total	Trade with the United States Value	U.S. % of Corr. Total	Trade with the United Kingdom Value	U.K. % of Corr. Total	Trade with Australia Value	Australia % of Corr. Total
1894																		
Imports	117,482	100.00	48,942	41.66	11,028	9.39	17,512	14.91	10,560	8.99			10,983	9.35	42,190	35.91	535	0.46
Exports	113,246	100.00	32,308	28.53	45,535	40.21	8,814	7.78	3,688	3.26	2,365	2.09	43,324	38.26	5,950	5.25	1,098	0.97
Total trade	230,728	100.00	81,250	35.21	56,563	24.52	26,326	11.41	14,248	6.18	2,365	1.02	54,307	23.54	48,140	20.86	1,633	0.71
Balance (a)	−4,232	1.83	−16,634	20.47	+34,507	61.01	−8,698	33.04	−6,872	48.23	+2,365	100.00	+32,341	59.55	−36,240	75.28	+563	34.48
1904																		
Imports	371,361	100.00	182,539	49.15	58,966	15.88	54,810	14.76	68,012	18.31	2,726	0.73	58,116	15.65	74,993	20.19	4,399	1.18
Exports	319,261	100.00	134,532	42.14	104,610	32.77	67,986	21.29	9,405	2.95	5,271	1.65	101,251	31.71	17,644	5.53	4,439	1.39
Total trade	690,622	100.00	317,071	45.91	163,576	23.69	122,796	17.78	77,417	11.21	7,997	1.16	159,367	23.08	92,637	13.41	8,838	1.28
Balance (a)	−52,100	7.54	−48,007	15.14	+45,644	27.90	+13,176	10.73	−58,607	75.70	+2,545	31.82	+43,135	27.07	−57,349	61.91	+40	0.45
1913																		
Imports	729,432	100.00	348,055	47.72	127,035	17.42	61,223	8.39	173,174	23.74	37,389	5.13	202,408	27.75	122,737	16.83	14,943	2.05
Exports	632,460	100.00	275,928	43.63	191,761	30.32	154,660	24.45	29,873	4.72	5,149	0.81	104,473	16.52	32,870	5.20	8,638	1.37
Total trade	1,361,892	100.00	623,983	45.82	318,796	23.41	215,883	15.85	203,047	14.91	42,538	3.12	306,881	22.53	155,607	11.43	23,581	1.73
Balance (a)	−96,972	7.12	−72,127	11.56	+64,726	20.30	+93,437	43.28	−143,301	70.58	−32,240	75.79	−97,935	31.91	−89,867	57.75	−6,305	26.74
Average per year 1929–1933																		
Imports	1,669,353	100.00	618,776	37.07	571,193	34.22	141,545	8.48	184,662	11.06	55,906	3.35	342,037	20.49	94,051	5.63	135,803	8.14
Exports	1,607,298	100.00	746,506	46.44	597,232	37.16	200,192	12.46	167,067	10.39	94,872	5.90	556,644	34.63	65,306	4.06	35,256	2.19
Total trade	3,276,631	100.00	1,365,282	41.67	1,168,425	35.66	341,737	10.43	351,729	10.73	150,778	4.60	898,681	27.43	159,357	4.86	171,069	5.22
Balance (a)	−62,055	1.89	+127,730	9.36	+26,039	2.23	+58,647	17.16	−17,595	5.00	+38,956	25.84	+214,607	23.88	−28,745	18.04	−100,547	58.78
1934																		
Imports	2,282,531	100.00	812,020	35.58	848,294	37.16	119,562	5.24	291,960	12.79	63,464	2.78	769,357	33.71	70,037	3.07	197,758	8.66
Exports	2,171,925	100.00	1,169,503	53.85	512,367	23.59	117,063	5.39	258,011	11.88	158,451	7.30	398,928	18.37	109,270	5.03	64,462	2.97
Total trade	4,454,456	100.00	1,981,523	44.48	1,360,661	30.55	236,625	5.31	549,971	12.35	221,915	4.98	1,168,285	26.23	179,307	4.03	262,220	5.89
Balance (a)	−110,606	2.48	+357,483	18.04	−335,927	24.69	−2,499	1.06	−33,949	6.17	+94,987	42.80	−370,429	31.71	+39,233	21.88	−133,296	50.83

Source:
Calculated from data in the Financial and Economic Annual of Japan, annual volumes.

Notes:
(a) Balance percents are of the corresponding total trade. + and − indicate export and import surplus, respectively.
(b) Including Manchuria, until 1932.
(c) Ceylon not included before 1913.

TABLE XXXVI
FOREIGN TRADE OF JAPAN PROPER, 1927-1930 AND 1932-1935
A—Absolute Figures
Merchandise—Gross Trade. Values in 1,000's of Yen

In the four years after her drive into Manchuria started in 1931 (1932-1935), Japan's trade with all the world was 325 million yen larger than in 1927-1930. Exports were up 359 million yen, and imports were down 34 million yen. But deducting the amounts for Manchuria (including the Kwantung Leased Territory), and Manchuria and China Proper together from these world totals gives a series of quite different pictures. Excluding Manchuria, Japan's exports were down 282 million yen and the imports were up 118 million yen. Excluding Manchuria and China Proper, both imports and exports were up 304 million yen, total trade with the non-Chinese parts of the world increased 608 million yen, and the balance remained "unfavorable" at 880 million yen, between 1927-1930 and 1932-1935.

With China Proper and Manchuria, Japan's trade decreased, between these periods, 283 million yen, but the balance "improved" by 393 million yen. Exports to Manchuria increased 641 million yen, but they fell off 586 million yen to China Proper, leaving a net increase of only 55 million yen. Imports were down 152 million yen from Manchuria and 186 million yen from China Proper; a total decrease of 338 million yen. So Japan paid in China Proper for her gains in Manchuria.

Japan's exports to all of Asia increased 783 million yen between 1927-1930 and 1932-1935, but those to the United States decreased 1,209 million yen. Imports from Asia were down 475 million yen, but they were up from the United States 314 million yen. Taking all of Asia and the United States together, therefore, her exports decreased by 426 million yen, her imports by 161 million yen, and her total trade by 587 million yen. The balance was worse by 263 million yen.

	1927	1928	1929	1930	1927-1930	
					Total	Average
Trade with Manchuria						
Imports.	45,153	61,703	50,577	45,242	202,675	50,669
Exports.	55,317	69,128	64,772	35,576	224,793	56,198
Total.	100,470	130,831	115,349	80,818	427,468	106,867
Balance (a).	+ 10,169	+ 7,425	+ 14,195	− 9,666	+ 22,118	+ 5,529
Kwantung						
Imports.	132,448	150,439	166,322	121,405	570,614	142,653
Exports.	91,271	110,190	124,476	86,814	412,751	103,188
Total.	223,719	260,629	290,798	208,219	983,365	245,841
Balance (a).	− 41,177	− 40,249	− 41,846	− 34,591	− 157,863	− 39,465
Manchuria and Kwantung						
Imports.	177,601	212,142	216,899	166,647	773,289	193,322
Exports.	146,588	179,318	189,248	122,390	637,544	159,386
Total.	324,189	391,460	406,147	289,037	1,410,833	352,708
Balance (a).	− 31,013	− 32,824	− 27,651	− 44,257	− 135,745	− 33,936
North China Ports						
Imports.	74,616	68,067	61,857	52,155	256,695	64,174
Exports.	104,790	104,246	85,820	78,667	373,523	93,381
Total.	179,406	172,313	147,677	130,822	630,218	157,555
Balance.(a).	+ 30,174	+ 36,179	+ 23,963	+ 26,512	+ 116,828	+ 29,207
Manchuria,Kwantung,and N.China						
Imports.	252,217	280,209	278,756	218,802	1,029,984	257,496
Exports.	251,378	283,564	275,068	201,057	1,011,067	252,767
Total.	503,595	563,773	553,824	419,859	2,041,051	510,263
Balance (a).	− 839	+ 3,355	− 3,688	− 17,745	− 18,917	− 4,729
China,except Manchuria and Kwantung						
Imports.	180,882	172,812	159,399	116,459	629,552	157,388
Exports.	278,867	304,014	281,880	225,250	1,090,011	272,503
Total.	459,749	476,826	441,279	341,709	1,719,563	429,891
Balance (a).	+ 97,985	+ 131,202	+ 122,481	+ 108,791	+ 460,459	+ 115,115
All Asia						
Imports.	872,911	903,200	857,954	632,504	3,266,569	816,642
Exports.	844,534	834,935	915,233	704,030	3,298,732	824,683
Total.	1,717,445	1,738,135	1,773,187	1,336,534	6,565,301	1,641,325
Balance.	− 28,377	− 68,265	+ 57,279	+ 71,526	+ 32,163	+ 8,041
United States						
Imports.	673,685	625,503	654;060	442,883	2,396,131	599,133
Exports.	833,804	826,141	914,101	506,220	3,080,266	771,066
Total.	1,507,489	1,451,644	1,568,161	949,103	5,476,397	1,369,099
Balance (a).	+ 160,119	+ 200,638	+ 260,041	+ 63,337	+ 684,135	+ 171,033
Total trade						
Imports.	2,179,153	2,196,314	2,216,238	1,546,070	8,137,775	2,034,444
Exports.	1,992,317	1,971,955	2,148,618	1,469,852	7,582,742	1,895,685
Total.	4,171,470	4,168,269	4,364,856	3,015,922	15,720,517	3,930,129
Balance (a).	− 186,836	− 224,359	− 67,620	− 76,218	− 555,033	− 138,759

(Continued on next page)

TABLE XXXVI
FOREIGN TRADE OF JAPAN PROPER, 1927-1930 AND 1932-1935
A—Absolute Figures (Concluded)
Merchandise—Gross Trade. Values in 1,000's of Yen

	1932	1933	1934	1935	1932-1935		Change 1927-1930 to 1932-1935	
					Total	Average	Total	Average
Trade with Manchuria								
Imports.	51,569	147,897	164,211	107,153	470,828	117,707	+ 268,153	+ 67,038
Exports.	25,947	82,071	107,151	126,046	341,215	85,304	+ 116,422	+ 29,106
Total.	77,516	229,968	271,362	233,197	812,043	203,011	+ 384,575	+ 96,144
Balance (a). . . .	− 25,622	− 65,826	− 57,060	+ 18,895	− 129,613	− 32,403	− 151,731	− 37,932
Kwantung								
Imports.	76,720	20,161	27,279	25,517	149,677	37,419	− 420,937	− 105,234
Exports.	120,583	221,068	295,868	300,269	937,788	234,447	+ 525,037	+ 131,259
Total.	197,303	241,229	323,147	325,786	1,087,465	271,866	+ 104,100	+ 26,025
Balance (a). . . .	+ 43,863	+ 200,907	+ 268,589	+ 274,752	+ 788,111	+ 197,028	+ 945,974	+ 236,493
Manchuria and Kwantung								
Imports.	128,289	168,058	191,490	132,668	620,505	155,126	− 152,784	− 38,196
Exports.	146,530	303,139	403,019	426,315	1,279,003	319,751	+ 641,459	+ 160,365
Total.	274,819	471,197	594,509	558,983	1,899,508	474,877	+ 488,675	+ 122,169
Balance (a). . . .	+ 18,241	+ 135,081	+ 211,529	+ 293,647	+ 658,498	+ 164,625	+ 794,243	+ 198,561
North China Ports								
Imports.	38,833	45,057	46,732	49,290	179,912	44,978	− 76,783	− 19,196
Exports.	75,525	58,130	55,094	66,183	254,932	63,733	− 118,591	− 29,648
Total.	114,358	103,187	101,826	115,473	434,844	108,711	− 195,374	− 48,844
Balance (a). . . .	+ 36,692	+ 13,073	+ 8,362	+ 16,893	+ 75,020	+ 18,755	− 41,808	− 10,452
Manchuria, Kwantung, and N.China								
Imports.	167,122	213,115	238,222	181,958	800,417	200,104	− 229,567	− 57,392
Exports.	222,055	361,269	458,113	492,498	1,533,935	383,484	+ 522,868	+ 130,717
Total.	389,177	574,384	696,335	674,456	2,334,352	583,588	+ 293,301	+ 73,325
Balance (a). . . .	+ 54,933	+ 148,154	+ 219,891	+ 310,540	+ 733,518	+ 183,380	+ 752,435	+ 188,109
China, except Manchuria and Kwantung..								
Imports.	77,175	113,357	119,574	133,815	443,921	110,980	− 185,631	− 46,408
Exports.	129,479	108,253	117,062	148,789	503,583	125,896	− 586,428	− 146,607
Total.	206,654	221,610	236,636	282,604	947,504	236,876	− 772,059	− 193,015
Balance (a). . . .	+ 52,304	− 5,104	− 2,512	+ 14,974	+ 59,662	+ 14,916	− 400,797	− 100,199
All Asia								
Imports.	450,912	658,557	812,020	869,871	2,791,360	697,840	− 475,209	− 118,802
Exports.	677,613	930,636	1,169,503	1,304,433	4,082,185	1,020,546	+ 783,453	+ 195,863
Total.	1,128,525	1,589,193	1,981,523	2,174,304	6,873,545	1,718,386	+ 308,244	+ 77,061
Balance (a). . . .	+ 226,701	+ 272,079	+ 357,483	+ 434,562	+1,290,825	+ 322,706	+11258,662	+ 314,665
United States								
Imports.	509,873	620,788	769,359	809,645	2,709,665	677,416	+ 313,534	+ 78,383
Exports.	445,147	492,237	398,928	535,389	1,871,701	467,925	−1,208,565	− 302,141
Total.	955,020	1,113,025	1,168,287	1,345,034	4,581,366	1,145,341	− 895,031	− 223,758
Balance (a). . . .	− 64,726	− 128,551	− 370,430	− 274,256	− 837,964	− 209,491	−1,522,099	− 380,524
Total trade								
Imports.	1,431,461	1,917,219	2,282,601	2,472,236	8,103,517	2,025,879	− 34,258	− 8,565
Exports.	1,409,991	1,861,045	2,171,924	2,499,073	7,942,033	1,985,508	+ 359,291	+ 89,823
Total.	2,841,452	3,778,264	4,454,525	4,971,309	16,045,550	4,011,387	+ 325,033	+ 81,258
Balance (a). . . .	− 21,470	− 56,174	− 110,677	+ 26,837	− 161,484	− 40,371	+ 393,549	+ 98,388

Source:
Annual and Monthly Foreign Trade Returns of Japan.

Note:
(a) + and − indicate excess of exports and imports, respectively.

TABLE XXXVI
FOREIGN TRADE OF JAPAN PROPER, 1927-1930 AND 1932-1935
B—Percentages and Index Numbers
Average 1927-1930 = 100 for Index Numbers

Trade with	1927		1928		1929		1930		Total and Average 1927-1930		1932		1933		1934		1935		Total and Average 1932-1935		Change 1927-1930 to 1933-1935
	%	Index	%	Index	%	Index	%	Index	%	Index	%	Index	%	Index	%	Index	%	Index	%	Index	%
Manchuria																					
Imports	2.1	89	2.8	122	2.3	100	2.9	89	2.5	100	3.6	102	7.7	242	7.2	324	4.3	212	5.8	232	+132.3
Exports	2.8	98	3.5	123	3.0	115	2.4	63	3.0	100	1.8	46	4.4	146	4.9	191	5.1	224	4.3	152	+51.8
Total	2.4	94	3.1	122	2.6	108	2.7	76	2.7	100	2.7	73	6.1	215	6.1	254	4.7	219	5.1	190	+90.0
Balance (a)	+10.2		+5.7		+12.3		+12.0		+5.2		-33.5		-28.6		-21.0		+8.1		-16.0		
Kwantung																					
Imports	6.1	93	6.8	105	7.5	117	7.8	85	7.0	100	5.4	54	1.1	14	1.2	19	1.0	18	1.9	26	-73.9
Exports	4.6	88	5.6	107	5.8	120	5.9	84	5.4	100	8.6	117	11.9	214	13.6	286	12.6	313	11.8	227	+127.2
Total	5.3	91	6.3	106	6.7	118	6.9	85	6.3	100	6.9	80	6.4	99	7.3	132	6.8	133	6.8	111	+10.6
Balance (a)	-18.5		-15.4		-14.4		-16.6		-16.1		+22.2		+83.1		+83.1		+84.5		+72.5		
Manchuria and Kwantung																					
Imports	8.2	92	9.6	110	9.8	112	10.7	86	9.5	100	9.0	66	8.8	87	8.4	99	5.4	69	7.7	80	-19.7
Exports	7.4	92	9.1	113	8.8	119	8.3	77	8.4	100	10.4	92	16.3	190	18.5	253	17.1	268	16.1	201	+100.6
Total	7.7	92	9.4	111	9.3	115	9.6	82	9.0	100	9.7	78	12.5	134	13.4	169	11.3	158	11.9	135	+34.6
Balance (a)	-9.6		-8.4		-6.8		-15.3		-9.6		+6.6		+28.7		+35.5		+53.5		+34.6		
North China Ports																					
Imports	3.4	116	3.1	106	2.8	96	3.4	81	3.2	100	2.7	61	2.3	70	2.0	73	2.0	77	2.2	70	-29.9
Exports	5.2	112	5.3	112	4.0	93	5.4	84	4.9	100	5.4	81	3.1	62	2.5	59	2.6	71	3.2	68	-31.7
Total	4.3	114	4.1	109	3.4	94	4.3	83	4.0	100	4.0	73	2.7	65	2.3	65	2.3	73	2.7	69	-31.0
Balance (a)	+16.8		+21.0		+16.2		+20.3		+18.5		+32.0		+12.6		+8.2		+14.6		+17.3		
Manchuria, Kwantung, and North China																					
Imports	11.6	98	12.7	109	12.6	108	14.1	85	12.7	100	11.7	65	11.4	83	10.4	93	7.4	71	9.9	78	-22.3
Exports	12.6	99	14.4	112	13.7	109	13.7	80	13.3	100	15.8	88	19.4	143	21.0	181	19.7	195	19.3	152	+51.6
Total	12.0	99	13.5	110	12.7	108	13.9	82	13.0	100	13.7	76	15.2	112	15.7	136	13.6	132	14.5	114	+14.4
Balance (a)	-0.2		+0.6		-0.6		-4.2		+0.9		+14.1		+25.8		+31.4		+46.1		+31.4		
China, except Manchuria, and Kwantung																					
Imports	8.3	115	7.9	110	7.2	101	7.5	74	7.7	100	5.4	49	5.9	72	5.2	72	5.4	85	5.4	70	-29.5
Exports	14.0	102	15.4	112	13.1	103	15.3	83	14.4	100	9.2	47	5.8	40	5.4	43	5.9	55	6.3	46	-53.7
Total	11.0	107	11.4	111	10.1	103	11.3	79	10.9	100	7.2	48	5.9	52	5.3	52	5.7	66	5.9	55	-45.0
Balance (a)	+21.3		+27.5		+27.7		+31.8		+26.8		+25.3		-2.3		+1.1		+5.3		+6.3		
All Asia																					
Imports	40.0	107	41.1	111	38.7	105	40.9	78	40.2	100	31.4	55	34.0	81	35.8	99	35.2	106	34.4	85	-14.6
Exports	42.4	102	42.3	101	42.7	111	48.5	85	43.5	100	48.0	82	50.0	113	53.8	142	52.2	158	51.5	124	+23.7
Total	41.4	105	41.7	106	40.7	108	44.4	81	41.7	100	39.7	69	42.1	97	44.5	121	43.7	132	42.9	105	+4.7
Balance (a)	+1.7		-3.9		+3.2		+5.4		-0.5		+20.1		+17.1		+18.0		+20.0		+18.8		
United States																					
Imports	30.9	112	28.5	104	29.5	109	28.6	74	29.4	100	35.6	85	32.4	104	33.7	128	32.8	135	33.4	113	-13.1
Exports	41.8	108	41.8	107	43.1	119	34.5	66	40.6	100	31.6	58	26.4	64	18.3	52	21.4	70	23.6	61	-39.2
Total	36.1	110	34.8	106	36.0	114	31.5	69	34.8	100	33.6	69	29.5	81	26.2	85	27.1	98	28.6	84	-16.4
Balance (a)	+10.7		+13.8		+16.6		+6.7		+12.5		-6.8		-11.4		-31.8		-20.2		-18.3		
Total trade																					
Imports	100.0	107	100.0	108	100.0	109	100.0	76	100.0	100	100.0	70	100.0	94	100.0	112	100.0	122	100.0	100	-0.4
Exports	100.0	105	100.0	104	100.0	113	100.0	77	100.0	100	100.0	74	100.0	98	100.0	114	100.0	132	100.0	105	+4.7
Total	100.0	106	100.0	106	100.0	111	100.0	77	100.0	100	100.0	72	100.0	96	100.0	113	100.0	127	100.0	102	+2.1
Balance (a)	-4.5		-5.4		-1.6		-2.5		-3.5		-0.7		-1.5		+2.5		+0.5		-1.0		

Sources:
Calculated from data in the Annual and Monthly Foreign Trade Returns of Japan.

Note:
(a) Balance percents are of the corresponding total trade. + and - indicate excess of exports and imports, respectively.

TABLE XXXVI
FOREIGN TRADE OF JAPAN PROPER, 1927-1930 AND 1932-1935
C — Changes
Merchandise—Gross Trade. Value in 1,000,000's of Yen

	Total Trade	With Manchuria (a)	With China Proper	With Manchuria and China	With the World less Manchuria	With the World less Manchuria and China
Imports						
1927-1930	8,138	773	630	1,403	7,365	6,735
1932-1935	8,104	621	444	1,065	7,483	7,039
Change (b).	− 34	− 152	− 186	− 338	+ 118	+ 304
Exports						
1927-1930	7,583	638	1,090	1,728	6,945	5,855
1932-1935	7,942	1,279	504	1,783	6,663	6,159
Change (b).	+ 359	+ 641	− 586	+ 55	− 282	+ 304
Total trade						
1927-1930	15,721	1,411	1,720	3,131	14,310	12,590
1932-1935	16,046	1,900	948	2,848	14,146	13,198
Change (d).	+ 325	+ 489	− 772	− 283	− 164	+ 608
Balances						
1927-1930 (c)	− 555	− 135	+ 460	+ 325	− 420	− 880
1932-1935 (c)	− 162	+ 658	+ 60	+ 718	− 820	− 880
Change (d).	+ 393	+ 793	− 400	+ 393	− 400	− 0

Source:
Calculated from data in Annual and Monthly Returns of the Foreign Trade of Japan.

Notes:
(a) Includes Kwantung Leased Territory.
(b) + and - indicate increase and decrease, respectively.
(c) + and - indicate excess of exports and imports, respectively.
(d) + indicates more "favorable" or less "unfavorable" balance; - indicates less "favorable" or more "unfavorable" balance.

Japan's colonies, like Japan herself, regularly have had an "unfavorable" balance on their foreign trade. Even in 1914-1918 the foreign trade imports exceeded the foreign trade exports for all the colonies, though Formosa, like Japan Proper, showed an export surplus in these years. Korea's "unfavorable" balance in foreign trade, 1894-1934, has been especially heavy. She imported from foreign countries more than three times as much as she exported to them, while the excess of Formosa's foreign imports was just under a third of the foreign exports.

TABLE XXXVII
FOREIGN TRADE OF THE JAPANESE EMPIRE, 1868-1934
Merchandise—Gross Trade. Value in 1,000's of Yen

	1868-1893 Value	% of Total	1894-1903 Value	% of Total	1904-1913 Value	% of Total	1914-1918 Value	% of Total	1919-1928 Value	% of Total	1929-1934 Value	% of Total	1894-1934 Value	% of Total	1868-1934 Value	% of Total
Imports																
By Japan Proper	1,009,064	100.00	2,267,561	96.13	4,930,065	95.52	4,588,565	95.21	21,175,335	93.13	10,629,194	93.80	43,590,720	93.93	44,599,784	94.06
By Korea (a)	...	...	...	...	77,539	1.50	135,070	2.80	1,020,937	4.49	454,901	4.01	1,688,447	3.64	1,688,447	3.56
By Formosa (b)	...	...	91,295	3.87	153,912	2.98	95,877	1.99	530,058	2.33	245,080	2.16	1,116,222	2.41	1,116,222	2.35
By Colonies (c)	...	...	91,295	3.87	231,451	4.48	230,947	4.79	1,563,029	6.87	702,159	6.20	2,818,881	6.07	2,818,881	5.94
Total	1,009,064	100.00	2,358,856	100.00	5,161,516	100.00	4,819,512	100.00	22,738,364	100.00	11,331,353	100.00	46,409,601	100.00	47,418,665	100.00
Exports																
By Japan Proper	1,001,234	100.00	1,915,600	95.98	4,353,618	97.03	6,991,980	97.25	18,506,926	96.80	10,208,412	96.64	41,976,536	96.82	42,977,770	96.89
By Korea (a)	...	...	...	...	16,697	0.37	64,296	0.89	232,950	1.22	214,054	2.03	527,997	1.22	527,997	1.19
By Formosa (b)	...	...	80,215	4.02	116,483	2.60	133,673	1.86	372,397	1.95	137,675	1.30	840,443	1.94	840,443	1.89
By Colonies (c)	...	...	80,215	4.02	133,180	2.97	197,969	2.75	612,701	3.20	354,477	3.36	1,378,542	3.18	1,378,542	3.11
Total	1,001,234	100.00	1,995,815	100.00	4,486,798	100.00	7,189,949	100.00	19,119,627	100.00	10,562,889	100.00	43,355,078	100.00	44,356,312	100.00
Total Trade																
Of Japan Proper	2,010,298	100.00	4,183,161	96.06	9,283,683	96.22	11,580,545	96.43	39,682,261	94.80	20,837,606	95.17	85,567,256	95.32	87,577,554	95.43
Of Korea (a)	...	...	...	...	94,236	0.98	199,366	1.66	1,253,887	3.00	668,955	3.92	2,216,444	2.47	2,216,444	2.42
Of Formosa (b)	...	...	171,510	3.94	270,395	2.80	229,550	1.91	902,455	2.16	382,755	2.82	1,956,665	2.18	1,956,665	2.13
Of Colonies (c)	...	...	171,510	3.94	364,631	3.78	428,916	3.57	2,175,730	5.20	1,056,636	4.83	4,197,423	4.68	4,197,423	4.57
Total	2,010,298	100.00	4,354,671	100.00	9,648,314	100.00	12,009,461	100.00	41,857,991	100.00	21,894,242	100.00	89,764,679	100.00	91,774,977	100.00
Balance (d)																
Of Japan Proper	- 7,830	0.39	- 351,961	8.41	- 576,447	6.21	+ 2,403,415	20.75	- 2,668,409	6.72	- 420,782	2.02	- 1,614,184	1.89	- 1,622,014	1.85
Of Korea (a)	...	...	...	...	- 60,842	64.56	- 70,774	35.50	- 787,987	62.84	- 240,847	36.00	- 1,160,450	52.36	- 1,160,450	52.36
Of Formosa (b)	...	...	- 11,080	6.46	- 37,429	15.84	+ 37,976	16.47	- 157,661	17.47	- 107,405	28.06	- 275,779	14.09	- 275,779	14.09
Of Colonies (c)	...	...	- 11,080	6.46	- 98,271	26.95	- 32,978	7.69	- 950,328	43.68	- 347,682	32.90	- 1,440,339	34.31	- 1,440,339	34.32
Of Total	- 7,830	0.39	- 363,041	8.34	- 674,718	6.99	+ 2,370,437	19.74	- 3,618,737	8.65	- 768,464	3.51	- 3,054,523	3.40	- 3,062,353	3.34

Sources:
Calculated from data in the Financial and Economic Annual of Japan, annual volumes.

Notes:
(a) Records for Korea begin with 1911.
(b) Records for Formosa begin with 1897.
(c) Includes South Seas Mandate areas (Nanyo) beginning in 1920.
(d) + and - indicate export and import surplus, respectively.
Balance percentages are of total trade.

In the 60 years before the World War, the United Kingdom's trade with the overseas British countries remained steadily close to 25% of her total external trade. This trade, like that with foreign countries, showed an excess of imports over exports, though in a considerably smaller proportion than the foreign trade. With the World War, the British countries' proportion began to increase: it was 32% in 1914-1918, 33% in 1919-1928, and 36% in 1929-1934. (For 1894-1934 it was 31%.) In the war and post-war years, too, the "unfavorable" balance has been a considerably larger proportion of the total trade with the British overseas countries than before the war, though still not as large a proportion as that in the foreign trade. From 1894 to 1934, the excess of imports over exports in the foreign trade was £9,211 million, or 60% of the value of the exports. In the same period the "unfavorable" balance with the British countries was £1,616 million, or 20% of the export value.

TABLE XXXVIII
EXTERNAL TRADE OF THE UNITED KINGDOM, 1854-1863 AND 1894-1934
Merchandise. Values in £1,000,000's

Values shown as Net value (% of totals) / Gross value (% of totals).

Item	1854-1863	1894-1903	1904-1913	1914-1918	1919-1928	1929-1934	1919-1934	1904-1934	1894-1934
Imports — From Foreign countries									
Net (imports retained)	1,423.7 (74.82)	3,770.7 (76.73)	4,112.2 (74.29)	2,991.9 (66.72)	7,782.9 (66.99)	3,236.8 (67.11)	11,019.7 (67.03)	18,125.8 (68.49)	24,540.8 (71.43)
Gross			4,924.6 (76.24)	3,332.9 (68.34)	8,956.7 (68.91)	3,555.9 (67.93)	12,512.6 (68.63)	20,770.1 (70.24)	
From British Countries									
Net (imports retained)	479.0 (25.18)	1,018.6 (21.27)	1,423.1 (25.71)	1,492.5 (33.28)	3,834.9 (33.01)	1,586.2 (32.89)	5,421.1 (32.97)	8,336.7 (31.51)	9,817.0 (28.57)
Gross			1,534.8 (23.76)	1,544.3 (31.66)	4,040.4 (31.09)	1,678.9 (32.07)	5,719.3 (31.37)	8,798.4 (29.76)	
Total Net	1,902.7 (100.00)	4,789.3 (100.00)	5,535.3 (100.00)	4,484.4 (100.00)	11,617.8 (100.00)	4,823.0 (100.00)	16,440.8 (100.00)	26,460.5 (100.00)	34,357.8 (100.00)
Gross			6,459.4 (100.00)	4,877.2 (100.00)	12,997.1 (100.00)	5,234.8 (100.00)	18,231.9 (100.00)	29,568.5 (100.00)	
Exports — To Foreign countries									
Net (British produce)	1,085.6 (72.34)	2,216.4 (69.58)	2,665.0 (65.25)	1,493.1 (63.53)	4,747.7 (59.47)	1,661.6 (55.38)	6,309.3 (58.40)	10,467.4 (60.72)	15,330.1 (65.15)
Gross			3,477.4 (69.43)	1,834.1 (66.86)	5,921.5 (63.24)	1,880.7 (58.20)	7,802.2 (61.95)	13,113.7 (64.45)	
To British countries									
Net (British produce)	415.0 (27.66)	969.1 (30.42)	1,419.2 (34.75)	857.3 (36.47)	3,235.8 (40.53)	1,258.1 (44.62)	4,493.9 (41.60)	6,770.4 (39.28)	8,201.2 (34.85)
Gross			1,530.9 (30.57)	909.1 (33.14)	3,441.3 (36.76)	1,350.8 (41.80)	4,792.1 (38.05)	7,232.1 (35.55)	
Total Net	1,500.6 (100.00)	3,185.5 (100.00)	4,084.2 (100.00)	2,350.4 (100.00)	7,983.5 (100.00)	2,819.7 (100.00)	10,803.2 (100.00)	17,237.8 (100.00)	23,531.3 (100.00)
Gross			5,008.3 (100.00)	2,743.2 (100.00)	9,362.8 (100.00)	3,231.5 (100.00)	12,594.3 (100.00)	20,345.8 (100.00)	
Total Trade — With Foreign Countries									
Net	2,509.3 (73.73)	5,987.1 (75.08)	6,777.2 (70.45)	4,485.0 (65.62)	12,530.6 (63.93)	4,798.4 (62.78)	17,329.0 (63.61)	28,591.2 (65.43)	39,870.9 (68.87)
Gross			8,402.0 (73.27)	5,167.0 (67.80)	14,878.2 (66.54)	5,436.6 (64.21)	20,314.8 (65.90)	33,883.8 (67.88)	
With British Countries									
Net	894.0 (26.27)	1,987.7 (24.92)	2,842.3 (29.55)	2,349.8 (34.38)	7,070.7 (36.07)	2,844.3 (37.22)	9,915.0 (36.39)	15,107.1 (34.57)	18,018.2 (31.13)
Gross			3,065.7 (26.73)	2,453.4 (32.20)	7,481.7 (33.46)	3,029.7 (35.79)	10,511.4 (34.10)	16,030.5 (32.12)	
Total Net	3,403.3 (100.00)	7,974.8 (100.00)	9,619.5 (100.00)	6,834.8 (100.00)	19,601.3 (100.00)	7,642.7 (100.00)	27,244.0 (100.00)	43,698.3 (100.00)	57,889.1 (100.00)
Gross			11,467.7 (100.00)	7,620.4 (100.00)	22,359.9 (100.00)	8,466.3 (100.00)	30,826.2 (100.00)	49,914.3 (100.00)	
Balance (Net and Gross)									
With Foreign Countries	− 338.1 (13.47)	−1,554.3 (25.96)	−1,447.2 (17.22)	−1,498.8 (29.01)	− 3,035.2 (20.40)	−1,675.2 (30.81)	− 4,710.4 (23.19)	− 7,656.4 (22.60)	− 9,210.7 (23.10)
With British Countries	− 64.0 (7.16)	− 49.5 (2.49)	− 3.9 (0.13)	− 635.2 (25.89)	− 599.1 (8.01)	− 328.1 (10.83)	− 927.2 (8.82)	− 1,566.3 (9.77)	− 1,615.8 (8.97)
Total	− 402.1 (11.96)	−1,603.8 (20.11)	−1,461.1 (12.65)	−2,134.0 (31.22)	− 3,634.3 (16.25)	−2,003.3 (23.66)	− 5,637.6 (18.29)	− 9,222.7 (18.48)	−10,826.5 (18.70)

Source:
Calculated from data in *Statistical Abstract of the United Kingdom*, annual volumes.
Prior to 1923, Irish trade is included with the United Kingdom (British Isles).

Notes:
(a) Balance percents are of corresponding totals. + and − indicate export and import surplus, respectively.

TABLE XXXIX
EXTERNAL TRADE OF THE UNITED KINGDOM
A—With Foreign Countries
Merchandise. Value in £1,000's. Gross Trade

Until very recently, for half a century, the United Kingdom has done more business with the United States than with any other country, foreign or British, though the proportion has decreased fairly steadily – from 18% of the total in 1894, to 17% in 1904, to 14% in 1913, to 11% in 1929-1933, and to 9% in 1934. The shares of France, the Netherlands, and Russia in Britain's trade also have decreased through these years, and Germany's share has fallen off since the War, though it was increasing until 1913. Italy's share has remained fairly constant at about 1.5% of the total. Japan's share has increased a little, from 0.7% in 1894 to 1.3% in 1913 and 1.1% in 1934. Australia and New Zealand together consistently have been more important in British trade than Canada, and in recent years they have passed India, Ceylon, and British Malaya taken together. The antipodes Dominions have been especially significant as sources of supplies. The imports from these regions have been a larger share of Britain's total imports than the imports from India regularly since 1894. The United States still is well ahead of Australia and New Zealand as a source of British imports but it fell behind them as a market for British goods in 1934.

A considerable part of Britain's "unfavorable" balance of trade arises from her business with the United States – 44% in 1894, 43% in 1904, 53% in 1913, 25% in 1929-1933, and 21% in 1934. Only in the last few years have the imports from all the Dominions together exceeded the exports to them by anything like as much as the "unfavorable" balance with the United States. The trade with India showed a comparatively small but steady favorable balance, until 1934. With France, Germany, the Netherlands, and Russia, the excess has been on the imports side fairly consistently, but with Italy and Japan it has been the other way.

	Total Trade		Trade with Foreign Countries		Trade with France		Trade with Germany		Trade with Italy		Trade with Japan		Trade with the Netherlands		Trade with Russia		Trade with the United States	
	Value	% of Total	Value	% of Total	Value	% of Total	Value	% of Total	Value	% of Total	Value	% of Total	Value	% of Total	Value	% of Total	Value	% of Total
1894																		
Imports	408,300	100.00	314,400	77.00	43,450	10.64	26,874	6.58	3,129	0.77	959	0.23	27,606	6.76	23,599	5.78	89,607	21.95
Exports	273,800	100.00	195,400	71.29	19,751	7.21	29,217	10.67	6,190	2.26	3,919	1.43	13,879	5.07	10,115	3.69	30,775	11.24
Total	682,100	100.00	509,600	74.71	63,201	9.27	56,091	8.22	9,319	1.37	4,878	0.72	41,485	6.08	33,714	4.94	120,382	17.65
Balance (b)	– 134,500	19.72	– 119,200	23.39	–23,699	37.50	+ 2,343	5.18	3,061	32.85	2,960	60.68	–13,727	33.09	–13,484	40.00	–58,832	48.87
Balance % of total balance		100.00		88.62		17.62		1.74		2.28		2.20		10.21		10.03		43.74
1904																		
Imports	551,100	100.00	430,300	78.08	44,798	8.13	49,512	8.98	5,936	1.08	2,442	0.44	16,365	2.97	32,981	5.98	116,376	21.12
Exports	371,100	100.00	249,700	79.43	21,578	5.82	36,425	9.82	9,222	2.49	5,043	1.36	12,807	3.45	15,286	4.12	39,273	10.59
Total	922,100	100.00	680,000	73.74	66,376	7.20	85,937	9.43	15,158	1.64	7,485	0.81	29,172	3.16	48,267	5.23	155,649	16.88
Balance (b)	– 180,100	19.53	– 180,600	26.56	–23,220	34.98	–13,087	15.23	3,286	21.68	2,601	34.75	–3,558	12.20	–17,695	36.66	–77,103	49.54
Balance % of total balance		100.00		85.62		12.89		7.27		1.82		1.44		1.38		9.83		42.81
1913																		
Imports	768,700	100.00	577,200	75.09	46,353	6.03	80,411	10.46	8,127	1.06	4,388	0.57	23,578	3.07	40,271	5.24	130,331	16.95
Exports	634,800	100.00	425,900	67.09	40,882	6.44	60,499	9.53	15,622	2.46	14,827	2.34	20,522	3.23	27,694	4.36	59,454	9.37
Total	1,403,500	100.00	1,003,100	71.47	87,235	6.22	140,910	10.04	23,749	1.69	19,215	1.37	44,100	3.14	67,965	4.84	189,785	13.52
Balance (b)	– 133,900	9.54	– 151,300	15.08	–5,471	6.27	–19,912	14.13	7,495	31.56	10,439	54.33	–3,056	6.93	–12,577	18.51	–70,877	37.35
Balance % of total balance		100.00		112.99		4.09		14.87		5.60		7.80		2.28		9.39		52.93
Average per year, 1929-1933																		
Imports	900,500	100.00	619,000	68.74	36,979	4.11	51,757	5.75	13,387	1.49	7,005	0.78	31,545	3.50	26,029	2.89	122,586	13.61
Exports	556,800	100.00	326,000	58.55	35,591	6.39	37,265	6.69	12,475	2.24	7,755	1.39	19,115	3.43	7,991	1.44	35,039	6.29
Total	1,457,300	100.00	945,000	64.85	72,570	4.85	89,022	6.11	25,862	1.77	14,760	1.01	50,660	3.48	34,020	2.33	157,625	10.82
Balance (b)	– 343,700	23.58	– 293,000	31.01	–1,388	1.91	–14,492	16.28	–912	3.53	750	5.08	–12,430	24.54	–18,038	53.02	–87,547	55.54
Balance % of total balance		100.00		85.25		0.40		4.22		0.27		0.22		3.62		5.25		25.47
1934																		
Imports	732,400	100.00	460,900	62.93	19,258	2.63	30,575	4.17	8,458	1.15	9,100	1.24	20,973	2.86	17,277	2.35	82,042	11.20
Exports	447,400	100.00	250,700	56.03	23,479	5.25	22,925	5.12	10,536	2.35	4,353	0.97	14,084	3.15	7,563	1.69	23,212	5.19
Total	1,179,800	100.00	711,600	60.32	42,737	3.62	53,500	4.53	18,994	1.61	13,453	1.14	35,057	2.97	24,840	2.11	105,254	8.92
Balance (b)	– 285,000	24.16	– 210,200	29.54	+4,221	9.88	–7,650	14.30	2,078	10.94	–4,747	35.29	–6,889	19.65	–9,714	39.11	–58,830	55.89
Balance % of total balance		100.00		73.75		1.48		2.68		0.73		1.67		2.42		3.41		20.64

Sources:
1894-1933: Calculated from data in the Statistical Abstract of the United Kingdom, annual volumes.
1934: Calculated from data in Accounts Relating to Trade and Navigation of the United Kingdom, January 1935.

Notes:
(a) Japan includes Kwantung and Formosa.
(b) + and – indicate export surplus and import surplus, respectively. Balance percentages are of corresponding totals.

TABLE XXXIX
EXTERNAL TRADE OF THE UNITED KINGDOM
B—With British Countries
Merchandise. Values in £1,000's. Gross Trade

	Total Trade		Trade with British Countries		Trade with the Six Dominions		Trade with the Six Dominions and British India		Trade with British India, British Malaya and Ceylon		Trade with Canada and Newfoundland		Trade with Australia and New Zealand		Trade with Union of South Africa		Trade with British India	
	Value	% of Total	Value	% of Total	Value	% of Total	Value	% of Total	Value	% of Total	Value	% of Total	Value	% of Total	Value	% of Total	Value	% of Total
1894																		
Imports	408,300	100.00	93,900	23.00	49,731	12.18	79,161	19.39	36,335	8.90	12,908	3.16	31,833	7.80	4,990	1.22	27,649	6.77
Exports	273,800	100.00	78,600	28.71	34,645	12.65	64,760	23.65	38,801	14.17	7,380	2.70	17,929	2.90	9,355	3.42	30,115	11.00
Total	682,100	100.00	172,500	25.29	84,376	12.37	143,921	21.10	75,136	11.02	20,288	2.97	49,762	7.30	14,345	2.10	57,764	8.47
Balance (b)	- 134,500	19.72	- 15,300	8.87	- 15,086	17.88	- 14,401	10.01	+ 2,466	3.28	- 4,528	22.31	- 13,904	27.94	- 4,365	30.43	+ 2,466	4.27
Balance % of total balance		100.00		11.38		11.22		10.71		1.83		3.37		10.34		3.25		1.83
1904																		
Imports	551,100	100.00	120,800	21.92	65,686	11.92	102,159	18.54	46,837	8.50	23,821	4.32	36,427	6.61	5,438	0.99	36,473	6.62
Exports	371,000	100.00	121,300	32.70	58,914	15.88	100,458	27.08	46,193	12.45	12,805	3.45	26,738	7.21	19,371	5.22	41,544	11.20
Total	922,100	100.00	242,100	26.26	124,600	13.51	202,617	21.97	93,030	10.09	36,626	3.97	63,165	6.85	24,809	2.69	78,017	8.46
Balance (a)	- 180,100	19.53	+ 500	0.21	- 6,772	5.43	- 1,701	0.84	- 644	0.69	- 11,016	30.08	- 9,689	15.34	+ 13,933	56.16	+ 5,071	6.50
Balance % of total balance		100.00		0.28		3.76		0.94		0.36		6.12		5.38		7.74		2.82
1913																		
Imports	768,700	100.00	191,500	24.91	102,167	13.29	150,587	19.59	75,590	9.83	31,463	4.09	58,403	7.60	12,301	1.60	48,420	6.30
Exports	634,800	100.00	208,900	32.91	101,967	16.06	173,637	27.35	83,374	13.13	28,302	4.46	49,619	7.82	24,046	3.79	71,670	11.29
Total	1,403,500	100.00	400,400	28.53	204,134	14.54	324,224	23.10	158,964	11.33	59,765	4.26	108,022	7.70	36,347	2.59	120,090	8.56
Balance (a)	- 133,900	9.54	+ 17,400	4.35	- 200	0.10	+ 23,050	7.11	+ 7,784	4.90	- 3,161	5.29	- 8,784	8.13	+ 11,745	32.31	+ 23,250	19.36
Balance % of total balance		100.00		12.99		0.15		17.21		5.81		2.36		6.57		8.77		17.36
Average per year, 1929-1933																		
Imports	900,500	100.00	281,500	31.26	184,095	20.44	228,147	25.34	65,085	7.23	43,422	4.82	89,382	9.93	17,507	1.94	44,052	4.89
Exports	556,800	100.00	230,800	41.45	95,315	17.12	142,406	25.58	62,863	11.29	25,800	4.63	44,048	7.91	25,467	4.57	47,091	8.46
Total	1,457,300	100.00	512,300	35.15	279,410	19.17	370,553	25.43	127,948	8.78	69,222	4.75	133,430	9.16	42,974	2.95	91,143	6.25
Balance (a)	- 343,700	23.58	- 50,700	9.90	- 88,780	31.78	- 85,741	23.14	- 2,222	1.74	- 17,622	25.46	- 45,334	33.98	+ 7,960	18.52	+ 3,039	3.33
Balance % of total balance		100.00		14.75		25.83		24.95		0.65		5.13		13.19		2.32		0.88
1934																		
Imports	732,400	100.00	271,500	37.07	172,389	23.54	214,433	29.28	65,820	8.99	52,829	7.21	90,506	12.36	11,886	1.62	42,094	5.75
Exports	447,400	100.00	196,700	43.97	108,588	24.27	145,805	32.59	47,260	10.56	21,951	4.91	38,657	8.64	30,875	6.90	37,217	8.32
Total	1,179,800	100.00	468,200	39.68	280,977	23.82	360,288	30.54	113,080	9.58	74,780	6.34	129,163	10.95	42,761	3.62	79,311	6.72
Balance (a)	- 285,000	24.16	- 74,800	15.98	- 63,801	22.71	- 68,678	19.06	- 18,560	16.41	- 30,878	41.29	- 51,849	40.14	+ 18,989	44.41	- 4,877	8.15
Balance % of total balance		100.00		26.25		22.39		24.10		6.51		10.83		18.19		6.66		1.71

Sources:
1894-1933: Calculated from data in the Statistical Abstract of the United Kingdom, annual volumes.
1934: Calculated from data in Accounts Relating to Trade and Navigation of the United Kingdom, January 1935.

Note:
(a) + and - indicate export and import surplus, respectively. Balance percentages are of corresponding totals.

TABLE XL
TRADE OF THE OVERSEAS BRITISH COUNTRIES
A—The British Empire, Excluding the United Kingdom
Values in £1,000,000's

While the British countries overseas have taken a steadily increasing share in the United Kingdom's trade, the United Kingdom's share of the British countries' trade has decreased. Britain's share of the trade of the overseas countries under the British flag was 49% in 1854-1863, 47% in 1894-1903, 42% in 1913, 36% in 1929-1933, and 39% in 1934. From 1894 to 1913, Britain was relatively more important to the overseas British countries as a source of imports than as a market for exports. In recent years, the share of their total exports which these other countries have sent to Britain has been larger than the share of their total imports which they have taken from the mother country.

Regularly since 1854, the British Dominion areas have done a larger share of their trade with Britain than have the British countries as a whole,

and a larger share also than India since 1894. In other words, the greater political independence of the Dominions has been accompanied (though not caused) by a greater proportion of trade with the mother country.

In their trade with foreign countries, the Dominion areas have had an "unfavorable" balance regularly since 1894, but a "favorable" balance with the United Kingdom. From 1854-1863 both balances were "unfavorable." India, on the other hand, regularly through the whole 80 years since 1854 has sold more to foreign countries than she has bought from them, and bought more from Britain than she has sold to her. Thus, Britain has been more a market than a source of supplies for the self-governing British areas, but in the India-Britain trade the opposite relation has prevailed.

	British Countries		United Kingdom		Foreign Countries		United States		Total	
	Value	% of Total	Value	% of Total	Value	% of Total	Value	% of Total	Value	% of Total
1913 (a)										
Imports from	332.3	57.96	242.9	42.37	241.0	42.04	117.2	20.44	573.3	100.00
Exports to	326.8	56.87	238.1	41.44	247.8	43.13	63.8	11.10	574.6	100.00
Total trade with	659.1	57.42	481.0	41.90	488.8	42.58	181.0	15.77	1,147.9	100.00
Balance (b).	− 5.5	0.83	− 4.8	1.00	+ 6.8	1.39	− 53.4	29.50	+ 1.3	0.11
Average, 1929 – 1933 (a)										
Imports from	326.4	48.06	237.3	34.94	352.7	51.94	151.5	22.31	679.1	100.00
Exports to	307.5	50.24	238.3	38.93	304.6	49.76	116.4	19.02	612.1	100.00
Total trade with	633.9	49.09	475.6	36.06	657.3	50.91	267.9	20.75	1,291.2	100.00
Balance (b).	− 18.9	2.98	+ 1.0	0.21	− 48.1	7.32	− 35.1	13.10	− 67.0	5.19
1934 (a)										
Imports from	281.7	48.15	202.4	34.59	303.4	51.85	102.8	17.57	585.1	100.00
Exports to	295.8	55.14	233.7	43.56	240.7	44.86	90.0	16.78	536.5	100.00
Total trade with	577.5	51.49	436.1	38.88	541.1	48.51	192.8	17.19	1,121.6	100.00
Balance (b).	+ 14.1	2.44	+ 31.3	7.18	− 62.7	11.52	− 12.8	6.64	− 48.6	4.33

For source and notes, see Table XL K.

TABLE XL
TRADE OF THE OVERSEAS BRITISH COUNTRIES
B—Canada and Newfoundland
Values in £1,000,000's

	British Countries		United Kingdom		Foreign Countries		United States		Total	
	Value	% of Total	Value	% of Total	Value	% of Total	Value	% of Total	Value	% of Total
1913 (a)										
Imports from	33.8	25.30	28.1	21.03	99.8	74.70	91.8	68.71	133.6	100.00
Exports to	51.9	51.13	46.4	45.71	49.6	48.87	34.7	34.19	101.5	100.00
Total trade with	85.7	36.45	74.5	31.69	149.4	63.55	126.5	53.81	235.1	100.00
Balance (b)	+ 18.1	21.12	+ 18.3	24.56	− 50.2	33.60	− 57.1	45.14	− 32.1	13.65
Average, 1929 – 1933 (a)										
Imports from	38.6	25.46	27.0	17.81	113.0	74.54	93.6	61.74	151.6	100.00
Exports to	62.2	38.80	48.9	30.51	98.1	61.20	63.3	39.49	160.3	100.00
Total trade with	100.8	32.32	75.9	24.33	211.1	67.68	156.9	50.30	311.9	100.00
Balance (b)	+ 23.6	23.41	+ 21.9	28.85	− 14.9	7.06	− 30.3	19.31	+ 8.7	2.79
1934 (a)										
Imports from	34.2	31.12	23.6	21.47	75.7	68.88	62.7	57.05	109.9	100.00
Exports to	70.8	51.45	57.2	41.57	66.8	48.55	46.0	33.43	137.6	100.00
Total trade with	105.0	42.42	80.8	32.65	142.5	57.58	108.7	43.92	247.5	100.00
Balance (b)	+ 36.6	34.86	+ 33.6	41.58	− 8.9	6.25	− 16.7	15.36	+ 27.7	11.19

For source and notes, see Table XL K.

TABLE XL
TRADE OF THE OVERSEAS BRITISH COUNTRIES
C—Australia
Values in £1,000,000's

	British Countries		United Kingdom		Foreign Countries		United States		Total	
	Value	% of Total	Value	% of Total	Value	% of Total	Value	% of Total	Value	% of Total
1913 (a)										
Imports from	50.3	63.11	41.3	51.82	29.4	36.39	9.5	11.92	79.7	100.00
Exports to	44.3	56.36	34.8	44.27	34.3	43.64	2.6	3.31	78.6	100.00
Total trade with	94.6	59.76	76.1	48.07	63.7	40.24	12.1	7.64	158.3	100.00
Balance (b)	− 6.0	6.34	− 6.5	8.54	+ 4.9	7.69	− 6.9	52.02	− 1.1	0.69
Average, 1929 – 1933 (a)										
Imports from	46.8	53.73	35.4	40.64	40.3	46.27	18.4	21.13	87.1	100.00
Exports to	50.2	54.80	40.5	44.21	41.4	45.20	2.9	3.17	91.6	100.00
Total trade with	97.0	54.28	75.9	42.47	81.7	45.72	21.3	11.92	178.7	100.00
Balance (b)	+ 3.4	3.51	+ 5.1	6.72	+ 1.1	1.35	− 15.5	72.77	+ 4.5	2.52
1934 (a)										
Imports from	34.7	58.22	25.9	43.46	24.9	41.78	7.8	13.09	59.6	100.00
Exports to	49.2	55.28	42.4	47.64	39.8	44.72	1.9	2.13	89.0	100.00
Total trade with	83.9	56.46	68.3	45.96	64.7	43.54	9.7	6.53	148.6	100.00
Balance (b)	+ 14.5	17.28	+ 16.5	24.16	+ 14.9	23.03	− 5.9	60.82	+ 29.4	19.78

For source and notes, see Table XL K.

TABLE XL
TRADE OF THE OVERSEAS BRITISH COUNTRIES
D—New Zealand
Values in £1.000,000's

	British Countries		United Kingdom		Foreign Countries		United States		Total	
	Value	% of Total	Value	% of Total	Value	% of Total	Value	% of Total	Value	% of Total
1913 (a)										
Imports from	18.4	82.51	13.3	59.64	3.9	17.49	2.1	9.42	22.3	100.00
Exports to	21.3	73.45	18.1	62.41	7.7	26.55	0.9	3.10	29.0	100.00
Total trade with	39.7	77.39	31.4	61.21	11.6	22.61	3.0	5.85	51.3	100.00
Balance (b).	+ 2.9	7.30	+ 4.8	15.29	+ 3.8	32.76	- 1.2	40.00	+ 6.7	13.06
Average, 1929 - 1933 (a)										
Imports from	22.3	69.69	15.3	47.81	9.7	30.31	5.3	16.56	32.0	100.00
Exports to	34.3	90.50	31.7	83.46	3.6	9.50	1.5	3.96	37.9	100.00
Total trade with	56.6	80.97	47.0	67.24	13.3	19.03	6.8	9.73	69.9	100.00
Balance (b).	+ 12.0	21.20	+ 16.4	34.89	- 6.1	45.86	- 3.8	55.88	+ 5.9	8.44
1934 (a)										
Imports from.	18.5	73.71	12.6	50.20	6.6	20.29	3.0	11.95	25.1	100.00
Exports to	31.8	87.36	29.9	82.14	4.6	12.64	1.0	2.75	36.4	100.00
Total trade with	50.3	81.79	42.5	69.11	11.2	18.21	4.0	6.50	61.5	100.00
Balance (b).	+ 13.3	26.44	+ 17.3	40.71	- 2.0	17.86	- 2.0	50.00	+ 11.3	18.37

For source and notes, see Table XL K.

TABLE XL
TRADE OF THE OVERSEAS BRITISH COUNTRIES
E—Union of South Africa
Values in £1,000,000's

	British Countries		United Kingdom		Foreign Countries		United States		Total	
	Value	% of Total	Value	% of Total	Value	% of Total	Value	% of Total	Value	% of Total
1913 (a)										
Imports from . . ·.	28.9	67.52	23.9	55.84	13.9	32.48	3.7	8.64	42.8	100.00
Exports to	61.2	91.75	59.0	88.46	5.5	8.25	0.5	0.75	66.7	100.00
Total trade with	90.1	82.28	82.9	75.71	19.4	17.72	4.2	3.84	109.5	100.00
Balance (b).	+ 32.3	35.85	+ 35.1	42.34	- 8.4	43.30	- 3.2	76.19	+ 23.9	21.83
Average, 1929 - 1933 (a)										
Imports from	33.9	57.36	27.3	46.19	25.2	42.64	8.8	14.89	59.1	100.00
Exports to	17.1	58.56	13.2	45.21	12.1	41.44	1.0	3.42	29.2	100.00
Total trade with	51.0	57.76	40.5	45.87	37.3	42.24	9.8	11.10	88.3	100.00
Balance (b).	- 16.8	32.94	- 14.1	34.81	- 13.1	35.12	- 7.8	79.59	- 29.9	33.86
1934 (a)										
Imports from	38.8	58.61	32.3	48.79	27.4	41.39	10.8	16.31	66.2	100.00
Exports to	12.8	55.65	9.3	40.43	10.2	44.35	0.6	2.61	23.0	100.00
Total trade with	51.6	57.85	41.6	46.64	37.6	42.15	11.4	12.78	89.2	100.00
Balance (b).	- 26.0	50.39	- 23.0	55.29	- 17.2	45.74	- 10.2	89.47	- 43.2	48.43

For source and notes, see Table XL K.

TABLE XL
TRADE OF THE OVERSEAS BRITISH COUNTRIES
F—Irish Free State
Values in £1,000,000's

	British Countries		United Kingdom		Foreign Countries		United States		Total	
	Value	% of Total	Value	% of Total	Value	% of Total	Value	% of Total	Value	% of Total
Average, 1929 – 1933 (a)										
Imports from	40.0	80.97	38.3	77.53	9.4	19.03	2.6	5.26	49.4	100.00
Exports to	32.8	95.07	32.4	93.91	1.7	4.93	0.6	1.74	34.5	100.00
Total trade with	72.8	86.77	70.7	84.27	11.1	13.23	3.2	3.81	83.9	100.00
Balance (b)	- 7.2	9.89	- 5.9	8.35	- 7.7	69.37	- 2.0	62.50	- 14.9	17.76
1934 (a)										
Imports from	28.4	72.63	26.1	66.75	10.7	27.37	1.9	4.86	39.1	100.00
Exports to	17.3	94.54	17.1	93.44	1.0	5.46	0.1	0.55	18.3	100.00
Total trade with	45.7	79.62	43.2	75.26	11.7	20.38	2.0	3.48	57.4	100.00
Balance (b)	- 11.1	24.29	- 9.0	20.83	- 9.7	82.91	- 1.8	90.00	- 20.8	36.24

For source and notes, see Table XL K.

TABLE XL
TRADE OF THE OVERSEAS BRITISH COUNTRIES
G—The Self-Governing Dominions
Values in £1,000,000's

	British Countries		United Kingdom		Foreign Countries		United States		Total	
	Value	% of Total	Value	% of Total	Value	% of Total	Value	% of Total	Value	% of Total
1913 (a)										
Imports from	131.4	47.20	106.6	38.29	147.0	52.80	107.1	38.47	278.4	100.00
Exports to	178.7	64.79	158.3	57.40	97.1	35.21	38.7	14.00	275.8	100.00
Total trade with	310.1	55.95	264.9	47.80	244.1	44.05	145.8	26.31	554.2	100.00
Balance (b)	+ 47.3	15.25	+ 51.7	19.52	- 49.9	20.44	- 68.4	46.91	- 2.6	0.47
Average, 1929 – 1933 (a)										
Imports from	181.6	47.89	143.3	37.79	197.6	52.11	128.7	33.94	379.2	100.00
Exports to	196.6	55.62	166.7	47.16	156.9	44.38	69.3	19.60	353.5	100.00
Total trade with	378.2	51.62	310.0	42.31	354.5	48.38	198.0	27.02	732.7	100.00
Balance (b)	+ 15.0	3.97	+ 23.4	7.55	- 40.7	11.48	- 59.4	30.00	- 25.7	3.51
1934 (a)										
Imports from	154.6	51.55	120.5	40.18	145.3	48.45	86.2	28.74	299.9	100.00
Exports to	181.9	59.78	155.9	51.23	122.4	40.22	49.6	16.30	304.3	100.00
Total trade with	336.5	55.69	276.4	45.75	267.7	44.31	135.8	22.48	604.2	100.00
Balance (b)	+ 27.3	8.11	+ 35.4	12.81	- 22.9	8.55	- 36.6	26.95	+ 4.4	0.73

For source and notes, see Table XL K.

TABLE XL
TRADE OF THE OVERSEAS BRITISH COUNTRIES
H—The Dominions and India
Values in £1,000,000's

	British Countries		United Kingdom		Foreign Countries		United States		Total	
	Value	% of Total	Value	% of Total	Value	% of Total	Value	% of Total	Value	% of Total
1913 (a)										
Imports from	244.4	55.28	209.1	47.30	197.7	44.72	110.8	25.06	442.1	100.00
Exports to	246.1	54.43	199.5	44.13	206.0	45.57	51.3	11.35	452.1	100.00
Total trade with	490.5	54.85	408.6	45.69	403.7	45.15	162.1	18.13	894.2	100.00
Balance (b)	+ 1.7	0.35	- 9.6	2.35	+ 8.3	2.06	- 59.5	36.71	+ 10.0	1.12
Average, 1929 - 1933 (a)										
Imports from	240.8	48.15	192.1	38.41	259.3	51.85	138.4	27.67	500.1	100.00
Exports to	255.9	51.30	203.5	40.80	242.9	48.70	83.5	16.74	498.8	100.00
Total trade with	496.7	49.72	395.6	39.60	502.2	50.28	221.9	22.21	998.9	100.00
Balance (b)	+ 15.1	3.04	+ 11.4	2.88	- 16.4	3.27	- 54.9	24.74	- 1.3	0.13
1934 (a)										
Imports from	205.0	51.15	162.0	40.42	195.8	48.85	92.6	23.10	400.8	100.00
Exports to	234.1	56.02	192.2	45.99	183.8	43.98	59.4	14.21	417.9	100.00
Total trade with	439.1	53.63	354.2	43.26	379.6	46.37	152.0	18.57	818.7	100.00
Balance (b)	+ 29.1	6.63	+ 30.2	8.53	- 12.0	3.16	- 33.2	21.84	+ 17.1	2.09

For source and notes, see Table XL K.

TABLE XL
TRADE OF THE OVERSEAS BRITISH COUNTRIES
I—British India
Values in £1,000,000's

	British Countries		United Kingdom		Foreign Countries		United States		Total	
	Value	% of Total	Value	% of Total	Value	% of Total	Value	% of Total	Value	% of Total
1913 (a)										
Imports from	113.0	69.03	102.5	62.61	50.7	30.97	3.7	1.65	163.7	100.00
Exports to	67.4	38.23	41.2	23.37	108.9	61.77	12.6	7.15	176.3	100.00
Total trade with	180.4	53.06	143.7	42.26	159.6	46.94	16.3	4.79	340.0	100.00
Balance (b)	- 45.6	25.28	- 61.3	42.66	+ 58.2	36.47	+ 8.9	55.28	+ 12.6	3.71
Average, 1929-1933 (a)										
Imports from	59.2	48.97	48.8	40.36	61.7	51.03	9.7	8.02	120.9	100.00
Exports to	59.3	40.81	36.8	25.33	86.0	59.19	14.2	9.77	145.3	100.00
Total trade with	118.5	44.52	85.6	32.16	147.7	55.48	23.9	8.98	266.2	100.00
Balance (b)	+ 0.1	0.08	- 12.0	14.02	+ 24.3	16.45	+ 4.5	18.83	+ 24.4	9.17
1934 (a)										
Imports from	50.4	49.95	41.5	41.13	50.5	50.05	6.4	6.34	100.9	100.00
Exports to	52.2	45.95	36.3	31.95	61.4	54.05	9.8	8.63	113.6	100.00
Total trade with	102.6	47.83	77.8	36.27	111.9	52.17	16.2	7.55	214.5	100.00
Balance (b)	+ 1.8	1.75	- 5.2	6.68	+ 10.9	9.74	+ 3.4	20.99	+ 12.7	5.92

For source and notes, see Table XL K.

TABLE XL
TRADE OF THE OVERSEAS BRITISH COUNTRIES
J—British Malaya
Values in £1,000,000's

	British Countries		United Kingdom		Foreign Countries		United States		Total	
	Value	% of Total	Value	% of Total	Value	% of Total	Value	% of Total	Value	% of Total
1913 (a)										
Imports from	42.6	64.55	8.0	12.12	23.4	35.45	0.7	1.06	66.0	100.00
Exports to	41.7	66.51	13.9	22.17	21.0	33.49	5.3	8.45	62.7	100.00
Total trade with	84.3	65.50	21.9	17.02	44.4	34.50	6.0	4.66	128.7	100.00
Balance (b)	- 0.9	1.07	+ 5.9	26.94	- 2.4	5.41	+ 4.6	76.69	- 3.3	2.56
Average, 1929-1933 (a)										
Imports from	20.9	32.01	9.5	14.55	44.4	67.99	2.1	3.22	65.3	100.00
Exports to	16.4	26.03	7.7	12.22	46.6	73.97	22.2	35.24	63.0	100.00
Total trade with	37.3	29.07	17.2	13.41	91.0	70.93	24.3	18.94	128.3	100.00
Balance (b)	- 4.5	12.06	- 1.8	10.47	+ 2.2	2.42	+ 20.1	82.72	- 2.3	1.79
1934 (a)										
Imports from	16.0	29.52	7.8	14.39	38.2	70.48	1.0	1.85	54.2	100.00
Exports to	18.5	29.04	10.7	16.80	45.2	70.96	22.0	34.54	63.7	100.00
Total trade with	34.5	29.26	18.5	15.69	83.4	70.74	23.0	19.51	117.9	100.00
Balance (b)	+ 2.5	7.25	+ 2.9	15.68	+ 7.0	3.39	+ 21.0	91.30	+ 9.5	8.06

For source and notes, see Table XL K.

TABLE XL
TRADE OF THE OVERSEAS BRITISH COUNTRIES
K—British India, Ceylon, and British Malaya
Values in £1,000,000's

	British Countries		United Kingdom		Foreign Countries		United States		Total	
	Value	% of Total	Value	% of Total	Value	% of Total	Value	% of Total	Value	% of Total
1913 (a)										
Imports from	167.0	68.72	114.4	47.08	76.0	31.28	4.5	6.82	243.0	100.00
Exports to	118.2	46.41	62.1	24.38	136.5	53.59	20.5	8.05	254.7	100.00
Total trade with	285.2	57.30	176.5	35.46	212.5	42.70	25.0	5.02	497.7	100.00
Balance (b)	- 48.8	17.11	- 52.3	29.63	+ 60.5	28.47	+ 16.0	64.00	+ 11.7	2.35
Average, 1929-1933 (a)										
Imports from	93.4	45.41	62.2	30.24	112.3	54.59	12.4	6.03	205.7	100.00
Exports to	87.5	38.60	53.1	23.42	139.2	61.40	39.1	17.25	226.7	100.00
Total trade with	180.9	41.84	115.3	26.67	251.5	58.16	51.5	11.91	432.4	100.00
Balance (b)	- 5.9	3.26	- 9.1	7.89	+ 26.9	10.70	+ 26.7	51.84	+ 21.0	4.86
1934 (a)										
Imports from	76.3	44.52	52.3	30.51	95.1	55.48	7.8	4.55	171.4	100.00
Exports to	82.9	42.45	56.3	28.83	112.4	57.55	34.0	17.41	195.3	100.00
Total trade with	159.2	43.41	108.6	29.62	207.5	56.59	41.8	11.40	366.7	100.00
Balance (b)	+ 6.6	4.15	+ 4.0	3.68	+ 17.3	8.34	+ 26.2	62.68	+ 23.9	6.52

Source:
Calculated from data in the Statistical Abstract of the United Kingdom and the Statistical Abstract of the British Empire, annual volumes.

Notes:
(a) 1913 figures include coins and bullion. For the other periods, the figures cover merchandise only. Exports are of domestic produce. Calendar years.
(b) Balance percents are of total trade. + and - indicate export and import surplus, respectively.

TABLE XL
TRADE OF THE OVERSEAS BRITISH COUNTRIES
L-Totals 1854-1863 and 1894-1903
Gross Trade—Merchandise and Bullion. Values in £1,000's

	IMPORTS					EXPORTS					TOTAL TRADE					BALANCE (b)			
	Total Imports		Imports from U.K.			Total Exports		Exports to U.K.			Total Trade		Total Trade with U.K.			Total Trade		Trade with U.K.	
	Value	% of Total	Value	% of Total Imports	% of Imports from U.K.	Value	% of Total	Value	% of Total Exports	% of Exports to U.K.	Value	% of Total	Value	% of Total Trade	% of Total Trade with U.K.	Value	% of Total	Value	% of Total Trade with U.K.
1854-1863 (a)																			
British North America	134,954	13.73	53,164	39.39	11.27	104,286	11.73	33,365	31.99	7.58	239,240	12.78	86,529	36.17	9.49	− 30,668	12.82	− 19,799	22.88
Australia and New Zealand	282,380	28.73	151,081	53.50	32.03	240,201	27.03	130,106	54.17	29.54	522,581	27.92	281,187	53.79	30.82	− 42,179	7.88	− 20,975	7.46
British South Africa	26,781	2.73	21,081	78.72	4.47	20,447	2.30	15,589	76.24	3.54	47,228	2.52	36,670	77.64	4.02	− 6,334	13.41	− 5,492	14.98
Total Self-governing Countries	444,115	45.19	225,326	50.74	47.77	364,934	41.06	179,060	49.07	40.65	809,049	43.23	404,386	49.98	44.33	− 79,181	9.79	− 46,266	11.44
India	339,577	34.55	189,905	55.92	40.25	345,081	38.83	166,717	48.31	37.85	684,658	36.58	356,622	52.10	39.09	+ 5,504	0.80	− 23,188	6.50
Other British Countries	199,094	20.26	56,528	28.39	11.98	178,703	20.11	94,679	52.98	21.50	377,797	20.19	151,207	40.02	16.58	− 20,391	5.40	+ 38,151	25.23
Total British Countries	982,786	100.00	471,759	48.00	100.00	888,718	100.00	440,456	49.56	100.00	1,871,504	100.00	912,215	48.74	100.00	− 94,068	5.03	− 31,303	3.43
1894-1903 (a)																			
British North America	344,436	15.52	86,232	25.04	7.89	351,693	15.13	196,672	55.92	18.60	696,129	15.32	282,904	40.64	13.16	+ 7,257	1.04	+110,440	39.04
Australia and New Zealand	426,770	19.24	266,804	62.52	24.40	527,381	22.70	323,916	61.42	30.64	954,151	21.01	590,720	61.91	27.47	+100,611	10.54	+ 57,112	9.67
British South Africa	297,931	13.43	197,389	66.25	18.05	198,407	8.54	179,573	90.51	16.99	496,338	10.93	376,962	45.95	17.53	− 99,524	20.05	− 17,816	4.73
Total Self-governing Countries	1,069,137	48.19	550,425	51.48	50.35	1,077,481	46.37	700,161	64.98	66.23	2,146,618	47.26	1,250,586	56.16	58.16	+ 8,344	0.39	+149,736	11.97
India	674,133	30.38	426,210	63.22	38.98	829,915	35.71	243,338	29.32	23.02	1,504,048	33.11	669,548	44.52	31.13	+155,782	10.36	−182,872	27.31
Other British Countries	475,422	21.43	116,660	24.54	10.67	416,366	17.92	113,697	27.31	10.75	891,788	19.63	230,357	25.83	10.71	− 59,056	6.62	− 2,963	1.29
Total British Countries	2,218,692	100.00	1,093,295	49.28	100.00	2,323,762	100.00	1,057,196	45.50	100.00	4,542,454	100.00	2,150,491	47.34	100.00	+105,070	2.31	− 36,099	1.68

Source:
Calculated from data in: For 1854-1863, Statistical Abstract, for the Several Colonies and Other Possessions of the United Kingdom.
For 1894-1903, Statistical Abstract for the British Colonies, Possessions, and Protectorates.

Notes:
(a) The several British countries used different fiscal years in these periods. The data used are those for the fiscal year corresponding more nearly to the calendar year, e.g., the fiscal year May 1,1854, to April 30,1855, is taken as 1854.
(b) + and − indicate excess of exports and imports, respectively. Balance percents are of corresponding total trade.

TABLE XLI
PERCENTAGES OF TRADE OF CERTAIN COUNTRIES, BY COMMODITY CLASSES
Percentages of Values

This table brings together for convenient comparison the percentage figures showing the proportions of British, French, Italian, and Japanese trade in the three main classes of commodities: Class I, foodstuffs, tobacco, drinkables, etc., grouped as comestibles; Class II, raw materials and partly manufactured goods; Class III, finished manufactured goods. The figures shown the proportions of total imports, total exports, and total trade in each class for these four countries. For France and the United Kingdom, they show also for the imports, exports, and total trade the proportions of the trade in each class with foreign countries and overseas territories (including the Dominions, for Britain). The balance percentages show the ratio of the net balance, "favorable" (+) or "unfavorable" (-) to the corresponding total trade. The record for each country is analyzed in the following tables (Tables XLII-A, B, and C; Table XLIII; Table XLIV, Tables XLV-A, B, and C; and Table XLVI).

	Imports				Exports				Total Trade				Balance (a)			
	1904	1913	Average 1929-1933	1934(e)	1904	1913	Average 1929-1933	1934(e)	1904	1913	Average 1929-1933	1934(e)	1904	1913	Average 1929-1933	1934(e)
Class I Trade																
Total external trade (b):																
France	18.15	21.59	28.21	32.31	15.57	11.77	13.45	14.40	16.87	17.18	21.81	24.50	- 8.21	- 38.36	- 46.54	- 48.77
Italy (e)	18.42	19.18	22.64	15.38	24.35	30.33	28.13	32.91	21.12	23.79	25.00	23.21	+ 5.08	+ 4.03	- 3.00	+ 26.64
Japan (foreign trade)	(f)	16.53	11.64	7.64	(f)	9.83	8.13	7.92	(f)	13.42	9.92	7.78	(f)	- 31.98	- 19.59	- 0.73
United Kingdom	41.86	37.75	47.53	47.43	5.53	6.21	8.26	7.69	29.03	24.95	33.79	33.48	- 86.56	- 79.80	- 82.89	- 83.87
With foreign countries (c):																
France	59.24	72.39	56.85	36.97	84.99	83.21	66.54	57.01	71.06	75.72	59.44	42.11	- 9.79	- 32.26	- 40.16	- 30.63
United Kingdom	75.32	73.82	60.83	55.21	50.77	60.87	44.53	51.99	73.67	72.51	59.44	54.96	- 90.79	- 83.05	- 87.18	- 84.74
With overseas territories (c):																
France	40.76	27.61	43.15	63.03	15.01	16.79	33.46	42.99	28.94	24.28	40.56	57.89	- 52.40	- 57.37	- 55.91	- 61.96
United Kingdom	24.68	26.18	39.17	44.79	49.23	39.13	55.47	48.01	26.33	27.49	40.56	45.04	- 74.86	- 71.25	- 76.60	- 82.81
Class II Trade																
Total external trade (b):																
France	63.37	58.73	52.33	49.32	27.43	26.72	24.16	28.89	45.50	44.37	40.12	40.41	- 40.06	- 45.81	- 47.78	- 37.67
Italy (e)	60.60	57.38	56.88	63.96	49.52	37.90	30.57	29.97	55.55	49.43	45.53	48.78	- 18.73	- 37.45	- 42.11	- 45.14
Japan (foreign trade)	(f)	65.87	72.60	79.56	(f)	59.99	39.55	27.36	(f)	63.14	56.39	54.11	(f)	- 11.75	- 31.19	- 50.69
United Kingdom	33.01	36.66	24.61	28.63	12.13	13.31	11.52	12.19	25.64	27.18	20.03	22.86	- 66.58	- 60.25	- 59.74	- 62.57
With foreign countries (c):																
France	94.88	94.36	94.24	90.96	96.31	95.43	89.31	87.67	95.31	94.65	92.95	89.93	- 39.43	- 45.37	- 49.83	- 39.24
United Kingdom	73.30	67.52	63.96	61.50	90.51	94.51	86.77	86.78	76.17	72.85	68.55	66.24	- 60.29	- 48.52	- 49.04	- 80.96
With overseas territories (d):																
France	5.12	5.64	5.76	9.04	3.69	4.57	10.69	12.33	4.69	5.35	7.05	10.07	- 52.88	- 53.72	- 20.78	- 23.63
United Kingdom	26.70	32.48	36.04	38.05	9.49	5.49	13.23	13.22	23.83	27.15	31.45	33.76	- 86.69	- 91.73	- 83.06	- 80.76
Class III Trade																
Total external trade (b):																
France	18.48	19.68	19.46	18.37	57.00	61.51	62.39	56.71	37.63	38.49	38.07	35.09	+ 50.61	+ 43.73	+ 42.08	+ 40.92
Italy (e)	20.98	23.34	20.49	20.67	26.13	31.77	41.31	37.12	23.33	26.78	29.47	28.01	+ 2.11	+ 3.21	+ 20.88	+ 18.34
Japan (foreign trade)	(f)	17.00	14.83	12.10	(f)	29.24	48.44	61.95	(f)	22.68	31.32	36.41	(f)	+ 19.71	+ 51.74	+ 65.94
United Kingdom	24.74	25.18	26.92	23.41	80.84	78.32	76.83	76.98	44.54	46.75	34.39	42.21	+ 28.15	+ 36.00	+ 21.14	+ 28.03
With foreign countries (c):																
France	99.04	99.03	98.56	97.90	83.88	84.05	74.00	62.76	87.62	88.27	81.82	73.14	+ 44.17	+ 36.86	+ 29.92	+ 30.92
United Kingdom	89.16	87.94	88.08	81.00	59.37	57.74	53.06	48.63	70.07	67.41	66.87	60.28	+ 8.57	+ 16.50	+ 3.87	+ 3.29
With overseas territories (c):																
France	0.96	0.97	1.44	2.10	16.12	15.95	26.00	37.24	12.38	11.73	18.88	26.86	+ 96.18	+ 95.37	+ 95.60	+ 95.38
United Kingdom	10.84	12.06	11.92	19.00	40.63	42.26	46.94	51.37	29.93	32.59	33.13	39.72	+ 73.98	+ 76.32	+ 71.62	+ 65.58

Sources:
See detailed trade by commodity classes tables.
Class I. Comestibles.
Class II. Raw materials and partly manufactured goods.
Class III. Manufactured goods.

Notes:
(a) + and - indicate export and import surplus, respectively. Percents are of corresponding totals.
(b) Percentages of total trade, i.e., of sum of Classes I, II and III, and, in the Japanese and British cases, Classes IV and V which are included in total.
(c) Percentages of each class total.
(d) Includes trade with the Dominions.
(e) Figures given under 1934 for Italy are for year 1933.
(f) Data not available.

TABLE XLII
EXTERNAL TRADE OF FRANCE, BY COMMODITY CLASSES
A—Total Trade
Merchandise—Special (Net) Trade. Value in 1,000,000's of Francs

Comestibles have formed a steadily increasing share of the total French imports, from less than a fifth in 1904 to nearly a third in 1934. Foreign countries have supplied a steadily decreasing share of these foodstuff imports, and the colonies an increasing share. Exports of comestibles have been a fairly unchanging share of the total exports, with a substantial decrease in the share of the total going to foreign countries, and an increase in the colonies' share. The "unfavorable" balance in the comestibles trade has increased very substantially.

Raw materials and partly manufactured goods form a smaller part of French imports than formerly; less than a half in 1934, as compared with nearly two-thirds in 1914. The share coming from foreign countries has decreased. Class II exports have remained somewhat more than a fourth of the total exports, with foreign countries taking a substantially decreasing share: 96% in 1904 and 88% in 1934. The balance remains "unfavorable," increasingly so.

Both the exports and imports of manufactured goods in 1934 were almost exactly the same proportion of the total as in 1904 (18% for imports and 57% for exports). In each case, the proportions were a little higher than in 1913 and 1929-1933. The "favorable" balance remains relatively large, but decreasingly so. The colonies have become increasingly important both as sources of and as markets for manufactured goods, the increase in exports being greater than in imports. In 1934, they supplied 9% of the manufactured goods imports and took 12% of these exports.

	Imports		Exports		Total Trade		Balance (a)	
	Value	% of Total Imports	Value	% of Total Exports	Value	% of Total Trade	Value	% of Class Total
1904								
Class I.	817	18.15	693	15.57	1,510	16.87	− 124	8.21
Class II	2,853	63.37	1,221	27.43	4,074	45.50	− 1,632	40.06
Class III.	832	18.48	2,537	57.00	3,369	37.63	+ 1,705	50.61
Total trade.	4,502	100.00	4,451	100.00	8,953	100.00	− 51	0.57
1913								
Class I.	1,818	21.59	810	11.77	2,628	17.18	− 1,008	38.36
Class II	4,946	58.73	1,838	26.72	6,784	44.34	− 3,108	45.81
Class III.	1,657	19.68	4,232	61.51	5,889	38.49	+ 2,575	43.73
Total Trade.	8,421	100.00	6,880	100.00	15,301	100.00	− 1,541	10.65
Average per year, 1929-1933								
Class I.	11,914	28.21	4,346	13.45	16,260	21.81	− 7,568	46.54
Class II	22,100	52.33	7,809	24.16	29,909	40.12	− 14,291	47.78
Class III.	8,220	19.46	20,163	62.39	28,383	38.07	+ 11,943	42.08
Total trade.	42,234	100.00	32,318	100.00	74,552	100.00	− 9,916	13.30
1934								
Class I.	7,451	32.31	2,566	14.40	10,017	24.50	− 4,885	48.77
Class II	11,373	49.32	5,149	28.89	16,522	40.41	− 6,224	37.67
Class III.	4,237	18.37	10,107	56.71	14,344	35.09	+ 5,870	40.92
Total trade.	23,061	100.00	17,822	100.00	40,883	100.00	− 5,239	12.81

For sources and note, see Table XLII C.

TABLE XLII
EXTERNAL TRADE OF FRANCE, BY COMMODITY CLASSES
B—With Foreign Countries
Merchandise—Special (Net) Trade. Value in 1,000,000's of Francs

	Imports			Exports			Total Trade			Balance (a)	
	Value	% of Class Total Imports	% of Total Foreign Imports	Value	% of Class Total Exports	% of Total Foreign Exports	Value	% of Total Foreign Trade	% of Class Total	Value	% of Class Total with Foreign Countries
1904											
Class I.	484	59.24	12.05	589	84.99	15.13	1,073	13.57	71.06	+ 105	9.79
Class II	2,707	94.88	67.42	1,176	96.31	30.21	3,883	49.10	95.31	- 1,531	39.43
Class III.	824	99.04	20.52	2,128	83.88	54.66	2,952	37.33	87.62	+ 1,304	44.17
Total trade. . . .	4,015	89.18	100.00	3,893	87.46	100.00	7,908	100.00	88.33	- 122	1.54
1913											
Class I.	1,316	72.39	17.26	674	83.21	11.26	1,990	14.62	75.72	- 642	32.26
Class II	4,667	94.36	61.21	1,754	95.43	29.31	6,421	47.18	94.65	- 2,913	45.37
Class III.	1,641	99.03	21.52	3,557	84.05	59.43	5,198	38.20	88.27	+ 1,916	36.86
Total trade. . . .	7,624	90.54	100.00	5,985	86.99	100.00	13,609	100.00	88.94	- 1,639	11.99
Average per year, 1929-1933											
Class I.	6,773	56.85	18.97	2,892	66.54	11.67	9,665	15.98	59.44	- 3,881	40.16
Class II	20,827	94.24	58.34	6,974	89.31	28.14	27,801	45.96	92.95	-13,853	49.83
Class III.	8,102	98.56	22.69	14,921	74.00	60.20	23,023	38.06	81.12	+ 6,819	29.62
Total trade. . . .	35,702	84.53	100.00	24,787	76.70	100.00	60,489	100.00	81.14	-10,915	18.04
1934											
Class I.	2,755	36.97	15.97	1,463	57.01	11.87	4,218	14.26	42.11	- 1,292	30.63
Class II	10,345	90.96	59.98	4,514	87.67	36.64	14,859	50.25	89.93	- 5,831	39.24
Class III.	4,148	97.90	24.05	6,343	62.76	51.49	10,491	35.48	73.14	+ 2,195	30.92
Total trade. . . .	17,248	74.79	100.00	12,320	69.13	100.00	29,568	100.00	72.32	- 4,928	16.67

For sources and note see Table XLII C.

TABLE XLII
EXTERNAL TRADE OF FRANCE, BY COMMODITY CLASSES
C—With Colonies and Protectorates
Merchandise—Special (Net) Trade. Value in 1,000,000's of Francs

	Imports			Exports			Total Trade			Balance (a)	
	Value	% of Class Total Imports	% of Colonial Imports Total	Value	% of Class Total Exports	% of Colonial Exports Total	Value	% of Total Trade with Colonies	% of Class Total	Value	% of Class Total with Colonies
1904											
Class I	333	40.76	68.38	104	15.01	18.64	437	41.82	28.94	− 229	52.40
Class II	146	5.12	29.98	45	3.69	8.06	191	18.28	4.69	− 101	52.88
Class III	8	0.96	1.64	409	16.12	73.30	417	39.90	12.38	+ 401	96.16
Total trade. . . .	487	10.82	100.00	558	12.54	100.00	1,045	100.00	11.67	+ 71	6.79
1913											
Class I	502	27.61	62.99	136	16.79	15.20	638	37.71	24.28	− 366	57.37
Class II	297	5.64	35.01	84	4.57	9.39	363	21.45	5.35	− 195	53.72
Class III	16	0.97	2.01	675	15.95	75.42	691	40.84	11.73	+ 659	95.37
Total trade. . . .	797	9.46	100.00	895	13.01	100.00	1,692	100.00	11.06	+ 98	5.79
Average per year, 1929-1933											
Class I	5,141	43.15	78.70	1,454	33.46	19.31	6,595	46.90	40.56	− 3,687	55.91
Class II	1,273	5.76	19.49	835	10.69	11.09	2,108	14.99	7.05	− 438	20.78
Class III	118	1.44	1.81	5,242	26.00	69.61	5,360	38.11	18.88	+ 5,124	95.60
Total Trade. . . .	6,532	15.47	100.00	7,531	23.30	100.00	14,063	100.00	18.86	+ 999	7.10
1934											
Class I	4,696	63.03	80.78	1,103	42.99	20.05	5,799	51.25	57.89	− 3,593	61.96
Class II	1,028	9.04	17.68	635	12.33	11.54	1,663	14.70	10.07	− 393	23.63
Class III	89	2.10	1.53	3,764	37.24	68.41	3,853	34.05	26.86	+ 3,675	95.38
Total trade. . . .	5,813	25.21	100.00	5,502	30.87	100.00	11,315	100.00	27.68	− 311	2.75

Sources:
Calculated from data in the Tableau général du commerce (et de la navigation) extérieur, annual volumes for 1904-1932;
Statistique mensuelle du commerce extérieur, for 1933 and 1934.
   Class I. "Objets d' alimentation" (comestibles).
   Class II. "Matieres nécéssaires a l'industrie" (raw materials and partly manufactured goods).
   Class III. "Objets fabriqués" (manufactured goods).

Note:
(a) + and − indicate export and import surplus, respectively. Balance percents are of corresponding total trade.

TABLE XLIII
EXTERNAL TRADE OF ITALY, BY COMMODITY CLASSES
Special (Net) Trade. Merchandise. Values in 1,000,000's of Lire

Raw materials and partly manufactured goods have formed distinctly more than half of Italy's imports. Imports of manufactured goods have been slightly more than those of comestibles, with the proportions being a little more and a little less than a fifth each. On the export side, however, the proportion of manufactured goods to the total has shown a substantial increase - from 26% in 1904 to 41% in 1929-1933. Foodstuffs also have increased their share of Italy's exports somewhat, but the raw materials proportion has dropped sharply - 50% in 1904 to 31% in 1929-1933. After a small export surplus in manufactured goods in 1904, Italy had an import surplus in this class of commodities in 1913, but for 1929-1933, the export margin was quite substantial. The raw materials balance has been heavily and increasingly "unfavorable." Foodstuffs have shifted from the "favorable" to the "unfavorable" side in the trade balance, but the margin is comparatively small.

	Imports		Exports		Total Trade		Balance	
	Value	% of Total	Value	% of Total	Value	% of Total	Value	% of Total
1904:								
Class I...............	346	18.42	383	24.35	729	21.12	+ 37	5.08
Class II...............	1,138	60.60	779	49.52	1,917	55.55	- 359	18.73
Class III...............	394	20.98	411	26.13	805	23.33	+ 17	2.11
Total trade.............	1,878	100.00	1,573	100.00	3,451	100.00	- 305	8.84
1913:								
Class I...............	703	19.28	762	30.33	1,465	23.79	+ 59	4.03
Class II...............	2,092	57.38	952	37.90	3,044	49.43	- 1,140	37.45
Class III...............	851	23.34	798	31.77	1,649	26.78	- 53	3.21
Total trade.............	3,646	100.00	2,512	100.00	6,158	100.00	- 1,134	18.42
Average per year, 1929-1933:								
Class I...............	2,987	22.64	2,813	28.13	3,800	25.00	- 174	3.00
Class II...............	7,505	56.88	3,057	30.57	10,562	45.53	- 4,448	42.11
Class III...............	2,704	20.49	4,131	41.31	6,835	29.47	+ 1,427	20.88
Total trade.............	13,196	100.00	10,001	100.00	23,197	100.00	- 3,195	13.77
1933:								
Class I...............	1,140	15.38	1,968	32.91	3,108	23.21	+ 828	26.64
Class II...............	4,741	63.96	1,792	29.97	6,533	48.78	- 2,949	45.14
Class III...............	1,532	20.67	2,220	37.12	3,752	28.01	+ 688	18.34
Total trade.............	7,413	100.00	5,980	100.00	13,393	100.00	- 1,433	10.70

Source:
Calculated from data in the Movimento commerciale del Regno d'Italia, annual volumes.
    Class I.   "Generi Alimentari" (Commestibles).
    Class II.   Sum of "Materia prime greggi" (raw materials) and "Prodotti semi-lavorati" (semi-manufactures).
    Class III. "Prodotti finiti" (Manufactured goods).

Note:
(a) + and - indicate export and import surplus, respectively. Percents are of corresponding total trades.

TABLE XLIV
FOREIGN TRADE OF JAPAN PROPER, BY COMMODITY CLASSES
Merchandise—Gross Trade. Value in 1,000's of Yen

Japan's notable industrial development is clearly reflected in her trade figures. Comparing 1913 with 1929-1933 and 1934, the proportions of raw materials in the total imports have increased from 66% to 73% and then to 80%, while the share of manufactured goods has decreased from 17% to 15% and to 12%. The change shows correspondingly in the export figures. For 1913, 1929-1933, and 1934, the proportions of total exports were: raw materials, 60%, 40%, and 27%; manufactured goods, 29%, 48%, and 62%. The balance in raw materials has been unfavorable, but its ratio to the total trade in this class of commodities has increased very substantially. The "favorable" manufactured goods balance also has increased largely, both in value and in ratio to the total trade in manufactured goods. In 1913, the import surplus in raw materials was just over a fourth (27%) of the exports of this class. In 1929-1933, Japan imported more than she exported of these goods by 91% of the value of the exports. In 1934, the imports of raw materials were more than the exports by over twice (206%) the value of the exports. The

ratio of export surpluses to the value of imports in manufactured goods was 49% in 1913, 210% in 1929-1933, and 387% in 1934.

Japan's foodstuffs imports have decreased considerably in their proportions of Japan's total imports. Their absolute value also was substantially lower in 1934 than on the average for 1929-1933, though the total imports had increased considerably. Value figures for 1913 and 1934 show an increase in comestibles imports of 45%, while exports of comestibles increased 176% (total imports increased 213%; total exports 243%). The foodstuffs balance continued to be "unfavorable," but in 1934 it was only 2.5 million yen instead of 58.4 million in 1913. In other words, Japan now is very much less dependent on food supplies from foreign sources than she was before the war, and the excess of imports over exports has become a very minor item both in the total foreign trade and in the food supply of the people.

	Imports		Exports		Total Trade		Balance (a)	
	Value	% of Total Imports	Value	% of Total Exports	Value	% of Total Trade	Value	% of Class Total
1904:								
Class I (b).	. . . .	. . .	. . . .	. . .	. . . .	. . .	. . . .	. . .
Class II (b).	. . . .	. . .	. . . .	. . .	. . . .	. . .	. . . .	. . .
Class III (b).	. . . .	. . .	. . . .	. . .	. . . .	. . .	. . . .	. . .
Total.	371,361	100.00	319,261	100.00	690,622	100.00	52,100	7.54
1913:								
Class I	120,582	16.53	62,142	9.83	182,724	13.42	- 58,440	31.98
Class II	480,469	65.87	379,424	59.99	859,893	63.14	- 101,045	11.75
Class III.	124,029	17.00	184,914	29.24	308,943	22.68	+ 60,885	19.71
Total.	729,432	100.00	632,460	100.00	1,361,892	100.00	- 96,972	7.12
Average per year, 1929-1933:								
Class I	194,384	11.64	130,710	8.13	325,094	9.92	- 63,674	19.59
Class II	1,211,948	72.60	635,716	39.55	1,847,664	56.39	- 576,232	31.19
Class III.	247,577	14.83	778,502	48.44	1,026,079	31.32	+ 530,925	51.74
Total.	1,669,333	100.00	1,607,298	100.00	3,276,631	100.00	- 62,035	1.89
1934:								
Class I	174,449	7.64	171,931	7.92	346,380	7.78	- 2,518	0.73
Class II	1,816,051	79.56	594,268	27.36	2,410,319	54.11	-1,221,783	50.69
Class III.	276,219	12.10	1,345,512	61.95	1,621,731	36.41	+1,069,293	65.94
Total.	2,282,531	100.00	2,171,925	100.00	4,454,456	100.00	- 110,606	2.48

Source:
Calculated from data in the Financial and Economic Annual of Japan, annual volumes.
Class I.   Foodstuffs, comestibles.
Class II.   Raw materials and partly manufactured goods.
Class III.   Manufactured goods.
Other minor items included in total.

Notes:
(a) + and - indicate export and import surplus respectively. Balance percents are of the corresponding total trade.
(b) Data not available.

TABLE XLV
EXTERNAL TRADE OF THE UNITED KINGDOM, BY COMMODITY CLASSES
A—Total Trade
Merchandise—Total Imports—Exports of British Produce. Value in £1,000's

The total trade record for the United Kingdom shows remarkably little variation in the proportions of the imports and exports formed by each of the three principal classes of goods. But there have been significant changes in the proportions in each class of the trade with foreign and British countries.

In the total trade: a little less than half of the gross imports are comestibles, roughly a third in raw materials and partly manufactured goods, and about a fourth in finished manufactures. Distinctly less than a tenth of the exports of British goods are comestibles, about an eighth are raw materials and partly manufactured goods, and between three-fourths and four-fifths are finished manufactures. The "unfavorable" balance on raw materials runs somewhat, but not much, larger than the "favorable" balance on manufactured goods, so that the import surplus in comestibles is only a little less than the total import surplus in value, though its ratio to the total trade in foodstuffs is very much greater than the corresponding ratio for the total trade. The "unfavorable" balances in foodstuffs were 1,288% of the total exports of this class of goods in 1904, 790% in 1913, 969% in 1929-1933, and 1,040% in 1934. The total "unfavorable" balances in

the same years were 83%, 46%, 86%, and 85% of the total exports.

The remarkable lack of change in the proportion of Britain's trade in each class to the total trade is striking evidence of the fundamental stability which has been reached in the British economic system. In France, Italy, and Japan economic equilibrium has not been reached, as the changes in the foreign trade show (Tables XLVII, XLVIII, and XLIX).

A breakdown of the British figures shows that in both the exports and the imports in each class there has been a shift from foreign to British countries corresponding to the shift in the total trade already discussed (Tables XXXVIII and XXXIX).

Comparing 1904 with 1913, 1929-1933, and 1934, the shares taken by the British countries were: comestibles imports, 25%, 26%, 39%, 45%; raw materials and partly manufactured goods imports, 27%, 32%, 36%, 39%; manufactured goods exports, 41%, 42%, 47%, 51%; total trade, 27%, 30%, 36%, 41%. The increase in the British countries' share of Britain's trade thus is not the result of a lop-sided large expansion in any one kind of goods, but of a shift in all parts of that trade.

	Imports		Exports		Total Trade		Balance (a)	
	Value	% of Total Imports	Value	% of Total Exports	Value	% of Total Trade	Value	% of Class Total
1904								
Class I	230,645	41.86	16,622	5.53	247,267	29.03	-214,023	86.56
Class II	181,886	33.01	36,488	12.13	218,374	25.64	-145,398	66.58
Class III	136,299	24.74	243,080	80.84	379,379	44.54	+106,781	28.15
Total trade (a)	551,039	100.00	300,711	100.00	851,750	100.00	-250,328	29.39
1913								
Class I	290,203	37.75	32,596	6.21	322,799	24.95	-257,607	79.80
Class II	281,823	36.66	69,905	13.31	351,728	27.18	-211,918	60.25
Class III	193,602	25.18	411,368	78.32	604,970	46.75	+217,666	36.00
Total trade (a)	768,735	100.00	525,254	100.00	1,293,989	100.00	-243,481	18.82
Averages per year,1929-1933								
Class I	428,028	47.53	40,038	8.26	468,066	33.79	-387,990	82.89
Class II	221,615	24.61	55,859	11.52	277,474	20.03	-165,756	59.74
Class III	242,437	26.92	372,442	76.83	614,879	34.39	+130,005	21.14
Total trade (a)	900,536	100.00	484,732	100.00	1,385,268	100.00	-415,804	30.02
1934								
Class I	347,336	47.43	30,465	7.69	377,801	33.48	-316,871	83.87
Class II	209,679	28.63	48,270	12.19	257,949	22.86	-161,409	62.57
Class III	171,404	23.41	304,938	76.98	476,342	42.21	+133,534	28.03
Total trade (a)	732,331	100.00	396,108	100.00	1,128,439	100.00	-336,223	29.80

For sources and note see Table XLV C.

TABLE XLV
EXTERNAL TRADE OF THE UNITED KINGDOM, BY COMMODITY CLASSES
B—With Foreign Countries
Merchandise—Total Imports—Exports of British Produce. Value in £1,000's

	Imports			Exports			Total Trade			Balance (a)	
	Value	% of Class Total Imports	% of Imports from Foreign Countries	Value	% of Class Total Exports	% of Exports from Foreign Countries	Value	% of Class Total	% of Total Foreign Trade	Value	% of Class Total with Foreign Countries
1904											
Class I	173,733	75.32	40.37	8,439	50.77	4.48	182,172	73.67	29.45	-165,294	90.74
Class II	133,318	73.30	30.98	33,026	90.51	17.54	166,344	76.17	26.89	-100,292	60.29
Class III. . . .	121,526	89.16	28.24	144,318	59.37	76.65	265,844	70.07	42.98	+ 22,792	8.57
Total trade. . .	430,253	78.08	100.00	188,287	62.61	100.00	618,540	72.62	100.00	-241,966	39.12
1913											
Class I	214,227	73.82	37.11	19,840	60.87	6.01	234,067	72.51	25.80	-194,387	83.05
Class II	190,284	67.52	32.97	65,956	94.51	19.99	256,240	72.85	28.25	-124,328	48.52
Class III. . . .	170,257	87.94	29.50	237,540	57.74	71.99	407,797	67.41	44.95	+ 67,283	16.50
Total trade. . .	577,219	75.09	100.00	329,942	62.82	100.00	907,161	70.11	100.00	-247,277	27.26
Averages per year, 1929-1933											
Class I	260,374	60.83	42.06	17,827	44.53	6.60	278,201	59.44	31.28	-242,547	87.18
Class II	141,738	63.96	22.90	48,468	86.77	17.94	190,206	68.55	21.39	- 93,270	49.04
Class III. . . .	213,533	88.08	34.50	197,622	53.06	73.13	411,155	66.87	46.24	- 15,911	3.87
Total trade. . .	619,024	68.74	100.00	270,232	55.75	100.00	889,256	64.19	100.00	-348,792	39.22
1934											
Class I	191,792	55.21	41.62	15,840	51.99	7.53	207,632	54.96	30.93	-175,952	84.74
Class II	128,962	61.50	27.98	41,891	86.78	19.90	170,853	66.24	25.45	- 87,071	80.96
Class III. . . .	138,841	81.00	30.13	138,841	48.63	65.96	287,125	60.28	42.77	+ 9,443	3.29
Total trade. . .	460,864	62.93	100.00	210,483	53.14	100.00	671,347	59.49	100.00	-250,381	37.30

For sources and note, see Table XLV C.

TABLE XLV
EXTERNAL TRADE OF THE UNITED KINGDOM, BY COMMODITY CLASSES
C—With British Countries
Merchandise—Total Imports—Exports of British Produce. Value in £1,000's

	Imports			Exports			Total Trade			Balance (a)	
	Value	% of Class Total	% of Imports from British Countries	Value	% of Class Total Exports	% of Exports to British Countries	Value	% of Class Total	% of Total Trade with British Countries	Value	% of Class Total with British Countries
1904											
Class I	56,912	24.68	47.11	8,183	49.23	7.28	65,095	26.33	27.91	- 48,729	74.86
Class II	48,568	26.70	40.21	3,462	9.49	3.08	52,030	23.83	22.31	- 45,106	86.69
Class III.	14,773	10.84	12.23	98,762	40.63	87.85	113,535	29.93	48.68	+ 83,989	73.98
Total trade. . . .	120,786	21.92	100.00	112,424	37.39	100.00	233,210	27.38	100.00	- 8,362	3.59
1913											
Class I	75,976	26.18	39.67	12,756	39.13	6.53	88,732	27.49	22.94	- 63,220	71.25
Class II	91,539	32.48	47.80	3,949	5.49	2.02	95,488	27.15	24.68	- 87,590	91.73
Class III.	23,345	12.06	12.19	173,828	42.26	89.00	197,173	32.15	50.97	+150,483	76.32
Total trade. . . .	191,516	24.91	100.00	195,311	37.18	100.00	386,827	29.89	100.00	+ 3,795	0.98
Averages per year, 1929-1933											
Class I	167,654	39.17	59.55	22,211	55.47	10.35	189,865	40.56	38.28	-145,443	76.60
Class II	79,877	36.04	28.37	7,391	13.23	3.45	87,268	31.45	17.59	- 72,486	83.06
Class III.	28,904	11.92	10.27	174,820	46.94	81.50	203,724	33.13	41.07	+145,916	71.62
Total trade. . . .	281,512	31.26	100.00	214,590	44.25	100.00	496,012	35.81	100.00	- 67,012	13.51
1934											
Class I	155,544	44.79	57.30	14,625	48.01	7.88	170,169	45.04	47.23	-140,919	82.81
Class II	80,717	38.50	29.73	6,379	13.22	3.44	87,096	33.76	19.05	- 74,338	80.76
Class III.	32,563	19.00	12.00	156,654	51.37	84.39	189,217	39.72	41.40	+124,091	65.58
Total trade. . . .	271,467	37.07	100.00	185,625	46.86	100.00	457,092	40.51	100.00	- 85,842	18.78

Sources:
For 1904,1913,1929-1933,calculated from data in the Annual Statement of Foreign Trade of the United Kingdom, annual volumes.
For 1934, calculated from data in Accounts Relating to the Trade and Navigation of the United Kingdom, December, 1934.

Class I. Food, drink, and tobacco (comestibles).
Class II. Raw materials and materials mainly unmanufactured.
Class III. Articles wholly or mainly manufactured.
Classes IV and V in the British records are parcel post and other minor items. Included in totals.

Note:
(a) + and - indicate export and import excess, respectively. Balance percents are of corresponding total trade.

TABLE XLVI
EXTERNAL TRADE OF THE UNITED KINGDOM WITH PARTICULAR COUNTRIES
By Commodity Classes

Merchandise—Total Imports—Exports of British Produce. Value in £1,000's

This table shows in more detail than the preceding ones (Tables XLV-A, B, and C) the sources of Britain's imports of the commodities in the three principal classes, and the destinations of the exports. The introductory note to Table XLIV-A should be consulted.

Australia and New Zealand have more than doubled their proportion of Britain's foodstuffs imports since 1913, and they now supply more than half of all the comestibles which Britain gets from the Dominions. The shares of the other Dominions in this class of imports also have increased somewhat, while those of India, Ceylon, and British Malaya has decreased. (Part of the sharp increase in the total Dominions' share which the figures show is due to the inclusion of the Irish Free State in this group for 1929-1933 and 1934.) The United States, on the other hand, in 1934 supplied only a little more than half the proportion of Britain's comestibles imports which she furnished in 1913.

As sources of raw materials and partially manufactured goods, all the Dominions together held practically the same relative position in 1929-1933 and 1934 as in 1913 (allowing for the inclusion of the Irish Free State in recent years). In spite of the development of rubber production in India and British Malaya, these two areas and Ceylon, taken together, were only slightly more important, relatively, as raw materials sources in 1934 than in 1913, and they were distinctly less important on the average in 1929-1933.

Australia and New Zealand increased their share. The United States' share in 1934 was only half its 1913 proportion.

India, Ceylon, and British Malaya were distinctly less important, relatively, as a market for British manufactures in 1934 than in 1913; their share of these exports dropped from 18% in 1913 to 14% in 1929-1933, and to 13% in 1934. Australia and New Zealand took a slightly larger proportion of these exports. Canada's share decreased a little. That of the Union of South Africa nearly doubled; in 1934, in fact, the Union's purchases of British manufactures were close to those by Australia and New Zealand combined and by India, and not much less than three times those by the United States.

	CLASS I (a) Imports from Value	% of Class Total	Exports to Value	% of Class Total	Balance (b) Value	% of Class Total	CLASS II (a) Imports from Value	% of Class Total	Exports to Value	% of Class Total	Balance (b) Value	% of Class Total	CLASS III (a) Imports from Value	% of Class Total	Exports to Value	% of Class Total	Balance (b) Value	% of Year Total
Trade with Canada and Newfoundland																		
In 1913	20,968	7.23	2,038	6.25	− 18,930	82.28	8,207	2.91	546	0.78	− 7,661	87.52	2,112	1.09	20,774	5.05	+ 18,662	81.54
Average per year 1929-1933	26,203	6.12	1,894	4.73	− 24,309	86.52	5,761	2.60	2,837	4.00	− 3,524	44.06	10,780	4.45	19,128	5.14	+ 8,348	27.91
In 1934	27,283	7.85	931	3.06	− 26,352	93.40	9,087	4.33	2,731	5.66	− 6,356	53.79	13,910	8.12	14,952	4.90	+ 1,042	3.61
Australia and New Zealand																		
In 1913	24,331	8.42	3,239	9.94	− 21,092	76.50	29,810	10.58	490	0.70	− 29,320	96.77	5,101	2.12	40,857	9.93	+ 35,756	77.80
Average per year 1929-1933	58,040	13.56	2,665	6.65	− 55,375	91.22	27,956	12.61	446	0.80	− 27,510	96.86	3,137	1.29	38,462	10.33	+ 35,325	84.92
In 1934	59,489	17.13	1,730	5.68	− 57,759	94.35	27,400	13.07	41	0.08	− 27,359	99.70	2,716	1.58	34,511	11.32	+ 31,795	85.41
British India																		
In 1913	20,635	7.11	1,984	6.09	− 18,651	82.44	20,721	7.35	547	0.78	− 20,174	94.85	6,935	3.58	66,982	16.28	+ 60,047	81.24
Average per year 1929-1933	19,777	4.62	3,000	7.49	− 16,777	73.66	14,595	6.59	441	0.79	− 14,154	94.13	9,363	3.86	41,608	11.17	+ 32,245	63.26
In 1934	18,695	5.36	1,956	6.42	− 16,739	81.08	15,442	7.36	343	0.71	− 15,099	95.06	7,458	4.35	33,218	10.89	+ 25,760	63.33
Union of South Africa																		
In 1913	229	0.08	1,724	5.29	+ 1,496	76.55	11,242	3.99	294	0.42	− 10,948	94.90	766	0.40	19,583	4.76	+ 18,817	92.47
Average per year 1929-1933	5,928	1.38	1,159	2.89	− 4,769	87.29	10,988	4.96	214	0.38	− 10,774	96.18	386	0.16	21,880	5.87	+ 21,494	96.53
In 1934	4,468	1.29	1,140	3.74	− 3,328	59.34	6,485	3.10	85	0.18	− 6,400	97.41	330	0.19	27,762	9.10	+ 27,432	97.68
Canada, Newfoundland, Australia, New Zealand, Union of South Africa, Irish Free State.																		
In 1913	45,628	15.72	7,001	21.48	− 38,627	73.59	49,259	17.48	1,330	1.90	− 47,929	94.74	6,979	3.60	81,214	19.74	+ 74,235	84.17
Average per year 1929-1933	118,372	27.66	11,290	28.20	−107,082	82.59	45,800	20.67	5,543	9.92	− 40,257	78.41	15,889	6.55	98,215	26.37	+ 82,326	72.15
In 1934	105,515	30.38	5,304	17.41	−100,211	90.43	43,615	20.80	4,098	8.49	− 39,517	82.82	17,357	10.13	92,242	30.25	+ 74,885	68.33
India, British Malaya, Ceylon.																		
In 1913	26,201	9.03	2,787	8.55	− 23,414	80.77	33,795	11.99	651	0.93	− 33,144	96.22	15,441	7.98	73,297	17.82	+ 57,856	65.20
Average per year 1929-1933	32,160	7.51	5,687	14.20	− 26,473	89.95	21,324	9.62	655	1.17	− 20,669	94.04	11,184	4.61	50,471	13.55	+ 39,287	63.72
In 1934	30,683	8.83	4,291	14.09	− 26,392	75.46	25,437	12.13	343	0.71	− 25,094	97.34	8,621	5.02	39,038	12.80	+ 30,417	63.82

(Continued on next page)

TABLE XLVI
EXTERNAL TRADE OF THE UNITED KINGDOM WITH PARTICULAR COUNTRIES
By Commodity Classes (Concluded)
Merchandise—Total Imports—Exports of British Produce. Value in £1,000's

	CLASS I (a)						CLASS II (a)						CLASS III (a)					
	Imports from		Exports to		Balance		Imports from		Exports to		Balance		Imports from		Exports to		Balance	
	Value	% of Class Total	Value	% of Class Total	Value	% of Class Total (b)	Value	% of Class Total	Value	% of Class Total	Value	% of Class Total (b)	Value	% of Class Total	Value	% of Class Total	Value	% of Class Total (b)
Six Dominions and India																		
In 1913	66,263	22.83	8,985	27.56	− 57,278	76.12	69,980	24.83	1,877	2.69	− 68,103	94.78	13,914	7.19	148,196	36.03	+134,282	82.83
Average per year 1929–1933	138,149	32.28	14,290	35.69	−123,859	81.25	60,395	27.25	5,984	10.71	− 54,411	81.97	25,252	10.42	139,823	37.54	+114,571	69.41
In 1934	124,210	35.76	7,260	23.83	−116,950	88.96	59,057	28.17	4,441	9.20	− 54,616	86.01	24,815	14.48	125,460	41.14	+100,645	66.97
Other British Countries																		
In 1913	4,147	1.43	2,968	9.11	− 1,179	16.57	8,485	3.01	1,968	2.82	− 6,517	62.35	925	0.48	19,317	4.70	+ 18,392	90.86
Average per year 1929–1933	17,122	4.00	5,234	13.07	− 11,888	53.18	12,753	5.75	1,193	2.14	− 11,560	82.89	1,831	0.76	26,134	7.02	+ 24,303	86.91
In 1934	19,346	5.57	5,030	16.51	− 14,316	58.73	11,665	5.56	1,938	4.02	− 9,727	71.51	6,585	3.84	25,374	8.32	+ 18,789	58.79
France																		
In 1913	9,248	3.19	1,105	3.39	− 8,143	78.65	6,878	2.44	9,484	13.57	+ 2,606	15.93	29,550	15.26	17,426	4.24	− 12,124	25.81
Average per year 1929–1933	8,091	1.89	936	2.34	− 7,155	79.26	4,426	2.00	10,818	19.37	+ 6,392	41.93	24,326	10.03	11,765	3.16	− 12,561	34.80
In 1934	5,038	1.45	568	1.86	− 4,470	79.74	3,173	1.51	8,916	18.47	+ 5,743	47.51	10,056	5.87	6,678	2.19	− 3,378	19.05
Germany																		
In 1913	16,461	5.67	4,013	12.31	− 12,448	60.80	7,106	2.52	8,400	12.02	+ 1,294	8.35	56,143	29.00	27,007	6.57	− 29,136	35.04
Average per year 1929–1933	3,847	0.90	2,539	6.34	− 1,308	20.48	3,454	1.56	5,246	9.39	+ 1,792	20.60	43,965	18.13	13,908	3.73	− 30,057	51.94
In 1934	1,846	0.53	1,199	3.94	− 647	21.25	1,997	0.95	4,489	9.30	+ 2,492	38.42	26,013	15.18	7,727	2.53	− 18,286	54.20
United States																		
In 1913	51,551	17.76	2,008	6.16	− 49,543	92.50	57,781	20.50	8,176	11.70	− 49,605	75.21	32,058	16.56	10,036	2.44	− 22,022	52.32
Average per year 1929–1933	44,201	10.33	1,053	2.63	− 43,148	95.35	31,623	14.27	3,595	6.44	− 28,028	79.58	45,379	18.72	19,446	5.22	− 25,933	40.00
In 1934	33,519	9.65	496	1.63	− 33,023	97.08	21,982	10.48	1,487	3.08	− 20,495	87.33	25,294	14.75	11,502	3.77	− 13,792	37.48
Other Foreign Countries																		
In 1913	136,967	47.20	12,714	39.00	−124,253	83.01	118,519	42.06	39,896	57.07	− 78,623	49.63	52,506	27.12	183,071	44.50	+130,554	55.42
Average per year 1929–1933	204,235	47.72	13,299	33.22	−190,936	87.77	102,235	46.13	28,809	51.57	− 73,426	56.03	99,863	41.19	152,503	40.95	+ 52,640	20.86
In 1934	151,389	43.59	13,577	44.57	−137,812	83.54	101,810	48.56	26,999	55.93	− 74,811	58.08	77,478	45.20	122,377	40.13	+ 44,899	22.47

Sources:
For 1913 and 1929–1933, calculated from data in Statistical Abstract of the United Kingdom, annual volumes.
For 1934, calculated from data in Accounts Relating to the Trade and Navigation of the United Kingdom, December, 1934.

Notes:
(a) Class I. Comestibles.
Class II. Raw materials and partly manufactured goods.
Class III. Manufactured goods.
(b) Balance percents are of the sum of imports and exports in the corresponding class and period.
+ and − indicate excess of exports and imports, respectively.

TABLE XLVII
JAPANESE TRADE IN COMMODITIES
A—Rice and Paddy Imports
Values in 1,000's Yen

The completeness with which expansion of rice production in Korea and Formosa has freed Japan from dependence on sources outside the Empire is clearly shown in the figures below. Unfortunately, Japanese statistics are not available covering rice imports from the colonies in 1913, but the fairly substantial amounts, both in value and in proportion to total imports, of rice imports from foreign countries in that year show that the colonial imports could not have been large. Of all Japan's foreign imports in 1913, rice was 6.7% — a larger share of the total imports than the colonial and foreign rice imports together formed in 1934. In 1929-1933, the foreign proportion was down to 0.87%, and in 1934 it had dropped to 0.03%.

Korea supplies only a little less than three-fourths of Japan's colonial rice imports, and this amount is nearly a third of all Japan's imports from that colony. Formosa's share in the rice total has been increasing recently, however, as has the share of rice in the total imports from the colonies.

	1913			Average per Year, 1929-1933				1934			
	Value	% of Foreign Rice Imports	% of Total Imports from Foreign Countries	Value	% of Foreign or Colonial Rice Imports	% of Total Imports of Rice	% of Total Imports from Foreign Countries or Colonies or Both Together	Value	% of Foreign or Colonial Rice Imports	% of Total Imports of Rice	% of Total Imports from Foreign Countries or Colonies or Both Together
Foreign Imports:											
From British-India	20,031	41.32	2.75	57	0.39	0.03	0.00	328	49.70	0.10	0.01
From China	845	1.74	0.12	2	0.01	0.00	0.00	. . .	. . .	. . .	. . .
From Siam	5,206	10.74	0.71	12,511	85.66	6.15	0.75	. . .	. . .	. . .	. . .
From French Indo-China . .	22,268	45.94	3.05	20	0.14	0.01	0.00	332	50.45	0.10	0.01
Total foreign imports . .	48,427	100.00	6.65	14,604	100.00	7.18	0.87	660	100.00	0.21	0.03
Colonial Imports:											
From Korea	(a)	. . .	. . .	138,796	73.55	68.27	27.65	222,289	70.31	70.16	32.25
From Formosa	(a)	. . .	. . .	49,901	26.45	24.55	9.94	93,881	29.69	29.63	13.66
Total colonial imports . .	(a)	. . .	. . .	188,697	100.00	92.82	37.59	316,170	100.00	99.79	46.01
Total rice and paddy imports . .	(a)	. . .	. . .	203,301	. . .	100.00	4.85	316,830	. . .	100.00	5.50

Source:
Calculated from data in the Financial and Economic Annual of Japan, annual volumes.

Note:
(a) Data not available.

TABLE XLVII
JAPANESE TRADE IN COMMODITIES
B—Wheat and Flour Imports and Exports
In Quintals. Flour to Grain: 1 Quintal Flour: 1.333 Quintals Grain

The figures for Japan's trade in wheat and wheat flour, like those for the trade in rice, show strikingly how Japan is becoming less dependent on outside sources of food supply, in this case on the colonies as well as on foreign countries. In 1925-1929, she imported on the average 4.4 million quintals more wheat and wheat flour than she exported. In 1933, the excess of these imports over the exports had fallen to 325,000 quintals. The drop came chiefly between 1932 and 1933, however. Japan regularly has bought substantially more wheat and wheat flour from foreign countries than she has sold to them, but in the wheat and wheat flour trade with the colonies the balance has been the other way.

	1925-1929 Average		1930		1931		1932		1933	
	Quantity	% of Total	Quantity	% of Total	Quantity	% of Total	Quantity	% of Total	Quantity	% of Total
Imports:										
Foreign.	6,174,328	99.27	5,097,953	99.87	7,300,224	99.92	7,499,259	97.86	5,124,207	96.37
Colonial	45,524	0.73	6,842	0.13	6,088	0.08	164,329	2.14	193,278	3.63
Total	6,219,852	100.00	5,104,795	100.00	7,306,312	100.00	7,663,588	100.00	5,317,485	100.00
Exports:										
Foreign.	1,524,599	83.93	1,599,003	68.05	1,801,605	71.21	2,955,899	80.11	4,243,388	85.50
Colonial	291,877	16.07	750,779	31.95	728,450	28.79	733,671	19.89	719,580	14.50
Total	1,816,476	100.00	2,349,782	100.00	2,530,055	100.00	3,689,570	100.00	4,962,968	100.00
Total Trade:										
Foreign.	7,698,927	95.80	6,696,956	89.84	9,101,829	92.53	10,455,158	92.09	9,367,595	91.12
Colonial	337,401	4.20	757,621	10.16	734,538	7.47	898,000	7.91	912,858	8.88
Total	8,036,328	100.00	7,454,577	100.00	9,836,367	100.00	11,353,158	100.00	10,280,453	100.00
Balance (a):										
Foreign.	− 4,649,729	60.39	− 3,498,950	52.25	− 5,498,619	60.41	− 4,543,360	43.46	− 880,819	9.40
Colonial	+ 246,353	73.01	+ 743,937	98.19	+ 722,362	98.34	+ 569,342	63.40	+ 526,302	57.65
Total	− 4,403,376	54.79	− 2,755,013	36.96	− 4,776,257	48.56	− 3,974,018	35.00	− 354,517	3.45

Source:
Calculated from data in the International Year Book of Agricultural Statistics 1933/34, Table 110.

Note:
(a) Balance percents are of corresponding totals. + and − indicate export and import surplus respectively.

TABLE XLVII
JAPANESE TRADE IN COMMODITIES
C—Raw Cotton Imports
Values in 1,000's of Yen

In 1934, Japan's imports of raw cotton were almost exactly the same proportion of her total imports as in 1913: 32.02% for 1913 and 32.04% for 1934. But the 1934 proportion was substantially larger than the 27% average for 1929-1933. The cotton imports from the United States have been distinctly more than half the total since 1929, but in 1913 they were only a little over a fourth. Indian cotton made up nearly two-thirds of the cotton imports in 1933; since 1929 it has been about a third. In quantity, however, the Indian share is larger than this. Japan has taken relatively little cotton from Egypt.

In the introductory note to Table XLVIII B, a comparison is made between the cotton imports of Britain and Japan, and the relation of the trade differences to the differences in production in the two countries is pointed out.

	1913			Average per Year 1929-1933			1934		
	Value	% of Cotton Imports from Foreign Countries	% of Total Imports from Foreign Countries	Value	% of Cotton Imports from Foreign Countries	% of Total Imports from Foreign Countries	Value	% of Cotton Imports from Foreign Countries	% of total Imports from Foreign Countries
From China	16,505	7.07	2.26	23,242	5.09	1.39	15,693	2.15	0.69
From British India	143,039	61.23	19.61	150,520	32.96	9.02	252,435	34.51	11.06
From the United States . .	64,220	27.49	8.80	261,852	57.33	15.69	400,919	54.81	17.56
From Egypt	6,236	2.67	0.85	16,153	3.54	0.97	39,787	5.44	1.74
Total from foreign countries	233,599	100.00	32.02	456,717	100.00	27.36	731,425	100.00	32.04

Source:
Calculated from data in the Financial and Economic Annual of Japan, annual volumes.

TABLE XLVII
JAPANESE TRADE IN COMMODITIES
D—Iron Imports
Values in 1,000's of Yen

The marked relative and absolute increase in Japanese pig iron imports from Manchuria, between an average for 1929-1933 and 1934, is shown in this table. In the latter year, Manchuria supplied 72% of all Japan's imports of pig iron from foreign countries, as against a 48% average for 1929-1933. Pig iron imports from Korea also have increased.

Japan's recent large imports of scrap iron from the United States explain the fact that in 1934 she got from that country 47% of all her foreign imports of iron other than pig iron, rails, and fish plates. In 1929-1933, the proportion was 28%.

	1913			Average per Year 1929-1933			1934		
	Value	% of Iron Imports from Foreign Countries	% of Total Imports from Foreign Countries	Value	% of Iron Imports from Foreign Countries	% of Total Imports from Foreign Countries	Value	% of Iron Imports from Foreign Countries	% of Total Imports from Foreign Countries
Pig Iron Imports:									
From Manchuria and Kwantung . .	(a)	. . .	. . .	8,882	47.79	0.53	18,980	71.55	0.83
From British India.	(a)	. . .	. . .	7,414	39.89	0.44	7,292	27.49	0.32
Total from foreign countries .	10,390	100.00	1.42	18,587	100.00	1.11	26,528	100.00	1.16
Imports of other Iron, except Rails and Fish Plates:									
From Great Britain.	(a)	. . .	. . .	14,933	18.47	0.89	11,491	7.95	0.50
From Germany.	(a)	. . .	. . .	19,638	24.29	1.18	23,593	16.31	1.03
From Belgium.	(a)	. . .	. . .	5,825	7.20	0.35	11,940	8.26	0.52
From the United States.	(a)	. . .	. . .	22,458	27.78	1.35	67,467	46.65	2.96
Total from foreign countries .	42,759	100.00	5.86	80,848	100.00	4.84	144,613	100.00	6.34

Source:
Calculated from data in the Financial and Economic Annual of Japan, annual volumes.

Notes:
(a) Data not available.

TABLE XLVII
JAPANESE TRADE IN COMMODITIES
E—Cotton Tissues and Yarns Exports
Values in 1,000's of Yen

As is well known, Japan's exports of cotton cloth have increased very remarkably in recent years. But the share going to the territory occupied by Chinese (China Proper, Manchuria, and the Kwantung Leased Territory) has decreased considerably, especially since 1931. In 1913, this region took 28.1 million yen's worth of cotton tissues from Japan, which was 85% of all Japanese exports of these goods. In 1929-1933, the average per year showed an increase to 86.7 million yen in value, but the proportion to the total cotton goods exports had dropped to 28%. In 1934, Chinese-occupied territory took only 72.5 million yen's worth of Japanese cotton goods, which was 15% of the total Japanese cotton tissues exports. Part of this sharp decrease is the result of the anti-Japanese feeling aroused by Japan's drive into Manchuria. A more important part has been caused by the development of cotton mills in China. The figures show that Chinese territory has ceased to be an important part of Japan's market for her principal industrial product.

Before the World War, Japan exported fairly large amounts of cotton yarn, the semi-manufactured article in the raw-cotton-to-cloth process. Since then, her home production of yarns has increased considerably, but her exports of this kind of goods have decreased. Japan is using the semi-manufactured article at home, and exporting the finished product. In 1913, only 5.3% of the total exports was cotton cloth, but 11.2% was cotton yarns. In 1929-1933, the cloth was 19.4% and the yarn only 1.09%. In 1934, the proportions were 22.7% and 1.08%. Cotton tissues have become the largest single item in Japan's exports. Cotton yarns, from being an important item, have dropped to a distinctly minor place.

The exports of yarns to Chinese-occupied territory have fallen off as sharply, absolutely and relatively, as the exports of tissues. In 1913, the 63.5 million yen's worth of cotton yarns sent to China, Manchuria, and Kwantung was 89% of the yarn exports. Only 3.3 million yen's worth was exported to these regions, on the average, in 1929-1933, and the proportion was 19.3%. In 1934, the Chinese regions took 4.3% million yen's worth of Japanese-made cotton yarns, or 18.4% of the total yarn exports from Japan.

	1913			Average per Year 1929-1933			1934		
	Value	% of Exports of Cotton Tissues or Yarns to Foreign Countries	% of Total Exports to Foreign Countries	Value	% of Exports of Cotton Tissues or Yarns to Foreign Countries	% of Total Exports to Foreign Countries	Value	% of Exports of Cotton Tissues or Yarns to Foreign Countries	% of Total Exports to Foreign Countries
Exports of Cotton Tissues:									
To Kwantung and Manchuria . . .	9,109	27.11	1.44	18,107	5.82	1.13	59,470	12.08	2.74
To China.	18,965	56.43	3.00	68,573	22.04	4.27	13,030	2.65	0.60
To British India.	1,032	3.07	0.16	74,407	23.92	4.63	66,814	13.57	3.08
To Netherlands Indies	233	0.69	0.04	45,469	14.62	2.83	82,828	16.82	3.81
To Egypt.	(a)	. . .	. . .	25,062	8.06	1.56	46,834	9.51	2.16
To Union of S. Africa	(a)	. . .	. . .	4,702	1.51	0.29	4,459	0.91	0.21
Total to foreign countries . .	33,606	100.00	5.31	311,096	100.00	19.36	492,352	100.00	22.67
Exports of Cotton Yarns:									
To Kwantung and Manchuria . . .	3,458	4.87	0.55	1,349	7.70	0.08	4,145	17.65	0.19
To China.	60,096	84.65	9.50	2,029	11.59	0.13	175	0.75	0.01
To British India.	(a)	. . .	. . .	9,513	54.32	0.59	11,112	47.31	0.51
To Netherlands Indies	(a)	. . .	. . .	851	4.86	0.05	1,695	7.22	0.08
Total to foreign countries . .	70,998	100.00	11.23	17,511	100.00	1.09	23,485	100.00	1.08

Source:
Calculated from data in the Financial and Economic Annual of Japan, annual volumes.

Notes:
(a) Data not available.

TABLE XLVII
JAPANESE TRADE IN COMMODITIES
F—Machinery and Iron Manufactures, Exports
Values in 1,000's of Yen

In 1934, Japan sold to Manchuria and the Kwantung Leased Territory nearly three-fourths of all her exports of machinery and parts to foreign countries, as compared with 45% in 1929-1933. But even so, these exports to Manchuria in 1934 were only a small fraction of Japan's total exports, though a larger proportion than in 1929-1933 - 1.97% as against 0.44%. The proportion of total machinery exports to total exports had increased from 0.97% to 2.66%.

Japan's exports of iron manufactures are more evenly distributed, though Manchuria takes a larger share than any other region - 22% in 1929-1933 and 34% in 1934. Iron manufactures are a very minor part of Japan's total exports, however - 1.00% in 1929-1933, and 1.62% in 1934.

	1913			Average per Year 1929-1933			1934		
	Value	% of Exports of Machinery and Parts, or of Iron Manufactures, to Foreign Countries	% of Total Exports to Foreign Countries	Value	% of Exports of Machinery and Parts, or of Iron Manufactures, to Foreign Countries	% of Total Exports to Foreign Countries	Value	% of Exports of Machinery and Parts, or of Iron Manufactures, to Foreign Countries	% of Total Exports to Foreign Countries
Exports of Machinery & Parts:									
To Kwantung and Manchuria . .	6,448	. . .	1.02	7,093	45.46	0.44	42,766	74.03	1.97
To China	(a)	. . .	. . .	5,277	33.82	0.33	9,691	16.78	0.45
To British India	(a)	. . .	. . .	957	6.13	0.06	2,273	3.93	0.10
To Asiatic Russia.	(a)	. . .	. . .	1,356	8.69	0.08	1,129	1.95	0.05
Total to foreign countries.	(a)	. . .	. . .	15,603	100.00	0.97	57,777	100.00	2.66
Exports of Iron Manufactures:									
To Kwantung and Manchuria . .	(a)	. . .	. . .	3,553	22.03	0.22	11,991	33.99	0.55
To China	(a)	. . .	. . .	1,839	11.40	0.11	2,012	5.70	0.09
To British India	(a)	. . .	. . .	2,850	17.67	0.18	4,985	14.13	0.23
To Netherlands Indies. . . .	(a)	. . .	. . .	2,108	13.07	0.13	5,055	14.33	0.23
To Asiatic Russia.	(a)	. . .	. . .	2,224	13.79	0.14	942	2.67	0.04
Total to foreign countries.	689	100.00	0.11	16,125	100.00	1.00	35,277	100.00	1.62

Source:
Calculated from data in the Financial and Economic Annual of Japan, annual volumes.

Notes:
(a) Data not available.

TABLE XLVIII
RAW MATERIALS IMPORTS BY THE UNITED KINGDOM
A—Wool
Quantities in Metric Tons

Even before the World War, Britain got most of her raw wool imports from the British countries (80% in 1913), and the bulk of these came from Australia and New Zealand (70% of the imports from British countries in 1913). The British countries' share of the total has increased somewhat since 1929, but the Australia-New Zealand share of the British areas' amount has remained about the same. South America has come to be relatively more important as a source of wool for Britain than it was before the War.

	1913			AVERAGE 1929-1933			1933		
	Quantity	% of Foreign or Colonial Wool Imports	% of Total Wool Imports	Quantity	% of Foreign or Colonial Wool Imports	% of Total Wool Imports	Quantity	% of Foreign or Colonial Wool Imports	% of Total Wool Imports
Foreign Imports:									
From France	11,110	14.86	3.04	8,203	11.30	2.09	10,699	13.75	2.47
From South America. . . .	45,577	60.98	12.46	58,989	81.23	14.99	61,762	79.35	14.23
Total foreign imports. .	74,744	100.00	20.43	72,621	100.00	18.46	77,831	100.00	17.93
Colonial Imports:									
From British South Africa	60,430	20.76	16.52	76,408	23.82	19.42	79,043	22.19	18.21
From Australia.	120,239	41.31	32.87	129,511	40.37	32.92	140,016	39.31	32.26
From New Zealand.	82,184	28.24	22.47	90,887	28.33	23.10	110,565	31.04	25.48
Total colonial imports .	291,034	100.00	79.57	320,778	100.00	81.54	356,171	100.00	82.07
Total Wool Imports	365,778	. . .	100.00	393,399	. . .	100.00	434,002	. . .	100.00

Source:
Calculated from data in the Statistical Abstract of the United Kingdom, annual volumes.

TABLE XLVIII
RAW MATERIALS IMPORTS BY THE UNITED KINGDOM
B—Raw Cotton
Quantities in Metric Tons

The British mills emphasize the production of the finer grades of cotton cloth. The Japanese make relatively more of the coarser grades. This difference is reflected in the figures showing the sources from which the two countries get their raw cotton (cf. Table XLVII-C). But Japan, in recent years, has been making proportionately more of the finer goods than she formerly did. This also shows in the raw cotton imports.

Indian cotton has a relatively short staple, and is not suitable for making the finer cloths. In 1913

and 1929-1933, the proportions of Indian cotton in Britain's raw cotton imports were 2.4% and 7.9%. The proportions for Japan were 61.2% and 33.0%. American cotton is better than Indian, though not the world's best. In 1913 and 1929-1933, the United States supplied 75.4% and 59.4% of Britain's raw cotton imports, and 27.5% and 54.8% of Japan's. Egyptian cotton is the world's best. Britain got 19.2% of her raw cotton from Egypt in 1913, and 18.1% in 1929-1933. Japan in these same years took from Egypt 7.1% and 5.1% of her raw cotton imports.

	1913			AVERAGE 1929-1933			1933		
	Quantity	% of Foreign or Colonial Raw Cotton Imports	% of Total Raw Cotton Imports	Quantity	% of Foreign or Colonial Raw Cotton Imports	% of Total Raw Cotton Imports	Quantity	% of Foreign or Colonial Raw Cotton Imports	% of Total Raw Cotton Imports
Foreign Imports:									
From Egypt.	182,651	19.15	18.52	214,613	18.14	15.66	145,097	25.02	21.51
From United States. . . .	718,852	75.38	72.89	702,111	59.35	51.23	364,310	62.81	54.01
Total foreign imports. .	953,642	100.00	96.69	1,182,906	100.00	86.32	580,036	100.00	85.99
Colonial Imports:									
From British India. . . .	23,271	71.34	2.36	108,528	57.87	7.92	54,345	57.52	8.06
Total colonial imports .	32,621	100.00	3.31	187,538	100.00	13.68	94,479	100.00	14.01
Total Raw Cotton imports .	986,261	. . . .	100.00	1,370,444	. . . .	100.00	674,516	. . . .	100.00

Source:
Calculated from data in the Statistical Abstract of the United Kingdom, annual volume.

TABLE XLVIII
RAW MATERIALS IMPORTS BY THE UNITED KINGDOM
C—Wheat
In 1,000's of Metric Tons

The British wheat imports show a very striking shift from foreign to British sources. The total quantity imported has remained nearly the same since 1913, but while foreign countries supplied 52% in 1913 and 48% in 1929-1933, their share was only 33% in 1933. The United States, which furnished 32% in 1913, sold not enough wheat to Britain in 1933 to be recorded in the British statistics. The Argentine's share in- creased from 14% to 22%. India also had dropped out of the picture in 1933, though she furnished 18% of the British wheat imports in 1913. Canada and Australia both increased their share substantially, Australia do- ing relatively better with an increase, 1913 to 1933, from 9.6% to 26.1% compared with Canada's increase from 20.6% to 40.6%.

	1913			Average 1929-1933			1933		
	Quantity	% of Foreign or Colonial Wheat Imports	% of Total Wheat Imports	Quantity	% of Foreign or Colonial Wheat Imports	% of Total Wheat Imports	Quantity	% of Foreign or Colonial Wheat Imports	% of Total Wheat Imports
Foreign Imports:									
From United States....	1,731	61.80	32.18	601	21.58	10.68	0	0.00	0.00
From Argentine......	750	26.78	13.94	1,286	46.18	22.85	1,255	66.54	21.99
From Russia.......	255	9.10	4.74	576	20.68	10.23	292	15.48	5.12
Total foreign imports. .	2,801	100.00	52.07	2,785	100.00	49.48	1,886	100.00	33.04
Colonial Imports:									
From British India....	953	36.98	17.72	36	1.27	0.64	....	....	....
From Australia......	514	19.95	9.56	1,039	36.55	18.46	1,488	38.93	26.07
From Canada.......	1,107	42.96	20.58	1,757	61.80	31.22	2,315	60.57	40.56
Total colonial imports .	2,577	100.00	47.91	2,843	100.00	50.52	3,822	100.00	66.96
Total Wheat imports....	5,379	....	100.00	5,628	....	100.00	5,708	....	100.00

Source:
Calculated from data in the Statistical Abstract of the United Kingdom, annual volumes.

TABLE XLIX
PERCENTAGES OF WORLD PRODUCTION OF FOODSTUFFS
A—Wheat

The figures in this and the following two tables (Tables XLIX-B and C) show that in the production of the important food stuffs, as in that of non-edible raw materials, the past 10 years have seen a distinct development away from the concentration of production in a few countries and a consequent increase in the international competition for world raw material markets (cf. introductory note to Table L).

The single important exception to this general trend is in sea products. Japan's share of the world's takings from the sea has increased until in 1933 her fishermen took 35% of the total sea fishery

production — a larger share than that of all Europe. The shares of the next three countries (Britain, Norway, and the United States) all decreased, between an average for 1925-1929 and 1933. Other records show that Japan exports from a fifth to a fourth of her takings from the sea. The Japanese people eat the rest — so in the past 10 years they have consumed roughly a fourth of all the sea products taken throughout the world. This consumption of sea products is the chief reason why Japan's imports of land-produced foodstuffs are so comparatively small in spite of the congestion of population in terms of arable land.

	Average 1925-1929	1930	1931	1932	1933	1934
Africa.	2.62	2.36	2.85	3.04	2.57	3.25
Algeria.	0.75	0.66	0.55	0.64	0.66	0.87
Egypt.	0.90	0.81	1.00	1.15	0.83	0.82
Union of South Africa.	0.18	0.19	0.30	0.23	0.24	0.34
North America	28.13	26.83	27.10	25.86	16.82	16.93
Canada	9.67	8.61	6.95	9.65	5.85	6.05
United States.	18.46	18.22	20.15	16.21	10.97	10.88
Latin America	6.85	5.84	6.10	6.50	7.50	6.59
Argentine.	5.45	4.76	4.75	5.25	5.94	5.22
Asia.	9.55	10.40	10.09	9.47	9.82	10.31
India.	7.19	8.00	7.51	7.34	7.31	7.66
Japan.	0.70	0.63	0.70	0.71	0.84	1.04
U.S.S.R	17.75	20.25	16.28	16.21	21.14	24.49
Europe.	31.89	29.78	33.32	34.01	38.32	35.32
Germany.	2.69	2.85	3.36	4.00	4.27	3.65
Spain.	3.28	3.00	2.91	4.01	2.87	3.81
France	6.54	4.67	5.71	7.27	7.52	7.25
Italy.	5.14	4.30	5.28	6.03	6.18	5.10
Roumania	2.37	2.68	2.92	1.21	2.47	1.68
Oceania	3.22	4.53	4.26	4.90	3.83	3.10
Australia.	3.05	4.37	4.12	4.66	3.64	2.96

Source:
Calculated from data in the League of Nations, Statistical Year-Book, 1934/35, Table 21.
Percentages are of quantities in metric tons.

TABLE XLIX
PERCENTAGES OF WORLD PRODUCTION OF FOODSTUFFS
B—Sugar

	Average 1925/26 1928/29	1929/30	1930/31	1931/32	1932/33	1933/34
Africa.	2.99	3.03	3.32	3.20	4.24	4.36
North America	4.33	4.38	4.94	5.09	6.80	7.64
United States.	4.20	4.26	4.78	4.89	6.53	7.38
Latin America	33.44	32.50	25.63	26.62	25.94	25.87
Cuba.	18.95	17.29	11.34	10.22	8.73	9.59
Puerto Rico.	2.34	2.87	2.55	3.48	3.27	4.18
Brazil	3.90	4.46	4.01	4.06	4.46	2.88
Asia.	24.80	25.14	25.06	29.89	28.70	25.80
Formosa.	2.44	3.16	3.04	4.09	2.91	2.87
India.	7.87	6.54	7.52	10.01	13.15	13.18
Java.	10.79	11.36	10.58	10.59	6.31	2.74
Philippines.	3.02	3.48	3.32	4.41	5.60	6.35
U.S.S.R	3.93	3.73	5.69	6.31	3.81	4.42
Europe.	24.85	25.62	29.56	22.26	23.10	24.38
Germany.	6.54	6.96	8.76	5.94	4.51	5.71
France	3.12	3.21	4.14	3.26	4.23	3.70
United Kingdom	0.63	1.14	1.65	1.03	1.52	2.07
Czechoslavakia	4.56	3.54	3.82	2.97	2.57	1.12
Oceania	5.68	5.59	5.81	6.66	7.38	7.51
Australia.	2.16	2.14	2.10	2.56	2.51	2.91
Hawaii	3.08	3.02	3.20	3.60	4.04	3.88

Source:
Calculated from data in the League of Nations, Statistical Year-Book, 1934/35, Table 31 (Beet sugar) and Table 32 (Cane sugar). Percentages are of quantities in quintals.

TABLE XLIX
PERCENTAGES OF WORLD PRODUCTION OF FOODSTUFFS
C—Sea Fishery Products

	Average 1925-1928	1929	1930	1931	1932	1933
Africa.	0.07	0.10	0.09	0.09	0.13	0.16
North America	19.21	18.40	16.20	13.76	12.91	12.20
Alaska	3.07	2.50	2.28	2.35	2.36	2.32
Canada	5.12	4.46	4.11	3.66	3.06	2.85
United States.	11.03	11.43	9.80	7.75	7.49	7.03
Asia.	37.71	34.51	34.48	37.37	39.22	43.49
Japan.	29.42	23.73	24.86	25.87	27.09	34.51
Korea.	6.83	8.37	7.62	9.42	10.48	7.86
U.S.S.R	. . . .	8.99	11.40	13.08	11.96	10.94
Europe.	42.53	37.52	37.40	35.29	35.39	32.83
Germany.	3.44	3.12	3.23	3.52	3.33	3.44
Spain.	3.08	2.61	2.51	2.80	2.87	2.71
France	3.06	2.65	2.55	2.61	2.68	2.51
Norway	10.66	10.26	9.77	7.45	9.01	8.45
United Kingdom	12.56	10.53	10.45	9.76	9.35	8.34
Oceania	0.48	0.48	0.44	0.41	0.39	0.38

Source:
Calculated from data in the League of Nations, Statistical Year-Book, 1934/35, Table 19. Percentages are of quantities in metric tons. Percentages are calculated to the sum of the amounts given for each continent in the Statistical Year-Book.

TABLE L
PERCENTAGES OF WORLD PRODUCTION OF RAW MATERIALS
A—Ginned Cotton

The detailed figures of each country's share in the world production of the principal raw materials, in the tables which follow, reveal a fact which bears directly and with great significance on the question of the relation between political control of territory and access to the minerals in it or the agricultural raw materials which can be produced on it. Without a single exception, the records show, the countries which were the leading producers in the years just prior to 1930 now produce a smaller share of the world's total than they then did, while the share of the less important producing countries has increased, or new sources have been developed, or both.

This means two things: (1) it is increasingly impracticable for any country to exercise anything approaching monopoly control of the production of any important raw material, either to keep supplies away from some other country or to get monopoly profits for its own nationals; (2) because the world market for raw materials is becoming increasingly competitive, political control of the sources of raw materials is becoming steadily less useful in providing advantages for nationals as against foreigners through the manipulation of tariffs or other trade barriers.

	Average 1925–1929	1930	1931	1932	1933	1934
Africa.	7.51	8.29	6.61	6.52	8.87	9.42
Egypt.	5.97	6.61	4.80	4.31	6.70	6.88
North America	57.39	53.71	62.30	54.56	49.22	41.01
United States.	57.37	53.71	62.30	54.56	49.22	41.01
Latin America	4.42	4.20	4.51	4.20	6.86	9.66
Argentine.	0.43	0.54	0.62	0.63	0.76	0.88
Brazil	1.97	1.77	2.10	1.91	3.91	5.50
Asia.	26.43	27.22	19.60	26.78	27.19	31.02
China.	7.74	9.47	6.50	9.48	10.28	13.26
India.	17.76	16.86	12.22	16.35	16.00	17.13
U.S.S.R	3.74	6.12	6.72	7.62	7.12	8.21
Europe.	0.46	0.41	0.25	0.26	0.66	0.67
Oceania	0.04	0.05	0.02	0.05	0.07	. . . .

Source:
Calculated from data in the League of Nations, Statistical Year-Book, 1934/35, Table 48.
Percentages are of quantites in quintals.

TABLE L
PERCENTAGES OF WORLD PRODUCTION OF RAW MATERIALS
B—Wool

	Average 1925–1928	1929	1930	1931	1932	1933
Africa.	10.01	10.92	10.90	10.43	11.38	10.37
Union of South Africa.	7.25	8.00	8.07	8.35	8.83	7.16
North America	10.08	10.89	12.12	12.79	12.19	12.85
United States.	9.58	10.36	11.56	12.24	11.64	12.32
Latin America	15.54	15.86	16.64	15.79	16.19	16.19
Argentine.	9.23	9.14	9.64	10.05	10.38	10.53
Uruguay.	3.72	4.14	4.33	3.06	3.21	3.01
Asia.	7.28	7.10	6.68	6.96	5.96	6.81
China.	1.90	2.09	1.51	1.73	0.80	1.68
India.	2.76	2.59	2.67	2.66	2.68	2.74
U.S.S.R	9.91	10.20	8.17	5.64	3.80	3.77
Europe.	15.24	13.70	13.89	14.08	14.35	14.71
Spain.	2.29	2.15	2.14	2.05	2.09	2.13
United Kingdom	3.05	2.90	2.96	3.01	3.19	3.28
Oceania	31.95	31.33	31.60	34.30	36.13	35.29
Australia.	24.68	24.27	24.36	26.77	28.41	27.08
New Zealand.	7.06	7.06	7.24	7.52	7.72	8.22

Source:
Calculated from data in the League of Nations, Statistical Year-Book, 1934/35, Table 51.
Percentages are of quantities in metric tons.

TABLE L
PERCENTAGES OF WORLD PRODUCTION OF RAW MATERIALS
C—Crude Rubber Shipments

	Average 1925-1929	1930	1931	1932	1933	1934
Africa.	1.22	0.60	0.49	0.28	0.23	0.29
Latin America	4.47	1.90	1.48	0.97	1.16	0.87
Asia.	94.16	97.38	97.91	98.61	98.49	98.74
British Borneo	2.56	2.15	2.09	1.81	2.20	2.81
Ceylon	9.02	9.18	7.76	6.93	7.53	7.76
India.	1.84	1.42	1.11	0.55	0.58	1.16
Netherlands Indies	33.50	29.20	32.14	29.68	33.02	37.25
French Indo-China.	1.30	1.19	1.35	1.94	1.85	1.94
British Malaya	45.25	53.64	52.96	57.28	52.49	46.07
Siam	0.69	0.60	0.49	0.42	0.82	1.75
Total British Areas.	58.67	66.39	63.92	66.57	62.80	57.80
Oceania						
Philippines.	0.15	0.12	0.12	0.14	0.12	0.10

Source:
Calculated from data in the League of Nations, Statistical Year-Book, 1934/35, Table 47.
Percentages are of quantities in metric tons.

TABLE L
PERCENTAGES OF WORLD PRODUCTION OF RAW MATERIALS
D—Petroleum

	1925	Average 1925-1929	1930	1931	1932	1933	1934
Africa.	0.12	0.13	0.15	0.15	0.15	0.12	0.11
North America	70.34	68.89	62.88	61.76	59.83	62.33	59.68
United States.	70.31	68.85	62.79	61.66	59.76	62.25	59.59
Latin America	15.73	15.58	17.07	15.49	16.04	15.11	16.63
Mexico	11.85	6.40	3.02	5.94	2.69	2.58	2.77
Venezuela.	1.92	6.03	10.28	9.09	9.39	8.88	9.83
Asia.	6.56	6.51	7.10	6.71	7.53	7.33	7.32
Netherlands Indies	2.06	2.23	2.82	2.48	2.83	2.81	2.93
Iran	3.13	3.01	3.08	3.09	3.64	3.66	3.36
Japan and Formosa.	0.18	0.15	0.15	0.14	0.13	0.10	0.10
U.S.S.R	5.03	6.24	9.37	11.80	11.87	10.89	11.70
Europe.	2.22	2.66	3.44	4.08	4.58	4.22	4.56
Roumania	1.56	2.12	2.95	3.57	4.08	3.75	4.10

Source:
Calculated from data in the League of Nations, Statistical Year-Book, 1934/35, Table 64.
Percentages are of quantities in metric tons. For 1934, no figure for Germany is given in the Year-Book; the 1933 figure has been used in 1934 calculations.

TABLE L
PERCENTAGES OF WORLD PRODUCTION OF RAW MATERIALS
E—Coal

	Average 1926-1929	1930	1931	1932	1933	1934
Africa.	1.13	1.12	1.10	1.11	1.14	1.20
North America	44.83	40.63	37.90	34.75	35.32	35.17
United States.	43.86	39.78	37.12	33.97	34.55	34.29
Latin America	0.26	0.29	0.26	0.26	0.29	0.30
Asia.	6.88	7.27	7.75	8.38	8.58	8.52
China (including Manchuria).	1.91	2.11	2.50	2.69	2.76	2.53
India.	1.79	1.98	2.04	2.13	2.00	2.01
Japan.	2.64	2.56	2.59	2.92	3.23	3.39
U.S.S.R	2.75	3.99	5.25	6.70	7.54	8.52
Europe.	43.06	45.80	46.35	47.79	46.13	45.37
Germany.	12.15	11.65	10.99	10.91	10.90	11.39
Belgium.	2.13	2.24	2.50	2.23	2.51	2.40
France	4.13	4.40	4.63	4.82	4.66	4.34
Poland	3.18	3.06	3.54	3.00	2.72	2.66
United Kingdom	17.57	20.24	20.65	22.09	20.91	20.46
Oceania	1.09	0.91	0.88	1.01	1.00	0.92

Source:
Calculated from data in the League of Nations, Statistical Year-Book, 1934/35, Table 61.
Percentages are of quantities in metric tons and are calculated against the sum of continental totals, which in turn are the sums of the figures for the individual countries as listed in the Year-Book, these totals not being shown separately. For 1934, the Year-Book does not give figures for China (including Manchuria), Oceania, or Australia. In these cases the 1933 figures have been used for 1934.

TABLE L
PERCENTAGES OF WORLD PRODUCTION OF RAW MATERIALS
F—Iron Ore

	Average 1925-1928	1929	1930	1931	1932	1933
Africa.	2.21	2.24	2.20	1.63	1.40	1.67
Algeria.	1.12	1.08	1.24	0.75	0.61	0.83
North America	40.69	37.97	34.04	27.28	13.35	19.96
United States.	39.13	37.21	33.37	26.68	13.16	19.66
Latin America	1.23	1.30	1.12	0.78	0.41	0.92
Asia.	2.74	3.18	3.22	4.50	7.04	5.75
China (including Manchuria).	1.04	1.20	1.28	2.01	2.99	2.62
India.	1.10	1.22	1.04	1.38	2.35	1.36
Japan.	0.08	0.09	0.14	0.17	0.30	0.35
U.S.S.R	2.55	3.93	5.90	8.83	15.80	15.83
Europe.	50.11	50.94	52.99	56.72	61.26	55.05
Germany.	3.62	3.14	3.18	2.19	1.74	2.83
Spain.	2.80	3.24	3.07	2.67	2.31	1.98
France .	25.76	25.03	26.95	32.23	36.20	32.98
Italy.	0.33	0.36	0.40	0.48	0.56	0.57
Luxemburg.	4.36	3.74	3.69	3.98	4.21	3.67
United Kingdom	5.67	6.63	6.56	6.48	9.77	8.27
Sweden .	4.70	5.66	6.23	5.91	4.33	2.94
Oceania .	0.47	0.43	0.54	0.26	0.73	0.82

Source:
Calculated from data in the League of Nations, Statistical Year-Book, 1934/35, Table 68.
Percentages are of quantities in metric tons. Percentages calculated against sum of continental totals, which in turn are the sums of the figures for the individual countries as listed in the Year-Book, these totals not being shown separately.

TABLE L
PERCENTAGES OF WORLD PRODUCTION OF RAW MATERIALS
G—Copper Ore: Metal Content

	Average 1925-1928	1929	1930	1931	1932	1933
Africa.	7.46	8.10	10.84	12.30	16.86	19.76
Belgian Congo.	6.00	6.68	8.71	8.58	5.89	6.35
North America	54.84	52.31	48.42	43.89	35.96	30.29
Canada	4.32	5.78	8.56	9.48	12.22	12.99
United States.	50.51	46.48	39.78	34.30	23.50	16.99
Latin America	23.31	24.81	22.53	24.28	18.22	22.65
Mexico	3.87	4.45	4.56	3.88	3.83	3.80
Chile.	15.01	16.47	13.70	15.98	11.23	15.60
Asia.	5.09	4.73	6.27	6.88	9.88	8.59
Japan.	4.36	3.88	4.91	5.42	7.82	6.61
U.S.S.R	1.29	1.69	2.12	2.22	3.48	3.01
Europe.	7.35	7.71	9.00	9.44	13.86	14.32
Germany.	1.71	1.49	1.68	2.13	3.34	2.81
Spain.	3.28	3.27	3.63	3.86	3.81	4.20
Norway	0.90	0.98	1.08	0.62	1.82	1.88
Yugoslavia	0.73	1.06	1.52	1.74	3.29	3.85
Oceania	0.66	0.67	0.82	0.99	1.73	1.39

Source:
Calculated from data in the League of Nations, Statistical Year-Book, 1934/35, Table 71B.
Percentages are of quantities in metric tons.

TABLE L
PERCENTAGES OF WORLD PRODUCTION OF RAW MATERIALS
H—Aluminum: Smelter Production

	Average 1925-1929	1930	1931	1932	1933	1934
North America	47.47	51.49	50.30	42.77	38.84	29.09
Canada	11.11	12.27	13.15	11.64	11.48	9.18
United States.	36.37	39.22	37.15	31.13	27.36	19.91
U.S.S.R	. . . .	. . . .	. . . .	0.59	3.12	8.53
Europe.	52.53	48.51	49.70	56.64	58.04	62.38
Germany.	13.70	11.40	12.41	12.43	13.04	22.04
France	8.47	9.29	8.40	9.42	10.13	9.66
Italy.	1.55	3.02	5.12	8.76	8.58	7.35
Norway	10.97	10.34	9.88	11.64	10.91	9.18
United Kingdom	4.14	4.98	6.55	6.67	7.80	7.41
Switzerland.	9.33	7.74	5.26	5.56	5.32	4.80

Source:
Calculated from data in the League of Nations, Statistical Year-Book, 1934/35, Table 80.
Percentages are of quantities in metric tons.

TABLE L
PERCENTAGES OF WORLD PRODUCTION OF RAW MATERIALS
I—Nickel

	Average 1925-1928	1929	1930	1931	1932	1933
North America	89.23	89.98	87.45	84.08	71.79	83.48
Canada	88.21	89.45	86.90	83.24	70.77	83.26
United States.	1.03	0.54	0.55	0.84	1.03	0.22
Asia (a).	. . . .	1.43	1.85	2.23	4.62	2.20
Europe (a).	. . . .	1.25	1.66	3.07	10.26	5.29
Greece	. . . .	0.54	. . . .	1.68	5.13	3.08
Norway	. . . .	0.72	1.66	1.40	5.13	2.20
Oceania (New Caledonia)	9.23	7.33	9.04	10.61	13.33	9.03

Source:
Calculated from data in the League of Nations, Statistical Year-Book, 1934/35, Table 81.
Percentages are of quantities in metric tons.

Note:
(a) 1925-1928 Percentages not calculated for Asia and Europe because the quantities were very small.

TABLE L
PERCENTAGES OF WORLD PRODUCTION OF RAW MATERIALS
J—Tin Ore: Metal Content

	Average 1925-1929	1930	1931	1932	1933	1934
Africa.	6.51	6.04	5.23	5.99	7.28	9.02
Nigeria.	5.08	4.76	4.64	4.29	3.98	4.43
Latin America	22.70	22.05	21.52	21.76	16.95	19.11
Bolivia.	22.58	21.71	20.93	21.66	16.72	19.03
Asia.	66.91	69.17	71.32	68.16	69.85	67.51
China.	5.14	3.53	3.91	7.09	8.76	6.32
Federated Malay States	33.15	35.31	35.96	27.25	26.17	30.02
Netherlands Indies	10.10	19.64	18.41	17.07	14.56	16.41
Siam	4.90	6.55	8.41	9.38	11.95	8.45
Europe.	2.15	1.90	0.73	1.90	2.62	2.13
Oceania	1.73	0.84	1.19	2.20	3.30	2.21

Source:
Calculated from data in the League of Nations, Statistical Year-Book, 1934/35, Table 77.
Percentages are of quantities in metric tons. For 1934, the Year-Book does not give a figure for Europe;
in this case the sum of the figures for the countries listed has been used.

TABLE L
PERCENTAGES OF WORLD PRODUCTION OF RAW MATERIALS
K—Zinc Ore: Metal Content

	Average 1925–1928	1929	1930	1931	1932	1933
Africa.	1.99	2.45	1.84	0.93	0.20	1.78
North America	47.13	44.91	44.39	43.46	42.71	43.84
Canada	4.49	5.22	7.79	8.92	8.27	7.63
United States.	42.64	38.35	34.67	30.85	27.40	29.88
Latin America	8.27	10.96	10.28	13.70	7.47	8.69
Asia.	6.29	5.43	6.01	5.80	6.51	6.42
India.	3.49	3.29	3.96	3.81	4.46	4.76
Japan.	0.68	0.58	0.64	0.83	1.06	0.84
U.S.S.R	0.27	0.62	1.16	1.66	2.12	1.69
Europe.	25.98	26.44	28.46	28.21	28.55	26.95
Germany.	7.45	8.32	8.90	8.72	7.97	8.82
Spain.	3.11	3.09	3.21	3.25	3.73	2.99
Italy.	5.10	5.08	5.11	3.90	3.41	2.46
Poland	7.48	6.13	6.42	4.97	2.65	2.96
Sweden	1.27	1.74	1.93	2.42	2.59	2.09
Yugoslavia	0.03	0.03	0.87	2.66	5.08	5.01
Oceania	10.08	9.18	7.86	6.25	12.44	10.62
Australia.	10.03	9.16	7.80	6.25	12.44	10.62

Source:
Calculated from data in the League of Nations, Statistical Year-Book, 1934/35, Table 75B.
Percentages are of quantities in metric tons. For 1932 and 1933 the Year-Book does not give figures for the U.S.S.R., in both cases the 1931 figure has been used.

POLITICAL STATUS OF
COLONIZED TERRITORIES, 1935

SECTION I. IN AFRICA

Region	Status	Date	Areas in 1000's Sq. Kms.
INTERNATIONAL AREAS			
Anglo-Egyptian Sudan	Joint Anglo-Egyptian administration established	1899	2,521
Tangier	Internationalization	1911–1912	0.6
BELGIAN AREAS			
Belgian Congo	Annexed by Belgium	1908	2,385
Ruanda-Urundi	Part of German East Africa	1884	55
	League mandate	1920	
BRITISH AREAS			
Union of South Africa	Organized	1909	1,222
	Statute of Westminster	1931	
Cape Colony	Ceded by Netherlands	1814	716
Bomvanaland, Emigrant Tombookieland, Gralekaland, Griqualand, Kaffraria, Pondoland, Xesibe	Acquired	1880–1881	
Natal	Conquered	1842	91
Zululand	Annexed to Natal	1897	
Orange Free State	Taken in Boer War	1902	129
Transvaal (South African Republic)	Taken in Boer War	1902	286
Walvis Bay	Annexed	1878	
British Areas in East Africa			
Kenya, Nyasaland, Somaliland, Uganda	Acquired	1884–1922	1,127
British Areas in South Africa			
Basutoland, Bechuanaland, Northern Rhodesia, Southern Rhodesia, Swaziland	Acquired	1871–1900	1,894

SECTION I. IN AFRICA (*continued*)

Region	Status	Date	*Areas in 1000's Sq. Kms.*
British Areas in West Africa			
Gambia, Nigeria (Banchi, Borim, Kano, Kantagora, Nufe, Sakoto, Yala in Northern Nigeria; Benin, Lagos, Oil River Protectorate in Southern Nigeria), Sierra Leone	Acquired	1788–1914	1,162
British Islands			
Damaraland Islands, Mauritius and dependencies, St. Helena and dependencies, Seychelles, Tristan de Cunha, Zanzibar, Pemba	Acquired	1814–1933	5.3
British Mandate areas			
Cameroons	Part of German Kamerun League mandate	1884 1920	89
Southwest Africa	German protectorate League mandate to Union of South Africa	1884 1920	835
Tanganyika	German protectorate League mandate	1884 1920	969
Togoland	Part of German Togoland League mandate	1884 1920	34
FRENCH AREAS			
Algeria	Conquered Part transferred to Italy	1830–1847 1919	2,227 81
French Equitorial Africa	Occupied	1839–1906	2,256
Gabon, Middle Congo, Ubangi-Chari, Tchad	Government-general established	1910	
French West Africa	Occupied	1817–1903	4,637
Dahomey, Guinea, Ivory Coast, Mauritania, Niger Colony, Senegal, Sudan	Government-general established	1913	
Morocco, French	Protectorate	1912	431
Somali Coast Ambabo, Gobad, Obock, Tojurah	Occupied	1862–1885	21
Tunis	Protectorate	1881	123

SECTION I. IN AFRICA (*continued*)

Region	Status	Date	Areas in 1000's Sq. Kms.
French Islands			
Kerguelen, Madagascar and dependencies, Comoro Islands, St. Marie, Reunion	Occupied	1643–1843	619
French Mandate areas			
Cameroons	Part of German Kamerun	1884	430
	League mandate	1920	
Togoland	Part of German Togoland	1884	52
	League mandate	1920	
ITALIAN AREAS			
Eritrea	Control taken	1883	120
Libya	Conquered from Turkey	1911–1912	1,761
	Acquired from France	1919	81
Somaliland	Protectorate	1891	358
	Acquired from Britain	1924	142
PORTUGUESE AREAS			
Angola	Occupied	1485	1,256
Cape Verde Islands	Occupied	1462	3.9
Guinea	Occupied	1650	36
Mozambique and dependencies	Occupied	1498	771
St. Thomé and Principe Islands	Occupied	1493	0.9
SPANISH AREAS			
Canary Islands	Occupied	1402–1482	7
	Made Spanish province	1927	
Guinea	Acquired	1778–1900	27
Annobon, Corisco, Elobey, Fernando Po, Rio Muni	Boundaries delimited	1901	
Morocco	Protectorate	1912	21
Rio de Oro	Occupied	1860–1900	285
Adrar, Ifni			
North African Areas			
Alhucemas, Ceuta, etc.	Occupied	1580–1844	0.2

Section II. In the Americas

Region	Status	Date	Areas in 1000's Sq. Kms.
British Areas			
Canada	Possession confirmed, Treaty of Paris	1763	9,542
	Dominion status		
	British North America Act	1867	
	Statute of Westminster	1931	
Newfoundland	Occupied	1583	111
	Possession confirmed, Treaty of Utrecht	1713	
	Self-government	1855	
	Statute of Westminster	1931	
	Special administration under British governor and commission	1933	
Labrador	Occupied	1759	311
	Boundaries redefined	1927	
British Islands			
Bahamas, Barbados, Bermudas, Jamaica (Cayman, Caicos, Turk Islands), Leeward Islands, Trinidad (Tobago), Windward Islands, Falkland Islands and dependencies	Occupied	1609–1814	48
Guiana	Ceded by Dutch, Treaty of Paris	1814	232
Honduras	Secured by treaties with Honduras and Nicaragua	1859–1860	22
Danish Areas			
Greenland	Acquired by ancient discovery		313
	Present administration set up	1921	
Virgin Islands	Purchased from France	1733	0.3
St. Croix, St. Johns, St. Thomas	Sold to United States	1917	
French Areas			
Guadaloupe and dependencies	Occupied	1634	1.8
	Occupation confirmed, treaty of Paris	1815	
	Regime established	1854	
Guiana, French	Occupied	1606	20
	Attached to France	1674	
	Represented in French Assembly	1848	

Section II. In the Americas (*continued*)

Region	Status	Date	*Areas in 1000's Sq. Kms.*
Inini	Part of Guiana in 1878		70
	Special administration	1930	
Martinique	Occupied	1635	1.0
	Occupation confirmed, treaty of Paris	1815	
	Regime established	1854	
St. Pierre and Miquelon	Occupied	1650	0.2
	Occupation confirmed, treaty of Paris	1815	
Netherlands Areas			
Curaçao	Treaty of Paris	1783	1.0
	Separate governor	1863	
Guiana, Dutch (Surinam)	Occupied	1667	150
	Occupation confirmed, treaty of Paris	1815	
	Separate governor	1863	
United States Areas			
Alaska	Purchased from Russia, created a territory	1867	1,519
Panama Canal Zone	Part of Nicaragua in 1878		1.4
	Perpetual lease from Panama	1904	
Porto Rico	Purchased from Spain	1898	
Virgin Islands	Purchased from Denmark	1917	

Section III. In Asia

British Areas

In the Far East
  In the Borneo region

Region	Status	Date	Areas
British North Borneo	Cessions by Brunei and Zulu Sultanates	1877–1878	76
	Protectorate	1888	
Brunei	Protectorate	1888	
Sarawak	Independent, (British subject as Sultan)	1842	109
	Protectorate	1888	

Section III. In Asia (*continued*)

Region	Status	Date	Areas in 1000's Sq. Kms.
In the China region			
Hongkong	Ceded by China, colony estab-lished	1841	0.9
Kowloon	Ceded by China	1860	
	Area extended	1898	
Leased territories, settlements, and concessions in China			
Amoy, Canton, Chinkiang, Hankow, Kiukiang, New-chwang, Tientsin, Weihai-wei	Concession acquired	1851–1898	
Chinkiang, Hankow, Kiuki-ang, Weihaiwei	Returned	1927–1930	
In the Malay regions			
Federated Malay States Negri-Sembilan, P a h a n g, Perak, Selangor	Acquired	1699–1895	72
Straits Settlements and de-pendencies C h r i s t m a s Island, Cocos Islands, Labuan, Malacca, Penang, (Dindings, Prov-ince Wellesley), Singapore	Occupied	1800–1888	4
Unfederated Malay States Johore, Kedah, Kelantoon, Perlis, Trengganu	Occupied	1895–1910	60
In the Middle East			
Burma	Parts occupied	1824–1852	650
	Provincial status under govern-ment of India	1923	
	Separate administration under India Act	1935	
Ceylon and dependencies	Occupied	1796	66
	Full possession	1815	
India			4,684
British provinces	Conquest, British East India Company	1772	2,839
	Transfer from British East India Company	1858	
	Indian Councils Act	1909	
	Government of India Act	1919	

Section III. In Asia (*continued*)

Region	Status	Date	Areas in 1000's Sq. Kms:
In the Middle East (continued)	Part of Federation of India; India Act	1935	
Indian States	May participate in government of all India; India Act	1935	1,845
Sikkim	Protectorate	1890	
In the Near East			
Aden and dependencies	Occupied	1839–1888	4.2
Kuria Muria Islands, Perim, Socotra			
Bahrein Islands	British treaty of support	1861	
	British political agent	1905	
Cyprus	Administrative control by treaty with Turkey	1878	9.3
	Annexed	1914	
British Mandate areas			
Iraq	Formerly Turkish		302
	Class A mandate	1922	
	Independent	1927	
Palestine	Formerly Turkish		26
	Class A Mandate	1922	
Trans-Jordan	Formerly Turkish		40
	Class A Mandate	1922	
FRENCH AREAS			
In the Far East			
Indo-China, French	Acquired	1863–1884	736
Annam, Cambodia, Cochin-China, Laos, Tonkin	Government general established	1898	
Leased territories, settlements, and concessions in China			
Canton, Hankow, Kwangchow-wan, Shanghai, Tientsin	Concessions acquired	1861–1899	
In the Middle East			
In India	Occupation	1674–1739	0.5
Chandernagore, Karikal, Mahé, Pondicherry, Yanaon			

Section III. In Asia (*continued*)

Region	Status	Date	Areas in 1000's Sq. Kms.
In the Near East			
Syria and Lebanon (including Syria, Jebel Drüze, Lattaquié, and Lebanese Republic)	Formerly Turkish Class A Mandate	1922	200
ITALIAN AREAS			
Aegean Islands	Occupied	1912	2.5
Concession in China			
Tientsin	Concession secured	1903	
JAPANESE AREAS			
Chosen (Korea)	Annexed	1910	221
Karafuto (Southern Saghalin)	Ceded by Russia	1905	36
Liuchiu Islands	Ceded by China	1879	
"Manchukuo"	Nominally independent but practically under Japanese control	1932	1,300
Taiwan (Formosa)	Ceded by China	1895	36
Pescadores Islands	Ceded by China	1895	
Settlements and concessions in China			
Amoy, Chungking, Hangchow, Hankow, Newchwang, Soochow, Tientsin	Concessions secured	1895–1906	
Kwantung Leased Territory and South Manchuria Railway Zone	Russian lease taken over Lease extended	1905–1907 1915	4
NETHERLANDS AREAS			
Netherlands East Indies	Acquired	1660–1844	1,904
Java and Madura, Sumatra, Outer Provinces (Borneo, Celebes Islands, Molucca Islands, New Guinea, Timor)	Re-organized	1925	
PORTUGUESE AREAS			
India, Portuguese	Occupied	1535	3.8
Macao	Occupied Sovereignty recognized	1557 1887	0.01
Timor, Portuguese	Occupied	1700	19
UNITED STATES AREAS			
Philippine and Sulu Islands	Purchased from Spain Independence arranged	1898 1935	296

Section IV. In Oceania

Region	Status	Date	Areas in 1000's Sq. Kms.
International Areas			
New Hebrides	Colonization begun	1875	12
	French-British Condominium	1906	
British Areas			
Australia, Commonwealth of	Commonwealth established	1900	7,704
	Statute of Westminster	1931	
New South Wales	Discovery	1770	801
Northern Territory	Transferred from New South Wales to South Australia	1863	1,356
Queensland	Discovery	1770	1,737
	Separated from New South Wales	1859	
South Australia	Colony founded	1836	984
Tasmania	Possession taken	1803	68
Victoria	Settlement	1834	228
Western Australia	Possession taken	1791	2,528
Federal Capital District	Created	1927	2
Islands administered by Australia			
Lord Howe Island, Macquarrie Island, Norfolk Island, Papua, (British New Guinea)	Occupied	1774–1888	235
New Zealand, Dominion of	Cessions by natives	1840	268
	Royal letters patent	1842	
	Dominion status	1907	
	Statute of Westminster	1931	
Areas administered by New Zealand			
Chatham, Cooke, Hervey, Union Islands, Ross Dependency	Taken over	1847–1925	
British Islands			
Fiji Islands	Colony	1874	19
Solomon Islands	Protectorate	1887	

SECTION IV. IN OCEANIA (*continued*)

Region	Status	Date	Areas in 1000's Sq. Kms.
Tongan Islands (Friendly Islands)	Annexed	1826	0.6
	Protectorate	1900	
Western Pacific, High Commissariat of Gilbert and Ellice Islands, Pitcairn Island, other small islands	Occupied	1790–1893	0.5
	Administration created	1893	
British Mandate areas			
Nauru	German protectorate	1885	0.02
	Mandate to Australia, New Zealand, and United Kingdom	1920	
New Guinea	German protectorate	1884	23.6
	Mandate to Australia	1920	
Western Samoa	German control under U. S.-British-German agreement	1899	2.9
	Mandate to New Zealand	1920	
FRENCH AREAS			
French Settlements (over 100 islands)	Administration organized	1861	4
Marquesas Islands	Occupied	1842	
Tahiti and Morea	Occupied, protectorate	1842	
New Caledonia and dependencies	Occupied	1853–1863	19
	Administration organized	1898	
JAPANESE MANDATE AREAS			
Caroline, Marianne and Palau Islands	German protectorate	1899	2.1
	Mandate to Japan	1920	
Marshall Islands	German protectorate	1885	
	Mandate to Japan	1920	
UNITED STATES AREAS			
Guam (in Marianne Islands)	Under Spain	1521	0.5
	Ceded by Spain	1898	
Hawaii	Annexed	1898	17
	Territory of United States	1900	

SECTION IV. IN OCEANIA (*continued*)

Region	Status	Date	*Areas in 1000's Sq. Kms.*
Samoa, American	U. S. control under United-States-British-German agreement	1899	0.2
Wake, Yap, and various other small islands in the Pacific			

Miscellaneous small islands elsewhere in the Pacific, not listed above, held by Britain, Chile, Ecuador, France, and Japan under mandate control.

Sources: In the main, the arrangement of countries by continents and political status in the League of Nations, *Statistical Year-Book*, 1934/35, has been followed, and the areas given are taken from this source. The data as to the pre-1935 changes in the status of different regions, and as to the subdivisions in many of the present divisions, have been gathered from various official and semi-official sources. Differences in spelling of the names of some of the regions, especially in Africa, are frequent. The English spelling used here follows the customary English usage.

PRINCIPAL TREATIES RELATING TO COLONIES

The selection is confined only to the more important instruments, particularly those establishing final allocations of territory. The significant steps of colonial development in Africa are in the record, but the boundary arrangements there have been omitted unless they were of high political consequence. The extent of the agreements underlying the colonial structure can be appreciated from the fact that over 300 treaties were made to effect the organization of French Equatorial and West Africa.

For simplicity and economy of space citations to texts have been confined so far as possible to *British and Foreign State Papers*. Texts are available in many places, and national treaty collections may be convenient to consult in many cases. Sir Edward Hertslet's *Map of Africa by Treaty* is a standard work. Hertslet's *Commercial Treaties* contains some texts not found elsewhere.

This list was prepared by Dr. Denys P. Myers, Research Director of the World Peace Foundation.

1763-1879

France—Great Britain—Spain. Treaty of peace, Paris, February 10, 1763; Martens, Recueil général de traités, 2d ed., I, 104.

Portugal—Spain. Preliminary treaty respecting boundaries in South America and Guinea, San Ildefonso, October 1, 1777; Martens, Recueil général de traités, 2d ed., II, 545.

Portugal—Spain. Treaty agreed to at El Pardo, March 24, 1778; Articles XIII-XV relate to Guinea; Peace Handbook No. 125, 49.

Great Britain—Netherlands. Preliminary articles of peace, Paris, September 2, 1783. Martens, Recueil général de traités, 2d ed., III, 514. Restored Dutch colonies.

Great Britain—Spain. Treaty of peace, Versailles, September 3, 1783; Martens, Recueil général de traités, 2d ed., II, 541; 1 State Papers, 647.

Austria—France—Great Britain—Prussia—Russia. Treaty of peace, Paris, May 30, 1814; Martens, Nouveau recueil général de traités, II, 1, 13.

Great Britain—Netherlands. Convention restoring Netherland colonies, London, August 13, 1814; Martens, Nouveau recueil général de traités, II, 57; 2 State Papers, 370.

France—Portugal. Convention respecting Guiana, Paris, August 28, 1817; Martens, Nouveau recueil général de traités, IV, 490; 4 State Papers, 818.

Great Britain—Tribes of Persian Gulf. 1820; Great Britain, Foreign Office, Peace Handbooks No. 76, p. 78.

Great Britain—Netherlands. Treaty respecting territory and commerce in East Indies, London, March 17, 1824; 11 State Papers, 194.

Great Britain—Tribes of Arabian Coast. Treaty of peace in perpetuity between chiefs, August 1853; Great Britain, Foreign Office, Peace Handbooks, No. 76, p. 80.

France—Great Britain. Declaration engaging to respect the independence of Muscat and Zanzibar, Paris, March 10, 1862; 57 State Papers, 785.

France—Siam. Treaty defining position of Kingdom of Cambodia, Paris, July 15, 1867; 57 State Papers, 1340.

Great Britain—Netherlands. Convention for the settlement of mutual relations in the island of Sumatra, November 2, 1871; Hertslet, Commercial Treaties, XIII, 665.

1880-1885

International convention on the right of protection in Morocco, Madrid, July 3, 1880; 71 State Papers, 639.

France—Tunis. Treaty of friendship, Casr Said, May 12, 1881; 72 State Papers, 247.

Great Britain—Transvaal. Convention for complete autonomy of Transvaal, Pretoria, August 3, 1881; 72 State Papers, 900.

Great Britain—South African Republic. Agreement modifying convention of August 3, 1881, London, February 27, 1884; 75 State Papers, 5.

Congo, International Association of. Declarations of mutual relations, United States, April 22,

1884; France, April 23,, 24, May 31, 1884; Great Britain, December 16, 1884; Italy, December 19, 1884; Austria—Hungary, December 24, 1884; Netherlands, December 27, 1884; Spain, January 7, 1885; Russia, February 5, 1885; Sweden and Norway, February 10, 1885; Portugal, February 14, 1885; Belgium, February 23, 1885; Denmark, February 23, 1885; 75 State Papers, *passim*.

General Act of Berlin concerning the Congo, trade, African settlement, etc., Berlin, February 26, 1885; 76 State Papers, 4.

Germany—Great Britain. Arrangement relative to respective spheres of action in portions of New Guinea, London, April 25, 29, 1885; 76 State Papers, 66.

Germany—Great Britain. Arrangement respecting boundaries in New Guinea, June 18, 1885; Hertslet, Commercial Treaties, XVII, 457.

France—Germany. Protocol on West African coast and Oceania, Berlin, December 24, 1885; 76 State Papers, 303.

1886-1887

Germany—Great Britain. Declaration on demarcation of spheres of influence in Western Pacific, Berlin, April 6, 1886; 77 State Papers, 42.

Great Britain—Socotra. Treaty of protectorate, Kishn, April 23, 1886; 77 State Papers, 1269.

France—Portugal. Convention on boundaries in Western Africa, Paris, May 12, 1886; 77 State Papers, 517.

Great Britain. Charter of Royal Niger Company, July 10, 1886; 77 State Papers, 1022.

Germany—Great Britain. Agreement concerning spheres of action in Gulf of Guinea, London, July 27, August 2, 1886; Martens, Nouveau recueil général de traités, 2d ser., XI, 503; XVI, 803.

Germany—Great Britain. Agreement on spheres of influence in Zanzibar and mainland, London, October 29, November 1, 1886; 77 State Papers, 1130.

Germany—Portugal. Declaration delimiting possessions and spheres of influence in southwest and southeast Africa, Lisbon, December 30, 1886; 77 State Papers, 603.

Great Britain—Somali Tribes. Treaties of protectorate, 1884-86; 76 State Papers, 99; 77 *idem*, 1263.

Great Britain. Proclamation of annexation of Zululand, Pietermaritzburg, May 14, 1887; 75 State Papers, 758.

British East African Association—Zanzibar. Concession of administration of mainland territory, Zanzibar, May 24, 1887; 3 Hertslet, Map of Africa, 946.

China—France. Convention delimiting frontier between China and Tonkin, Peking, June 26, 1887; 85 State Papers, 748.

Germany—Great Britain. Agreement concerning annexations in rear of spheres of influence in East Africa, London, July 2 and Berlin, July 8, 1887; 78 State Papers, 1047.

Great Britain. Notification of British protectorate over Niger districts, London, October 18, 1887; 78 State Papers, 42.

1888-1889

France—Great Britain. Agreement on boundary and rights on Somali coast, London, February 2, 8, 1888; 100 State Papers, 493.

German East African Association—Zanzibar. Concession ceding administration of territories, Zanzibar, April 28, 1888; 79 State Papers, 326.

Italy. Notification of protectorate over Zulu, Zulu, August 2, 1888; 79 State Papers, 749.

Great Britain. Royal charter of Imperial East Africa Company, Westminster, September 3, 1888; 79 State Papers, 641.

Zanzibar. Concession to Imperial British East Africa Company of right of administration of mainland territory, Zanzibar, October 9, 1888; 79 State Papers, 373.

Italy—Migertini. Treaty of protectorate, Bender Alula, April 7, 1889; 81 State Papers, 133.

Italy. Notification of protectorate over Sultanate of Oppia, May 20, 1889; 3 Hertslet, Map of Africa, 1124.

Germany—Great Britain—United States. Final act of conference concerning Samoa, Berlin, June 14, 1889; 81 State Papers, 1058.

France—Great Britain. Agreement on boundaries of West Africa, Paris, August 10, 1889; 81 State Papers, 1126.

Great Britain. Royal charter to British South Africa Company, Westminster, October 29, 1889; 81 State Papers, 617.

Italy. Notification of protectorate over Benadir Coast (Somaliland), London, November 19, 1889; 3 Hertslet, Map of Africa, 1125.

1890-1891

British East Africa Company—Zanzibar. Cession by Zanzibar of places on Benadir Coast, Zanzibar, March 4, 1890; 83 State Papers, 918.

Great Britain—Zanzibar. Agreement for British protectorate, Zanzibar, June 14, 1890; 82 State Papers, 653.

Germany—Great Britain. Agreement concerning spheres of influence in Africa, Berlin, July 1, 1890; 82 State Papers, 35.

General act of Brussels, slave trade, importation of firearms, ammunition and spirituous liquors in Africa, Brussels, July 2, 1890; 82 State Papers, 55, 80. Declaration of June 15, 1910; 103 State Papers, 255.

France—Great Britain. Declarations concerning possessions in Africa, London, August 5, 1890; 82 State Papers, 89.

France—Germany. Exchange of notes concerning Zanzibar, Berlin, November 17, 1890; 82 State Papers, 1085.

France—West African chiefs. Treaties concerning sovereignty, protection, 1819-90; 75 State Papers, 341; 2 Hertslet, Map of Africa, 634 (344 treaties are listed by Hertslet).

Great Britain—Italy. Protocols concerning demarcation of spheres of influence in eastern Africa, Rome, March 24, April 15, 1891; 83 State Papers, 19.

Great Britain. Announcement of protectorate over Nyasaland, London, May 14, 1891; 83 State Papers, 142.

Congo Free State—Portugal. Treaty delimiting frontiers, Lisbon, May 25, 1891; 83 State Papers, 913.

Great Britain—Portugal. Treaty defining spheres of influence in Africa, Lisbon, June 11, 1891; 83 State Papers, 27.

Great Britain—Netherlands. Convention defining boundaries in Borneo, London, June 20, 1891; 83 State Papers, 41.

France—Great Britain. Arrangement of delimitation in West Africa, Paris, June 26, 1891; 83 State Papers, 43.

1892-1894

British East Africa Company—Uganda. Treaty of protection, Kampala, March 30, 1892; 84 State Papers, 59.

Italy—Zanzibar. Convention, concession of Benadir ports, Zanzibar, August 12, 1892; 84 State Papers, 630.

Germany—Great Britain. Protocols concerning boundaries in East Equatorial Africa, Taveta, October 27, Zanzibar, December 24, 1892; 84 State Papers, 628.

Great Britain—Portugal. Agreement concerning spheres of influence north of Zambesi, London, May 31, June 5, 1893; 85 State Papers, 65.

France—Great Britain. Agreement concerning delimitation on Gold Coast, Paris, July 12, 1893; 83 State Papers, 31.

Germany—Great Britain. Agreement respecting boundaries in Africa, July 25, 1893; 85 State Papers, 39.

Germany—Great Britain. Agreement for delimitation of spheres of influence in Africa, Berlin, November 15, 1893; 85 State Papers, 41.

France—Germany. Boundary protocol, Kamerun and French Congo, Berlin, February 4, 1894; 86 State Papers, 974.

Germany—Great Britain. Convention concerning Togoland—Gold Coast customs union, Berlin, February 24, 1894; 86 State Papers, 37 (denounced by Germany, December 8, 1903).

France—Germany. Convention of delimitation, Congo and Kamerun, Berlin, March 15, 1894; 86 State Papers, 974.

Great Britain—Italy. Protocol, spheres of influence in East Africa, Rome, May 5, 1894; 86 State Papers, 55.

Congo Free State—Great Britain. Agreement for spheres of influence in East and Central Africa, Brussels, May 12, 1894; 86 State Papers, 19.

Great Britain—South African Republic. Convention of annexation of Swaziland by South African Republic, December 10, 1894; 86 State Papers, 61.

1895-1899

Belgium—Congo Free State. Treaty ceding Congo Free State to Belgium by King Leopold, Brussels, January 9, 1895; 90 State Papers, 1281.

France—Great Britain. Agreement delimiting possessions north and east of Sierra Leone, Paris, January 21, 1895; 87 State Papers, 4.

Great Britain—Netherlands. Convention delimiting boundaries in island of New Guinea, The Hague, May 16, 1895; 87 State Papers, 18.

China—France. Convention delimiting frontier of Tonkin, Peking, June 20, 1895; 87 State Papers, 523.

Egypt—Italy. Agreement on dependence of semi-nomadic tribes between Baraka and Red Sea, Cairo, June 28, Asmara, July 7, 1895; 95 State Papers, 459.

Great Britain—Venezuela. Treaty for arbitration of Guiana boundary, Washington, February 2, 1897; 89 State Papers, 57.

Ethiopia—Great Britain. Treaty concerning frontiers of British Somaliland, Addis Ababa, May 14, 1897; 89 State Papers, 31.

France—Germany. Conventions delimiting possessions of Togoland, Dahomey and Sudan, Paris, July 23, 1897; 89 State Papers, 584.

France—Great Britain. Convention concerning delimitation and spheres of influence in Africa, Paris, June 14, 1898; 91 State Papers, 38.

Egypt—Italy. Convention concerning boundaries of Sudan and Eritrea, Asmara, December 7, 1898; 95 State Papers, 459, 461.

Spain—United States. Treaty of peace, Cuba, Porto Rico, Guam, Philippines, Paris, December 10, 1898; 90 State Papers, 382.

Egypt—Great Britain. Agreement concerning joint rule in Sudan, Cairo, January 19, 1899; 91 State Papers, 19.

France—Great Britain. Declaration concerning Egypt and spheres of influence in Central Africa and Sudan, London, March 21, 1899; 91 State Papers, 55.

Germany—Spain. Treaty ceding Caroline, Palau (Pellew) and Marianne Islands to Germany, Madrid, June 30, 1899; 92 State Papers, 113.

Germany—Great Britain. Agreement concerning Samoan Islands, Tonga, Togoland and Zanzibar, London, November 14, 1899; 91 State Papers, 70.

Germany—Great Britain—United States. Convention effecting division of Samoan Islands, Washington, December 2, 1899; 91 State Papers, 75.

1900-1903

France—Italy. Protocol respecting boundary of Red Sea possessions, Rome, January 24, 1900; 94 State Papers, 588.

Great Britain—Tonga. Treaty establishing protectorate, Nukualofa, May 18, 1900; 107 State Papers, 521.

Great Britain. Proclamation of annexation of Orange Free State, May 24, 1900; 92 State Papers, 548.

Ethiopia—Italy. Treaty concerning boundary of Eritrea, Addis Ababa, July 10, 1900; 95 State Papers, 463.

France—Spain. Convention for delimitation of possessions in West Africa, Paris, June 27, 1900; 92 State Papers, 1014.

Great Britain. Proclamation of annexation of Transvaal, September 1, 1900; 92 State Papers, 547.

Spain—United States. Treaty ceding Cagayan Sulú and Sibutú, Washington, November 7, 1900; 92 State Papers, 814.

Germany—Great Britain. Agreement as to boundary of spheres of interest between Lakes Nyasa and Tanganyika, Berlin, February 23, 1901; 95 State Papers, 78.

Egypt—Italy. Agreement on frontier between Sudan and Eritrea, Todluc, April 16, 1901; 95 State Papers, 464.

France—Italy. Protocol respecting boundary of Red Sea possessions, Rome, July 10, 1901; 94 State Papers, 589.

Ankole—Great Britain. Agreement on administration, Entebbe, October 25, 1901; 94 State Papers, 461.

Great Britain—Italy. Declaration on Sudan-Eritrea frontier, Rome, November 22, 1901; 95 State Papers, 466.

Ethiopia—Great Britain—Italy. Treaty on frontier between Sudan and Eritrea, Addis Ababa, May 15, 1902; 95 State Papers, 467.

Great Britain—Orange Free State—South African Republic. Peace of Vereeniging, surrender of Boers, Pretoria, May 21, 1902; 95 State Papers, 160.

France—Netherlands. Convention on commercial relations between France and Netherland colonies, The Hague, August 13, 1902; 95 State Papers, 796.

Great Britain—Italy. Exchange of notes concerning southern frontier of Ethiopia, Rome, January 20, February 9, 1903; 98 State Papers, 682.

France—Great Britain. Agreement for lease of land on Niger, Paris, May 20, 1903; 97 State Papers, 929.

1904-1906

France—Great Britain. Convention concerning possessions in Newfoundland, West and Central Africa, London, April 8, 1904; 97 State Papers, 31.

France—Great Britain. Declaration regarding Egypt and Morocco, London, April 8, 1904; 97 State Papers, 39.

France—Great Britain. Declaration concerning Siam, Madagascar and New Hebrides, London, April 8, 1904; 97 State Papers, 53.

Germany—Great Britain. Exchange of notes on demarcation of spheres of influence in Western Pacific, London, March 7, May 9, 1904; 98 State Papers, 443.

Netherlands—Portugal. Convention on boundary in Island of Timor, The Hague, October 1, 1904; 101 State Papers, 497.

France—Spain. Declaration on integrity of Morocco, Paris, October 3, 1904; Martens, Nouveau recueil général de traités, 2d ser., XXXII, 57.

France—Great Britain. Exchange of notes on Morocco, London, October 6, 1904; 102 State Papers, 450.

Italy—Somali. Agreement of peace and protectorate over the Mullah, Illig, March 5, 1905; 100 State Papers, 547.

Japan—Korea. Agreement for protectorate, Seoul, November 17, 1905; 98 State Papers, 1139.

France—Great Britain. Protocol concerning New Hebrides, London, February 27, 1906; 99 State Papers, 230.

Germany—Great Britain. Agreement on boundaries from Yola to Lake Chad, London, March 19, 1906; 99 State Papers, 366.

General act concerning Morocco, Algeciras, April 7, 1906; 99 State Papers, 141.

France—Great Britain. Convention on delimitation of possessions east of Niger, London, May 29, 1906; 99 State Papers, 194.

France—Great Britain. Convention establishing New Hebrides condominium, London, October 20, 1906; 99 State Papers, 229.

France—Great Britain—Italy. Agreement concerning Ethiopia, London, December 13, 1906; 99 State Papers, 486.

1907-1911

Great Britain—Portugal. Exchange of notes concerning boundary in East Africa, Lisbon, June 3, 1907; 100 State Papers, 553.

Belgium—Congo Free State. Treaty of cession, Brussels, November 28, 1907; 100 State Papers, 705.

Ethiopia—Great Britain. Agreement as to frontiers, Addis Ababa, December 6, 1907; 100 State Papers, 459.

France—Germany. Convention for delimitation of French Congo and Kamerun, Berlin, April 18, 1908; 101 State Papers, 1003.

Ethiopia—Italy. Convention concerning frontiers of Somaliland and Eritrea, Addis Ababa, May 18, 1908; 101 State Papers, 1000.

Belgium—France. Agreement concerning preferential right of France over territories of Congo, Paris, December 23, 1908; 102 State Papers, 357.

France—Germany. Declaration concerning integrity of Morocco, Berlin, February 9, 1909; 102 State Papers, 435.

Great Britain—Siam. Treaty concerning cession of jurisdiction in Malay state, Bangkok, March 10, 1909; 102 State Papers, 126.

Great Britain—Trengganu. Agreement establishing protectorate, Singapore, August 22, 1910; 103 State Papers, 987.

France—Wallis Islands. Treaty declaring a protectorate, Matautu, May 19, 1910; 103 State Papers, 544.

Japan—Korea. Treaty of annexation, Seoul, August 22, 1910; 103 State Papers, 992.

Great Britain—Kelantan. Agreement respecting administration and position of the rajah, Kelantan, October 22, 1910; 103 State Papers, 518.

Great Britain—Italy. Exchange of notes, frontier at mouth of Juba River, Rome, July 8, 15, 1911; 104 State Papers, 158.

France—Germany. Convention concerning Morocco, Berlin, November 4, 1911; 104 State Papers, 948, 953.

France—Germany. Convention respecting Equatorial Africa, Berlin, November 4, 1911; 104 State Papers, 956.

1912-1923

France—Morocco. Treaty of protectorate, Fez, March 30, 1912; 106 State Papers, 1023.

France—Germany. Protocol delimiting boundaries in Africa, Paris, September 12, 1912; 106 State Papers, 1001.

Italy—Turkey. Peace preliminaries, cession of Cyrenaica and Tripoli, Lausanne, October 15, 1912; 106 State Papers, 1096.

France—Italy. Declaration, reciprocal relations in Libya and Morocco, Paris, October 28, 1912; 107 State Papers, 794.

France—Spain. Convention concerning Morocco, Madrid, November 27, 1912; 106 State Papers, 1025.

Italy—Spain. Agreement, reciprocal relations in Libya and Morocco, Rome, May 4, 1913; 107 State Papers, 947.

Great Britain. Order in Council annexing Cyprus, London, November 5, 1914; 108 State Papers, Pt. II, 165.

Great Britain. Proclamation of protectorate over Egypt, London, December 18, 1914; 109 State Papers, 437.

France—Great Britain—Italy—Russia. Agreement respecting Italy's entrance into the World War, London, April 26, 1915; 112 State Papers, 973.

Great Britain. Order in council annexing Gilbert and Ellice Islands, London, November 10, 1915; 109 State Papers, 352.

Australia—Great Britain—New Zealand. Agreement respecting administration of Nauru, July 2, 1919; 113 State Papers, 151.

Egypt—Great Britain. Negotiations for treaty of Egyptian independence, November, December 1921; 114 State Papers, 200; 119 *idem*, 186.

International Convention for Organization of the statute of the Tangier zone, Paris, December 18, 1923; 117 State Papers, 499; 119 *idem*, 480.

BIBLIOGRAPHY

To give a complete bibliography of all the works dealing with European expansion and with colonies, it would be necessary to include practically every book on the history and development of Europe and the Western countries which has been written in the past century or more. This impossible task has not been attempted. The effort has been simply to include the more important volumes, chiefly of relatively recent date though also a few of earlier periods, which deal with particular phases of expansion and colonies.

The grouping is roughly according to the principal subjects of the books, though of course many of the volumes cover material pertinent to two or more of the headings.

The official publications listed are mainly the periodic statistical volumes containing material bearing on colonies and related subjects, though a few special studies of particular importance have been included.

The more important official collections of pre-War documents have been listed, together with a few unofficial documentary collections, since this material throws light on the relation of colonies to developments in Europe and in international relations.

OFFICIAL PUBLICATIONS

Australian Government

Australian Statistics of Overseas Imports and Exports. Census and Statistics Bureau. Periodically.

Official Year Book of the Commonwealth of Australia. Census and Statistics Bureau. Annual. The volume for 1908 contains "authoritative statistics for the period for 1901 to 1907 and corrected statistics for the period of 1788 to 1900."

Quarterly Summary of Australian Statistics. Census and Statistics Bureau.

Belgian Government

Annuaire officiel. Ministère de Colonies. Annual.

Annuaire statistique de la Belgique et du Congo Belge. Administration de la statistique générale. Annual.

British Government

Accounts Relating to the Trade and Commerce of Certain Foreign Countries and British Possessions. Statistical Department. Annual.

Accounts Relating to the Trade and Navigation of the United Kingdom. Statistical Department. Annual.

Annual Reports of the Colonies. Colonial Office. Published annually for each principal colony and for some of the lesser colonies grouped together.

Annual Reports on the Mandated Territories. Published annually for each mandate area.

Annual Statement of the Trade of the United Kingdom with Foreign Countries and British Countries. Statistical Department.

British and Foreign State Papers. Vols. I to LXIV published by J. Ridgway & Sons, London. Subsequent volumes published by H. M. Stationery Office.

British Documents of the Origins of the War, 1898–1914. G. P. Gooch and Harold Temperely, eds. H. M. Stationery Office, London. 11 vols.

Colonial and Imperial Conferences, series of documents on. 1897 and later years. H. M. Stationery Office.

Colonial Office publications, in various series.

Department of Overseas Trade, various publications. Particularly the Reports dealing with economic conditions in British and other colonial territories.

Economic Survey of the Colonial Empire. Colonial No. 109. H. M. Stationery Office. 1935. Covers data for 1933.

Peace Handbooks. Series published by the Historical Section of the Foreign Office. H. M. Stationery Office. 1920. Especially those dealing with the British and other colonial possessions.

Statistical Abstract of the Several British Over-

British Government (Continued)
seas Dominions and Protectorates in Each Year. Statistical Department. H. M. Stationery Office. Annual. Earlier issues entitled Statistical Abstracts of the British Empire.

Statistical Abstract of the United Kingdom. Statistical Department. H. M. Stationery Office. Annual.

Canadian Government
The Canada Year Book. Statistics Bureau; General Statistics Branch. Annual.

Official Handbook of Present Conditions and Recent Progress. Statistics Bureau. Annual.

Trade of Canada. Statistics Bureau; External Trade Branch. Annual and Quarterly Reports.

Twelve Years of the Economic Statistics of Canada, 1919-1930. Statistics Bureau; General Statistics Branch.

French Government
Annales du commerce extérieur; commerce et navigation des principaux pays étrangers. Annual.

Annales du commerce extérieur; commerce et navigation de la France. Annual.

Annales maritimes et coloniales, 1816-1847. Imprimerie royale. Paris.

Annuaire colonial, administratif. Ministère des colonies.

Annuaire agricole, commercial et industriel des colonies français et pays de protectorat. Ministère des colonies.

Annuaire statistique de la France. Bureau de la statistique générale de la France.

Annuaire statistique; France et colonies. Bureau de la statistique générale de la France.

Documents diplomatiques français, 1871-1914. Imprimerie nationale. Paris, 1929. The official collection of pre-War documents.

Indices généraux du movement économique en France. 1901-1931. Bureau statistique générale de la France.

German Government
Deutsches Kolonial-Handbuch. Kolonialamt. Annual, prior to 1914.

Deutsches Kolonialblatt. Kolonialamt. Periodic issues, prior to 1914.

Deutschland und die Weltwirtschaftliche Lage. Auswärtiges Amt. 1920/21 to 1924/25.

Die Grosse Politik. The official collection of pre-War documents.

Handbuch für das deutsche Reich. Reichsamt des Inner. Annual.

Statistisches Jahrbuch für das deutsche Reich. Statistisches Amt. Annual.

Statistik des deutschen Reiches. Statistisches Amt. Annual.

Weissbuch. Auswärtiges Amt. Series of "white papers." C. Heyman. Berlin, 1885-1902.

Indian Government
Accounts Relating to the Trade by Land of British India with Foreign Countries. Statistics Department. Annual.

Accounts Relating to the Sea-borne Trade and Navigation of British India. Statistics Department. Annual and Monthly Reports.

Annual Statement of the Sea-borne Trade of British India with the British Empire and Foreign Countries. Statistics Department.

Financial and Commercial Statistics of British India. Statistics Department. Annual.

Statistical Abstract for British India. Statistics Department. Annual.

Institut Colonial International
Reports of the sessions of the Institut in 1894 and subsequent years. Published by the Institut at Brussels.

Institut Internationale de Statistique
Annuaire internationale de statistique. Published by the Permanent Office of the Institute. The Hague. Annual.

International Institute of Agriculture
International Yearbook of Agricultural Statistics. Published by the Institute at Rome. Annual.

International Labor Office
Migration Movements, 1920-1924; and Migration Movements, 1925-1927. International Labor Office. Geneva, 1926 and 1929. Series O, Nos. 2 and 4.

Migration in the Pacific Area. International

Labor Office. Geneva, 1931. Report prepared for the Institute of Pacific Relations.

The I. L. O. Yearbook. Geneva. Annual.

Consult lists of publications of the I. L. O. for other studies pertinent to the general subject of colonies.

Italian Government

Annali di Statistica. Direzione di Statistica. Annual.

Annuario delle Colonia Italiana. Direzione di Statistica.

Annuario Statistico Italiano. Direzione di Statistica.

Annuario Statistica delle Emigrazione Italiana, 1876-1925. Commissario del l'Emigrazione.

Les Colonies italiennes. Ministero delle colonie. 1930.

Statistica delle migrazioni da e per l'estro. Direzione di Statistica. Annual.

Japanese Government

Annual Return of the Foreign Trade of Japan. Ministry of Finance. Also monthly return.

Financial and Economic Annual of Japan. Ministry of Finance.

Résumé statistique de l'empire du Japon. Statistical Bureau. Annual.

League of Nations

The Official Journal, the reports of the Mandates Commission, and various other of the League publications contain a good deal of pertinent material. Consult the indices.

International Economic Conference, the; reports, documentation, resolutions, etc. Geneva, 1927. Particularly the volume on Population and Natural Resources. 1927 II 38. C.E.I. 39.

International Trade Statistics. Geneva. Annual.

Memorandum on Production and Trade. Geneva, 1926. 341.014 (00) II.

Report on Certain Aspects of the Raw Materials Problem. By the Provisional Economic and Financial Committee. 241.014 (00) II 13. Geneva, 1921. 2 vols. in 1.

Report on the Problem of Raw Materials and Foodstuffs. By Corrado Gini. 341.014 (00) B. Geneva, 1921. Also a preliminary edition which differs slightly from the final form.

Review of World Trade. Geneva. Annual.

Statistical Year Book. Geneva. Annual.

World Production and Prices, 1925-1934. (1935. II A. 15). Geneva, 1935.

Netherlands Government

Jaarcijvers; Kolonien. Centraal Bureau voor de Statistiek. Annual.

Jaarcijvers; Rijk in Europe. Centraal Bureau voor de Statistiek. Annual.

Statistich Overzicht van de Behandelde Zieken der Koloniale Troepen. Centraal Bureau voor de Statistiek. Annual.

New Zealand Government

The New Zealand Official Yearbook. Census and Statistics Office. Annual.

Statistics of the Dominion of New Zealand. Census and Statistics Office. Annual, 1853-1920. Continued as separate reports under population, trade, etc.

Union of South Africa Government

Official Year Book. Census and Statistics Office. Annual.

United States Government

Agriculture Year Book. Department of Agriculture. Annual.

Commerce Year Book. Department of Commerce. Annual.

Colonial Systems of the World. Statistics Bureau. Washington, 1898.

Colonial Tariff Policies. U. S. Tariff Commission. 1921.

Foreign Commerce and Navigation of the United States. Bureau of Foreign and Domestic Commerce. Annual.

Foreign Relations of the United States. State Department. The official collection of documents.

Geography of the World's Agriculture. Finch, V. C., and Baker, O. E., Department of Agriculture. Washington, 1917.

Statistical Abstract of the United States. Bureau of Foreign and Domestic Commerce. Annual.

World Atlas of Commercial Geology. Geological Survey.

World Economic Review. Department of Commerce. 1934 and previous issues.

BIBLIOGRAPHIES

General

Council on Foreign Relations, New York. Foreign Affairs Bibliography. William Leonard Langer and H. F. Armstrong, eds. Harper & Brothers, New York, 1933. For the Council on Foreign Relations.

Library of Congress, Washington. List of Books Relating to the Theory of Colonization, Government of Dependencies, Protectorates, and Related Topics. Government Printing Office, Washington, 1903.

Library of Congress. Mimeographed lists of references on colonial subjects. Issued in 1919, 1924, and from time to time subsequently.

Royal Empire Society. London. A Select Bibliography on Foreign Colonization. Aberdeen University Press, Aberdeen, 1915.

British

Royal Empire Society and Royal Institute of International Affairs. List of Publications on the Constitutional Relations of the British Empire, 1926-1932. London, 1933.

French

Catalogue méthodique de la bibliothèque du Ministère des Colonies. Imprimerie Administrative, Paris, 1905.

Société de l'histoire des colonies françaises. Bibliographie d'histoire colonial (1900-1930). Paris, 1932.

Italian

Catalogo delle publicazioni edite dall' Administrazione Coloniale, presente al' Espasizione Coloniale di Anversa. Rome, 1930.

Instituto Coloniale Fascista. Guide bibliographiche. Rome. Periodical issues, beginning 1928.

League of Nations

List of Works Relating to the Mandates System and the Territories under Mandate, Catalogued in the Library of the League of Nations. Geneva, 1930. First supplement. Geneva, 1934.

Netherlands

Hartmann, A. et al. Repertorium ap de literatuur betreffende de Nederlandsche Kolonën.

Nijhoff. 's Gravenhage, 1895 and subsequent years.

MANDATES

See, primarily, the publications of the Mandates Commission of the League of Nations and the reports of the several governments which hold mandates.

Bentwick, Norman de Mattos. The Mandates System. Longmans, Green, London, 1930.

Clyde, Paul Hibbert. Japan's Pacific Mandate. Macmillan, New York, 1935.

Comisetti, Louis. Mandats et souveraineté. Librairie du Recueil Sirey, Paris, 1934.

Gerig, Benjamin. The Open Door and the Mandates System. Allen & Unwin, London, 1930.

Rees, Daniel François Willem van. Les mandats internationaux. Rousseau & Co., Paris, 1927-28. 2 vols.

Schnee, Heinrich. Die deutschen Kolonien unter fremden Mandatherrschaft. Quelle & Meyer, Leipzig, 1922.

Wright, Philip Quincy. Mandates Under the League of Nations. University of Chicago Press, Chicago, 1930.

COLONIAL AND RELATED HISTORY

Abbott, W. C. The Expansion of Europe. H. Holt, New York, 1918. New ed., 1924. 2 vols.

Beer, George Louis. The old Colonial System. Macmillan, New York, 1912. 2 vols.

Bowman, Isaiah. The New World. World Book Co., New York, 1922. 4th ed., 1928.

Calenbrander, Herman Theodoor. Koloniale Geschiedenis. Nijhoff, 's Gravenhage, 1925. 3 vols.

Congrès international colonial (Paris, 1900); rapports, mémoires et procès verbaux des séances. H. Raberge, Paris, 1901.

Cooke, W. Henry, and Edith P. Stickney. Readings in European International Relations. Harper & Brothers, New York, 1931. A collection of documents.

Dubois, Marcel. Un Siècle d'expansion coloniale, 1800-1900. Challamel, Paris, 1902.

Fawcett, Charles B. Frontiers: a Study in Political Geography. Clarendon Press, Oxford, 1918.

Lane-Poole, S., ed. Thirty Years of Colonial Governments. Longmans, Green, New York, 1889. 2 vols.

Marvin, F. S. Western Races and the World. Oxford University Press, London, 1922.

Moon, Parker T. Imperialism and World Politics. Macmillan, New York, 1926.

Morris, Henry C. The History of Colonization from Earliest Times to the Present Day. Macmillan, New York, 1900. 2 vols.

Muir, Ramsay. The Expansion of Europe. Houghton Mifflin, Boston, 1917. New ed., 1924.

Raynal, G. T. F., Abbé. Histoire philosophique et politique des établissements et du commerce des Européens dans les deux Indes. Amsterdam, 1771. Burned by the public executioner. Reprinted at Geneva, 1780-81.

——— Same. Revised, augmented, and published in 10 volumes newly translated from the French by J. O. Justamond, F.R.S., with a new set of maps and copious index. W. Strahan, London, 1789. 8 vols.

——— Same. New translation in English with title A Philosophical and Political History of the Settlements and Trade of Europeans in the East and West Indies. Mundell & Son, Edinburgh, 1804. 3 vols.

Reinsch, Paul S. World Politics at the End of the Nineteenth Century. Macmillan, New York, 1904.

Royal Institute of International Affairs, London. Various periodical and other publications which contain considerable material pertinent to colonies.

Royal Empire Society, London. Various publications.

Siebert, B. Entente Diplomacy and the World: Matrix of the History of Europe, 1909-1914. Translated from the original texts. Arranged and annotated by George Abel Schreiner. The Knickerbocker Press, New York, 1921.

Temperley, H. W. V., A History of the Peace Conference. H. Froude, London, 1920-1924. For the Royal Institute of International Affairs. 6 vols.

Toynbee, Arnold J. Survey of International Affairs. H. Milford, London. Royal Institute of International Affairs. Annual volumes.

Zimmermann, Alfred. Die europaischen Kolonien. Mittler & Sohn, Berlin, 1896-1903. 5 vols.

COLONIAL POLICY

Brougham, Henry. An Inquiry into the Colonial Policy of the European Powers. Willison, Edinburgh, 1803. 2 vols.

Cesari, Cesare. Colonie e possedimente coloniale. Tipografia Regionale, Roma. 5th ed., 1930.

Folliet, Joseph. L droit de colonisation. Bloud & Gay, Paris, 1933.

Harmand, Jules. Domination et colonisation. Flammarion, Paris, 1910. New ed., 1919.

Joehlinger, Otto. Die koloniale Handelspolitik der Weltmächte. L. Simon, Berlin, 1914.

Key, Helmer. The New Colonial Policy. Translated by E. Classen. Methuen, London, 1927.

Lindley, Mark F. Acquisition and Government of Backward Territory in International Law. Longmans, Green, London, 1926.

Merivale, H. Lectures on Colonization and Colonies. Oxford University Press. London, 1928. Lectures originally delivered 1839, 1840, and 1841. Reprinted in 1861 by Herman Merivale.

Ram, V. Shiva. Comparative Colonial Policy. Longmans, Green, London, 1926.

Reinsch, Paul S. Colonial Administration. Macmillan, New York, 1905.

Talleyrand-Périgord, Charles Maurice de, Prince de Bénévent. Memoir . . . and Essay on the Advantages to be Derived from New Colonies. Translated into English. T. B. Wait, Boston, 1809.

Woolf, Leonard S. Imperialism and Civilization. Hogarth Press, London, 1928.

ECONOMIC AND OTHER SPECIAL PROBLEMS

American Academy of Political and Social Science. Economics of World Peace. Annals of the Academy. Vol. 150. July, 1930.

——— Raw Materials and Foodstuffs in the Commercial Policy of Nations. Annals of the Academy. Vol. 112. March, 1924.

Bain, H. Foster. Ores and Industry in the Far East. Council on Foreign Relations, New York, 1927. Revised ed., 1933.

Commission of Inquiry. International Economic Relations; Report of the Commission of Inquiry into National Policy in International Economic Relations. University of Minnesota Press, Minneapolis, 1934.

Culbertson, William S. International Economic Policies. Appleton, New York, 1925.

Denny, Ludwell. We Fight for Oil. Knopf, New York, 1928.

Donaldson, John. International Economic Relations. Longmans, Green, London, 1928.

Emeny, Brooks. Strategy of Raw Materials. Macmillan, New York, 1934.

Ferenczi, Imrie. International Migrations. National Bureau of Economic Research, New York, 1929. Data compiled on behalf of the International Labor Office, Geneva. Vol. I. Statistics; Vol. II. Interpretations.

Leith, C. K. Minerals and World Politics. McGraw-Hill Book Co., New York, 1931.

Penrose, E. F. Population Theories and Their Application, with Special Reference to Japan. Stanford University Press, 1934, for the Institute of Pacific Relations.

Smith, Joseph Russell. The World's Food Resources. Holt, New York, 1919.

Spurr, J. E., editor. Political and Commercial Geography and the World's Mineral Resources. McGraw-Hill Book Co., New York, 1920.

Thompson, Warren S. Danger Spots in World Population. Knopf, New York, 1929.

Wallace, Bruce and Lynn Ramsay Edminister. International Control of Raw Materials. The Brookings Institution, Washington, 1930.

Wilkinson, H. L. The World's Population Problems and a White Australia. P. S. King & Son, London, 1930.

World Economic Conference. Reports and Proceedings. League of Nations, Geneva. C.E.I. 46, 1927. 2 vols.

Woytinsky, Wl. Die Welt in Zahlen. Mosse, Berlin, 1927. 7 vols.

Zimmermann, Erich W. World Resources and Industries. Harper & Brothers, New York, 1933.

GENERAL DISCUSSIONS

Angell, Norman. The Great Illusion. G. P. Putnam's Sons, New York, 1910. Reprinted with additions and revision under the title The Great Illusion, 1933. Putnam, New York, 1933.

East, E. M. Mankind at the Crossroads. Charles Scribner's Sons, New York, 1923.

Hobson, John Atkinson. Imperialism, a Study. James Pott & Co., New York, 1902.

Nearing, Scott. The Twilight of Empire. Vanguard Press, New York, 1930.

Perla, Leo. What is National Honor? Macmillan, New York, 1918.

Simonds, Frank H., and Brooks Emeny. The Price of Peace. Harper & Brothers, New York, 1935.

Taylor, Griffith. Environment and Race. Oxford University Press, London, 1927.

AFRICA AND THE PACIFIC AREA

Barnes, Joseph, ed. Empire in the East. Doubleday, Doran, New York, 1934.

Buell, Raymond Leslie. The Native Problem in Africa. Macmillan, New York, 1928. 2 vols.

Clark, Grover. Economic Rivalries in China. Yale University Press, New Haven, 1932.

Field, F. V. Economic Handbook of the Pacific Area. Doubleday, Doran, New York, 1934.

Giffen, Morrison B. Fashoda, the Incident and Its Diplomatic Setting. University of Chicago Press, Chicago, 1930.

Hanotaux, Gabriel. Fachoda. E. Flammarion, Paris, 1909.

Herstlet, Edward. The Map of Africa by Treaty. 1909. 3 vols.

Institute of Pacific Relations. Problems of the Pacific and other publications. Honolulu and New York.

Johnston, Sir Harry. A History of the Colonization of Africa by Alien Races. Cambridge University Press, Cambridge, 1899. Revised ed., 1913.

MacCallum, Elizabeth P. Rivalries in Ethiopia. World Peace Foundation, New York, 1935.

Morse, H. B. and MacNair, Harley. Far Eastern International Relations. Houghton Mifflin, Boston, 1931.

Roosevelt, Nicholas. The Restless Pacific. Charles Scribner's Sons, New York, 1928.

Woolf, Leonard. Empire and Commerce in Africa. George Allen and Unwin, London.

THE BRITISH EMPIRE

Beer, George Louis. The Origin of the British Colonial System. Macmillan, New York, 1908.

Ward, A. W. and G. P. Gooch, editors. Cambridge History of British Foreign Policy. Vol. III. 1866-1919. Cambridge University Press, Cambridge, 1923.

Campbell, Persia Crawford. Chinese Coolie Emigration to the Countries within the British Empire. King and Son, London, 1923.

Colquhoun, Patrick. A Treatise on the Wealth, Power, and Resources of the British Empire. J. Mawman, London, 1815.

Curtis, Lionel. The Commonwealth of Nations. Macmillan, London, 1916.

Curtis, Lionel, and Margery Perham. The Protectorates of South Africa. Oxford University Press, London, 1935.

Dilke, Charles Wentworth. Problems of Greater Britain. Macmillan, London, 1890. 2 vols.

Egerton, Hugh E. British Colonial Policy in the XXth Century. Methuen, London, 1922.

——— A Short History of British Colonial Policy. Methuen, London, 1897. Revised ed., 1932.

Elliott, William Yandell. The New British Empire. McGraw-Hill Book Co., New York, 1932.

Fawcett, Charles Bungay. A Political Geography of the British Empire. University of London Press, London, 1933.

Federation of British Industries. The Resources of the Empire. Benn, London, 1924. 10 vols.

Gibbins, Henry de Beltgens. British Commerce and Colonies from Elizabeth to Victoria. Methuen, London, 1893.

Grey, Viscount, of Fallodon. Twenty-five years, 1892-1916. Stokes, New York, 1925. 2 vols.

Gunn, Hugh, ed. The British Empire. W. Collins Sons, London, 1924. 12 vols.

Herbertson, A. J. and O. J. R. Hawarth. The Oxford Survey of the British Empire. Oxford University Press, London, 1914. 6 vols.

Hirst, F. W. and J. E. Allen. British War Budgets. Oxford University Press, 1926. For the Carnegie Endowment for International Peace.

Keith, Arthur Berridale. The Constitution, Administration and Laws of the Empire. W. Collins & Sons, London, 1924.

——— The Governments of the British Empire. Macmillan, London, 1935.

——— Responsible Government in the Dominions. Clarendon Press, Oxford, 1912. 3 vols.

——— Selected Speeches and Documents on British Colonial Policy, 1763-1917. Oxford University Press, London, 1918. 2 vols.

Knowles, Lillian C. A. The Industrial and Commercial Revolutions in Great Britain. Routledge & Sons, London; Dutton, New York, 1926.

Lucas, C. P. Historical Geography of the British Colonies. Clarendon Press, Oxford, 1887-1924. 13 vols.

Palmer, Gerald Eustace Howell. Consultation and Cooperation in the British Commonwealth. Oxford University Press, London, 1934.

Porritt, Edward. The Fiscal and Diplomatic Freedom of the British Overseas Dominions. Clarendon Press, London, 1922. For the Carnegie Endowment for International Peace.

Scott, James Brown. Autonomy and Federation within the Empire. Carnegie Endowment for International Peace. Washington, 1921. Pamphlet No. 33.

Seeley, John R. The Expansion of England. Macmillan, London, 1884.

Trotter, R. G. The British Empire-Commonwealth. H. Holt, New York, 1932.

Williamson, J. A. A Short History of British Expansion. Macmillan, London, 1930. 2 vols.

FRANCE

Allain, Maurice. Encyclopédie pratique illustrée des colonies françaises. A. Quillet. Paris, 1932. 2 vols.

Ferdinand-Lop, Samuel. Les Colonies françaises. E. Molfère, Paris, 1931.

Girald, Arthur. The Colonial Tariff Policy of France. Clarendon Press, Oxford, 1916. For the Carnegie Endowment for International Peace.

——— Principes de colonisation et de legislation coloniale. L. Tenin, Paris, 1921-23. 3 vols.

Lebel, A. Roland. Histoire de la littérature coloniale en France. Libraire Larose, Paris, 1931.

Roberts, Stephen H. History of French Colonial Policy. 1870-1925. King & Son, London, 1929.

L'Union coloniale française. Le Domaine colonial français. Editions du Cygne, Paris, 1929. 2 vols.

GERMANY

Bülow, Bernhard, Prince von. Imperial Germany. Translated by Marie A. Lewenz. Dodd, Mead, New York, 1914.

———— Memoirs. Translated by F. A. Voight. Little, Brown, Boston, 1931. 2 vols.

Dawson, William Harbutt. Evolution of Modern Germany. Charles Scribner's, New York, 1919.

Dietzel, Karl H. and Hans Rudolphi, eds. Koloniale Studien. D. Reimer, Berlin, 1928.

Herrfurth, Kurt. Fürst Bismarck und die Kolonialpolitik. Trewendt's Nachfolger, Berlin, 1909.

Jacob, Ernst Gerhard. Deutsche Kolonialkunde, 1884-1934. Ehlermann, Dresden, 1934.

Kaiser-Wilhelm-Dank: Verein der Soldatenfreunde. Deutschland als Kolonialmacht. Wohlfahrtsgesellschaft, Berlin, 1914.

Le Sueur, Gordon. Germany's Vanishing Colonies. Everett & Co., London, 1915.

Lewin, Perry Evans. The Germans and Africa. Stokes, New York, 1915.

Mayer, Anton. Das Buch der deutschen Kolonien. Volk und Haimat, Potsdam, 1933.

Schnee, Heinrich. German Colonization, Past and Future. Allen and Unwin, London, 1926.

Townsend, Mary Evelyn. Origins of Modern German Colonialism. Columbia University Press, New York, 1921.

———— Rise and Fall of Germany's Colonial Empire. Macmillan, New York, 1930.

Wilhelm II, Kaiser. The Kaiser's Memoirs. Translated by Thomas R. Ybarra. Harper & Brothers, New York, 1922.

Winkler. Statistisches Handbuch des gesamten Deutschtums. Deutsche Rundschau, Berlin, 1927.

Zimmermann, Alfred. Geschichte der Deutschen Kolonialpolitik. Mittler und Sohn, Berlin, 1914.

ITALY

Cippico, Antonio. Italy, the Central Problem of the Mediterranean. Institute of Politics, New Haven, 1926.

Corni, Guido. Prolemi coloniali. Popolo d'Italia, Milano, 1933.

Glanville, James L. Colonialism in the New Italy. Arnold Foundation Studies in Public Affairs. Vol. II, No. 4. Spring, 1934.

Guyot, Georges. L'Italie devant le probleme coloniale. Challamel, Paris, 1927.

Mussolini, Benito. The Political and Social Doctrine of Fascism. Enciclopedia Italiana, 1931. Translated in International Conciliation. January, 1935.

Tabasso, Voltera E. Commercio e colonie. Instituto Coloniale Italiano, Milano, 1920.

Tittoni, Tommaso. Italy's Foreign and Colonial Policy. Smith, Elder & Co., London, 1914.

Villari, Luigi. The Expansion of Italy. Faber & Faber, London, 1930.

JAPAN

Asami, Noboru. Japanese Colonial Government. Privately printed, New York, 1924.

Ballard, George Alexander. The Influence of the Sea on the Political History of Japan. Murray, London; Dutton, New York, 1921.

Crocher, W. R. The Japanese Population Problem. Macmillan, 1931.

Foreign Trade of Japan, The; a Statistical Survey. Oriental Economist, Tokyo, 1936. A complete collection of all the Japanese official foreign trade statistics back to 1868.

Kobayashi, Ushisaburo. The Basic Industries and Social History of Japan. Yale University Press, New Haven, 1930. For the Carnegie Endowment for International Peace.

———— War and Armament Taxes of Japan. Oxford University Press, London, 1923. For the Carnegie Endowment for International Peace.

Mocharville, Maurice. Le Japon d'outre mer. A. Pedone, Paris, 1931.

Moulton, Harold G. Japan, an Economic and Financial Appraisal. The Brookings Institution, Washington, 1931.

Nasu, Shirosi. Land Utilization in Japan. Institute of Pacific Relations, 1931.

Ogawa, Gotaro. Expenditures of the Russo-Japanese War. Oxford University Press, London, 1923. For the Carnegie Endowment for International Peace.

Ono, Giichi. War and Armament Expenditures of Japan. Oxford University Press, London, 1922. For the Carnegie Endowment for International Peace.

THE NETHERLANDS

Kat Angelino, Arnold Dirk Adrian de. Colonial Policy. Translation by G. J. Renier. University of Chicago Press, 1931. For the Institute of Pacific Relations. 2 vols.

Koninklijke Koloniaal Instituut. Various publications, especially those of the Encyclopaedisch Bureau. Amsterdam.

Vuuren, L. van. Die Niederlande und Ihr Kolonialreich. Oasthoek, Utrecht, 1932.

Wijck, Jhr. van der. Onze Koloniale Staatkunde. Nijhoff, 's Gravenhage, 1865.

Date Due